ROLLS-ROYCE
FROM THE INSIDE
THE HUMOUR, THE MYTHS, THE TRUTHS

D1712669

ROLLS-ROYCE
FROM THE INSIDE
THE HUMOUR, THE MYTHS, THE TRUTHS

REG ABBISS

TEMPUS

For my children
Caroline and Christopher
Who have brought joy to my life

ACKNOWLEDGEMENTS

Picture credits: Rolls-Royce and Bentley Motor Cars.
Christopher Abbiss 62, 246; colour pictures 13, 14
Monte Shelton 74, 75, 76
Qantas Airways 224, 225

The names Rolls-Royce, Bentley, and the Rolls-Royce badge are registered trademarks.

Frontispiece: Henry Royce's masterpiece: the most valuable Rolls-Royce of all, the revered Silver Ghost, AX 201, chassis number 551, celebrated her centenary in 2007. This motor car, driven by both Henry Royce and Charles Rolls and technically superior to anything else on the road, established the Company's reputation for reliability, quality, silence and engineering excellence.

First published in the United Kingdom in 2007 by
Tempus Publishing, an imprint of NPI Media Group Limited
Cirencester Road · Chalford · Stroud · Gloucestershire · GL6 8PE

First published in the United States in 2007 by
The History Press, Charleston, SC   29403
www.historypress.net

British Library Cataloguing in Publication Data
A catalogue record for this book is available from the British Library.

Library of Congress CIP data applied for.

ISBN 978 0 7524 4324 9

Notice: The information in this book is true and complete to the best of our knowledge. It is offered without guarantee on the part of the author or The History Press. The author and The History Press disclaim all liability in connection with the use of this book.

Typesetting and origination by NPI Media Group Limited.
Printed and bound in England.

CONTENTS

ABOUT THE AUTHOR

British journalist and broadcaster, Reg Abbiss, brings a unique perspective to this book, viewing Rolls-Royce as both an inquisitive BBC reporter, and later, from the inside, as the company's spokesman in North America.

He had a teenage ambition to become a journalist and willingly suffered leg pulling as the only young man in a college class of twenty girls as he aimed for the 140 words a minute shorthand speed needed to land a job on a newspaper.

He managed it, despite the distractions, became a reporter on weekly and daily papers, and founded a freelance agency covering northern England for the nationals and wire services, before joining BBC News as a reporter in London.

TV and radio assignments ranged over the Alaskan oilfields and an earthquake in Japan, to war in Vietnam and stories in Germany, Italy, Scandinavia, North America and Hong Kong. Along the way he interviewed Muhammad Ali, the Beatles, Richard Nixon, Robert Kennedy and a few Prime Ministers.

Specialising in business coverage during a turbulent time in British politics, he anchored general election and financial broadcasts; reported several nights a week on BBC TV News and was a frequent broadcaster on the BBC World Service.

He became a 'poacher-turned gamekeeper' when he joined Rolls-Royce Motors International in the US to help persuade wealthy Americans that life was incomplete without the most luxurious of all British products.

After sixteen years as media strategist and spokesman, he couldn't resist the fun of poaching again and returned to broadcast journalism in 1996, with the US Speedvision TV Network, co-anchoring and reporting for *Aviation News* through its three-year run. He anchored programmes from the Farnborough and Paris International Air Shows with Apollo 12 commander, Pete Conrad.

Reg has also narrated fifty-two programmes in the *Great Cars* television series broadcast on 200 stations in North America, the UK and the Pacific Rim.

INTRODUCTION

There has never been anything quite like a Rolls-Royce – for 100 years the poster possession of the privileged and the acquisitive; triggering the gamut of emotions: envy, pride, avarice, the ideal mobile boudoir, royalty-on-wheels, engineering perfection and much admired, though out of reach for 99.99 per cent of those who gaze upon it. Conversely, some call it 'in your face conspicuous consumption'.

Rolls-Royce – a name with a touch of magic about it – stands for something special whether you are in Tokyo, Beverly Hills, New York, Monte Carlo, Frankfurt, London or Riyadh, and many places in between. Unless you have lived your life in the Himalayas without communication with the rest of the planet, you will recognize the name and its unique place in the lexicon.

It is a motor car crafted to provide luxurious travel for the very wealthy, who for most of the twentieth century were the only people able to afford one.

Henry Royce's legendary cars attracted an interesting mix of bedfellows – kings, queens and dukes juxtaposed with billionaires, screen idols, pop stars and the just plain rich. In later years, they have been joined by entrepreneurs in pimping, drug dealing and other shadowy business enterprises that prudently steer clear of the tax authorities, and tend not to make the RSVP list for Ivy-League events or Buckingham Palace garden parties.

But not all Rolls-Royce owners have the fat wallets of those who lord it over small countries or move in the lucrative world of wheeling and lobbying. There are many dedicated enthusiasts who devote evenings and weekends over years to rebuild engines, scouring around for parts, and lovingly restoring an old car.

Sixteen fascinating years as spokesman for Rolls-Royce and Bentley in North America, and regular forays to the Pacific Rim, gave me a graduate course in the idiosyncrasies of the rich and the indulgent. I met unusual and delightful people marching to their own drumbeat, particularly around Los Angeles, Newport Beach and San Francisco. Individualistic, laid-back Californians do a lot of things right and in terrific style, like buying one third of all the Rolls-Royce and Bentley motor cars sold in America. That makes them, as I would have said in my spin-days, consumers of perspicacity and fine judgment.

They are among the many that have been intrigued by the majestic motor cars of Rolls-Royce since the buggy gave way to the horseless carriage. Astonishing and funny stories about the mega-rich who owned, and still drive them, are the stuff of legend.

The Rolls-Royce universe teems with tales of extravagance, myths and humor that have been the norm since Henry Royce put his first car together eight years before the Titanic set sail.

What I have set out to do is lift the wraps on the rarified world of Rolls-Royce – its soul, flaws and the bizarre, quirky people who for decades have been dazzled and have lusted after the world's most expensive cars.

'The Rolls-Royce of Rolls-Royces' – a description often applied over the past century to the Silver Ghost, which turned out to be the greatest moble public relations tool of all. The six cylinder, 40/50hp open tourer holds many endurance records and with more than half a million miles under her wheels is regarded by Rolls-Royce engineers as 'just nicely run in.' She still goes out for regular runs in Britain and has also been driven in many other countries, usually getting there by new-fangled jet freighters.

We will look at the mistakes and misfortunes that led to Britain's most famous company falling into the hands of the Germans, following a donnybrook between the chief executives of Volkswagen and BMW that brought to mind Oscar Wilde's foxhunting quote about 'the unspeakable in pursuit of the uneatable'.

Rolls-Royce enjoyed holding on to an Edwardian aura in the modern world, but sharp perception lurked beneath the languid façade, and when danger or an opportunity was sensed, it could speedily cover the bases without spilling the drinks. It was a company of good, honest people committed to old-world values with an obsessive attention to detail, going to meticulous lengths to make its motor cars 'mobile Rembrandts' and unique in all the world.

It also artfully fed the egos of happy big bucks dreamers, some of whom believed that an ostentatious purchase was a ticket to social acceptability.

It skillfully applied a polished 'fact and mythology spin machine' to persuade the deep-pocketed to part with a fortune to acquire a symbol that for many decades has been held as the best in the world.

Just what is a Rolls-Royce? It is the most famous of all motor cars, instantly recognized by its radiator grille and statuesque Flying Lady bonnet mascot, and as the gold standard for quality, exquisite craftsmanship and luxury.

A Rolls-Royce lasts a long time. How long? Well, about three-quarters of all Rolls-Royce motor cars ever built are still on the road or in collections and able to fire up when the key is turned.

Ownership sometimes triggers curious behavior. How about these samples? A Californian hacked a hole in the roof of his Silver Shadow, stuck in a lemon tree and, causing uproar, angrily paraded the car through Beverly Hills, flanked by two cavorting blondes in bikinis to add spice to the scene for the television crews; English and Australian farmers chauffeured pigs and sheep to market in a Rolls; a New Yorker suggested that if he did not get a new engine, a Rolls-Royce manager would take the quick way down from his twenty-seventh floor balcony!; the followers of a cult leader in Oregon, with gun-toting bodyguards, shelled out many millions to buy ninety-three Rolls-Royce cars, aiming to provide one for each day of the year; the oil-rich Sultan of Brunei, the heaviest of hitters, and the guy with all the marbles, blew untold millions on hundreds of specially crafted Rolls and Bentleys and filled caverns beneath his palaces with hundreds more exotic motor cars; a young American millionaire bought a dozen – sometimes more – new Rolls a year, often trading them in after only a few hundred miles. Clutching a bag of washcloths and polishes, he would peer through the windows of a New York showroom, eagerly waiting for it to open and would insist on helping remove the protective shipping-wrapping.

As somebody else said – you can't make this stuff up!

Then, there is the pursuit of trademark infringers capitalizing on the Rolls-Royce name – opportunists running 'The Rolls-Royce of call-girl services…'; entrepreneurs' fitting fake

Charles Stewart Rolls

(1877-1910)

Frederick Henry Royce

(1863-1933)

Frederick Henry Royce, born in 1863, sold newspapers as a boy, left school at fourteen and taught himself electrical engineering. He became a great engineer and his name has symbolised excellence for more than a century. Yet he always signed his name: 'Henry Royce, mechanic.' He died Sir Henry Royce in 1933, having been knighted for his contribution to the British engineering industry.

Charles Stewart Rolls brought investment and marketing savvy to the Company. An aristocrat who loved to drive fast and to fly, he was among aviation's pioneers and made the first two-way crossing of the English Channel in 1910. A few weeks later he became the first Englishman to die in an aviation accident.

The *Spirit of Ecstasy* in sillouhette

radiators to try to make a Volkswagen or a Chevy look like a Rolls; the Queen's Phantoms – palaces on wheels with a special hydraulic seat to give the crowds a good view of the monarch; the school for gentlemen chauffeurs, who in these changed times are also taught kidnap-avoidance maneuvers; metal crafting – the 'black art'; haughty car salesmen in cathedrals of commerce and a British Lord's mistress, whose shapely figure in flowing chiffon has adorned the prow of every Rolls-Royce since before the First World War.

Rolls-Royce has always gone to expensive lengths to make cars to live up to its towering reputation, crafted by some of the finest artisans in the world who take tremendous pride in what they do. They have done unusual things to create 'The Rolls-Royce experience'. Some examples are: Putting a man in the trunk with his ear pressed to the carpet to find the source of a squeak as the car drives over bumpy roads; using a dipstick as a stethoscope to listen to the heartbeat of the engine; running fingertips over the paintwork as though reading Braille to seek the slightest imperfection; taking days to make a convertible top look like a solid roof; a self-leveling fluid suspension to compensate for the weight of passengers and luggage and even the emptying of the fuel tank and making wheel nuts and bolts of brass to ensure not only top quality, but to create left- and right-hand threads to run counter to the direction of travel, so they would never work loose.

That is attention to detail. They could have economized with less pricey outsourcing, but that was not the Rolls-Royce way. By making many components in the factory, piece by piece, the special character of the motor car was maintained, even though such extravagance defied the rules of economics.

There has long been a perception that Rolls-Royce motor cars were created by omnipotent engineers who guaranteed them for life. 'Whose life?' you may ask. When a car was less than perfect, owners were usually forgiving. One was even heard to sigh: 'Even their mistakes are beautifully done.'

But it must be conceded that the Company committed to perfection has produced a few cars of citrus quality, otherwise known as lemons. I'll talk about those.

And we'll look at: selling the sizzle and the magic; presentation, image burnishing, advertising; the collapse – how Rolls-Royce made it back from bankruptcy; freeloading automotive journalists, who live the high life at the expense of the car-makers, and respond by abusing their cars.

If some of the many Rolls-Royce owners I have known over the years suspect that they see themselves as I describe idiosyncrasies and messianic devotion to motor cars, be proud. You belong to a unique group, privileged to drive remarkable and wonderful carriages, whose like the world will probably not see again.

The sinews, the heart and the soul of Rolls-Royce, I do believe, could have sprung only from England, acknowledged the world over for its eccentricities, wry sense of fun and an inbuilt desire to get it right.

So, fasten the belts and let's be off. I hope you will have a few chuckles along the way, roll your eyes, chortle perhaps, and say: 'I had no idea! Is he serious? I can hardly believe it.'

Reg Abbiss
November 2007

1

CAN THOSE QUIRKY OWNERS
BE FOR REAL?

'Ass with class' the naked lady suggests as she straddles the hood of a Rolls-Royce, smiling seductively. Apart from going into near cardiac arrest, what should the Company do when an owner uses its revered product – the world's most prestigious motor car and carriage of kings, queens and heads of state – as a prop in a less than tasteful advertisement to sell pornographic magazines? The message delivered a non-too-subtle roadmap to take the mind swimming into areas that tub-thumping televangelists would most decidedly prefer that you did not stray. The advertisement sure got your attention.

The perpetrator of this 'heinous crime against morality' was the magazine publisher, Larry Flynt, whose literary preferences might offend many people, but whose taste in motor cars could not be faulted, or, indeed, his appreciation of nubile ladies. Flynt certainly knew how to produce a picture for the memory bank while jerking the strings of startled Rolls-Royce executives, whose sensitivities were deeply offended by the eye-popping ad. Right up front was Flynt's personal Rolls-Royce with the well-structured young woman bracing her shapely buttocks against the outstretched wings of the Flying Lady mascot.

Across the hallowed grille screamed the 'Ass with Class' message, providing a whole new take on the emblem's official name, the *Spirit of Ecstasy*. There was near apoplexy on the management corridor at the factory where the suits were unaware that the United States owner-list included one of the world's leading sex-mag publishers, whose raunchy publications enjoyed wide circulation but were unlikely to count conservatives like the Reverends Jerry Falwell or Pat Robertson among their readers.

I suspect that I was one of very few in the Company to see the comical and encouraging side to it, noting that apart from its intriguing creativity it was at least acknowledging the 'class' of a Rolls-Royce, rather than one of those German or Italian cars who names sometimes escape one. But proprieties had to be saluted and somebody had to remonstrate with Mr Flynt.

Whatever we said had to be carefully phrased so as not to sound pompous. Some might ask why an owner should not use his car to help his business along, an argument that would invoke the sanctity and protection of all three major trademarks – mascot, radiator shell and the distinctive RR badge.

What could we do to make the upsetting subject go away? We could not very well splutter that it was an outrage and leave it hanging. Ron Lehrman, the Rolls-Royce trademark lawyer in New York, and a noted international expert, approached the problem calmly. He figured that if we admonished Larry Flynt he would gleefully publish the letter and prolong the dialogue and the publicity by using the advertisement again.

Ron called Flynt's attorney, a classmate at law school, and, after exchanging pleasantries, advised him that his client had had his one bite of the cherry and a repetition of what amounted to a gross trademark infringement would have them both saying 'Good morning, your Honor'. This approach worked and Flynt, doubtless grinning mischievously, returned to the paths of trademark protocol, if not other morally righteous avenues.

Rolls-Royce owners are an eclectic lot and include doctors, lawyers and successful operators in finance and real estate who reward themselves with a car that speaks to their appreciation of the good things in life. There are rich, entrepreneurial egocentrics, many of them delightful people and a few that you might consider not to be among the brightest bulbs in the chandelier but who have a talent for making big money. Of course, the owner-body, as it is known, has always included substantial representation of the showbiz crowd whose highly strung, artistic temperament can propel them to the front page of the supermarket tabloids.

Zsa Zsa Gabor, noted for her colorful personality, ability to collect husbands and eye-watering alimony, was out with her Corniche convertible in Beverly Hills when she got into a parking row with a cop. The disagreement lit Zsa Zsa's fire and pursuing an inadvisable course, she slapped the cop, escalating the altercation to a whole new level. Attended by a publicity hullabaloo, she clicked for three days in the slammer for assaulting a bastion of Beverly Hills law.

After returning to the bosom of a law-abiding community more accustomed to the ambience of friendly watering holes like the Beverly Hills Hotel Polo Lounge than the distressingly spartan accommodations of the county jail, Miss Gabor disposed of the car and in classic Hollywood style drove it across the block at a Las Vegas auction, heading back to Los Angeles $90,000 richer.

Some time earlier, Zsa Zsa had decided she did not like the color of her Corniche and asked Tony Thompson, the English gentleman who ran Rolls-Royce of Beverly Hills, where she had bought the car, to repaint it. Cognizant that she would not expect to foot the bill, Tony pointed out 'there's nothing wrong with your magnificent coachwork' (he meant the car, I believe) 'and I can't justify spending several thousand dollars on a whim'. Though he repeated in his urbane and charming way that it was not on, she came back several times to berate him for his stubbornness. He stood his ground but Zsa Zsa ultimately got her re-spray. Tony told me after we had had a cocktail or two:

> She brought the car in with a dent in each door, telling me with a straight face that a terrible thing had happened. The engine stalled a moment after she pressed the button to close the electric gates of her mansion, the jaws closed in, and, presenting her dented car, Zsa Zsa smiled dazzlingly at me and cooed: 'Now can I have my new paint job, dahlink....?'

The somewhat reserved English are not inclined to throw public tantrums, but the odd one will erupt. A pistol-packing Rolls-driving businessman imploded in London, falling foul of the law through what the judge called 'a streak of arrogance'. The man drew up alongside a taxi in his gold-colored Rolls and terrified its passenger, a Dutch television soap-star actress. It was late at night in Mayfair when the Rolls caused the taxi to swerve. Gesticulations of complaint by the cabby resulted in the Rolls driver producing the pistol, which he said later he had forgotten about after a fancy dress party. He sped off, chased by the cab whose driver called the police, who in turn stopped the Rolls some miles away in North London.

Passing sentence, the judge said the pistol-waving was 'nasty and frightening' and four months in the pokey (he did not use quite that expression) was the price the Rolls-Royce owner would have to pay, along with about $1,000 prosecution costs.

Some Rolls enthusiasts will quietly shell out a fortune for a special car to add to their collection and any sibling of Henry Royce's legendary 1907 Silver Ghost, is special. One, made the same year, came up for auction at Sotheby's, in Palm Beach and a British businessman heard about it, paying $2.86 million, a world-record price for a Rolls-Royce. 'This is the best Rolls there is,' the new owner, Charles Howard, said of the cream-colored car that was once owned by the Rockefeller family.

Armored ghosts: 'A Rolls in the desert was above rubies,' said Lawrence of Arabia of his fleet of 40/50hp armored Rolls-Royce Ghosts.

GO FIRST CLASS. YOUR HEIRS WILL

This thought-provoking message, aimed directly at the wealthy elderly in Florida, is on the wall right behind Richard Kovacs's desk. Retirees, about to reward themselves with a Rolls-Royce after a lifetime's toil and respect for the value of the dollar, sometimes hesitate at the last minute about splashing out serious money – like $250,000 on a car.

Kovacs, who has successfully worked the lucrative markets of Miami, Palm Beach and Fort Lauderdale for many years, knows when to push the button. His casual glance toward the message underscores that they should enjoy what they have earned – while still able to. The buyer stares at all the zeros on the paperwork and, after agonizing further reflection, grits his teeth and says: 'Damn it, I'm going to have it. I earned it.'

People whose ages range from the early '20s to the late '80s, have 'kicked the tires' of highly polished carriages with gleaming radiator grilles in Rolls-Royce emporiums watched over by Richard Kovacs and his brethren in well-heeled markets extending to Texas, California and New York.

Wall Street bankers and yuppie traders were strongly represented in the client list before the dot-com bubble popped; also entrepreneurs from the heartland, the 'snowbirds' who flee south every winter. Others with an appreciation of the qualities of a Rolls or Bentley include those of a gambling persuasion, whose workplaces are many miles away in Atlantic City and Las Vegas, but always keep enough to maintain a home in Florida where no state income tax has long had additional appeal.

Some buyers are in what some euphemistically describe as 'the recreational pharmaceuticals business'; others manage a string of employees in the oldest profession and even men of the cloth spring for a Rolls – occasionally two or even more. Or maybe their churches do.

Above, opposite and overleaf: Owners polishing and pampering their cars.

A notable Rolls lover, the Right Reverend Dr Frederick Eikerenkoetter II – Reverend Ike to his flock and owner of a stable of Rolls-Royce cars – is one of the most flamboyant owners in New York. A powerful orator, and a jolly man with a mischievous twinkle in his eye, founded the United Church of Jesus Christ for All People in South Carolina and the United Christian Evangelistic Association in Boston. Reverend Ike uses a Rolls-Royce to spread his gospel of brotherly love and material success. Asked by reporters how he squared owning wildly expensive cars while ministering to hard-working people who struggled to meet the bills each week, he said they rejoiced that the Almighty had seen fit to bestow magnificent carriages on the parish to carry him around as he did the Lord's work.

A preacher for fifty years, Ike declared: 'Money is not the root of all evil. It is the absence of money that's evil. You must love yourself before you can love anyone else. Christ rode on the Rolls-Royce of his day – an ass.' Always upbeat, he quoted his philosophy: 'In my church, we do not teach poverty. We teach aiming for riches. These damn cars are the nearest things I've come across to the chariots of The Lord.'

He tells people to avoid negative thoughts that induce poverty and replace them with positive mind-power which produces unearned wealth. He underscored his philosophy in his inimitable way in an NBC interview:

> I have no right to teach success and prosperity unless I'm successful and prosperous myself. As far as Rolls-Royces go, I wish that the church had bought more because some that I bought for $25,000 are now going for over $100,000 on the collectors' market. Everybody in the church enjoys riding in those Rolls-Royces in the person of me. Would it help the poor if I got out of the Rolls and rode a bicycle?

Ike certainly has a way with words. For many years he has preached every Sunday at the United Church Center at Broadway and 175th Street in upper Manhattan and broadcast his message in the United States, Canada, Mexico and the Caribbean.

A gifted communicator with a sense of humor, he is credited with changing the face of television evangelism, and produced one of the most notable exhortations ever shouted to persuade people to peer into their souls and dig deep into their pockets. During a service televised to share the proceedings with an overflow congregation down the street, he was reported to have told the assembled throng: 'Now brothers and sisters, it is time for the offerings. And I do not want to hear any clinking in those plates. I wanna hear the rustle of green.'

In 1998, writer Ken Miller wrote: 'Far from being evasive about how much money he makes, he openly brags about having sixteen Rolls-Royces, wears $1,000 suits and diamond rings on both hands and enjoys luxury homes on each coast.'

Ike's old-time religion message, mailed to lots of folks out there, includes what amounts to a teach-in about accumulating wealth through faith and three weekly $20 contributions gets you what you want… Salvation on the installment plan. 'Forget about the pie in the sky. Get yours, here and now,' Ike says.

My old friend Warren Brown of *The Washington Post* grew up listening to Reverend Ike's broadcasts in New Orleans. 'The man talked sense to me. The first thing to do for the poor is not to become one of them, he would say. And I'd say "Amen to that".'

As he cruised a Bentley GT press car along Virginian roads, Warren contemplated the Reverend Ike's words on eternal justice. 'If it is that difficult for a rich man to get into Heaven, think how terrible it must be for a poor man to get in. He doesn't even have a bribe for the gatekeeper.'

The Right Reverend Dr Frederick Eikerenkoetter II is certainly one of a kind.

Some Rolls-Royce owners are so proud of their cars they have to tell the world, even if the expression of delight is a bit gauche. One license plate announced simply 'I'm Rich'. That gentleman's happy crowing was matched by an owner who sought to enhance his Corniche with this home truth: 'You need a lot of bread to own a Rolls.' These were not old-school Rolls-Royce owners.

In the Midwest, one owner who would have had difficulty denying that he conducted business on the periphery of the law, was so delighted by his Silver Shadow, he proclaimed in big lettering on the trunk 'The Crowd Pleaser'. The special décor was finished off with a red, white and black checkerboard roof. It disappeared when he left the scene for a while and the car was sold, but he did it again when he was back in business.

This expression of graphic design also sent a quiver through those at the Rolls-Royce headquarters who prided themselves on owners' appreciation of the aesthetics. There was a similar distressing reaction to the special paint job demanded by a Chicago lady. She ordered her car in three shades of purple. This unusual taste in colors, the Company decided, would require a substantial upfront deposit – which was forthcoming.

Rolls-Royce enthusiasts nurture their motor cars to the point of fanaticism. No devotion runs as deep or as pure as the affection of the aficionado for his Royce. If he is not driving it, he is polishing it or fiddling under the hood with screwdriver and spanner to seek out anything that might require tightening. He doesn't begrudge it his last penny. He will heat the garage better than his house and will drive about all week in an old wreck to have his days of glory at the weekend.

Eric Barrass, for many years the driving force in the Rolls-Royce Enthusiasts' Club in Britain – a quintessential English gentleman to whom I make reference elsewhere – tells us in his 'Source Book of Rolls-Royce' that some motor cars had drifted downward over the years, to perform menial tasks with dignity and total reliability.

Often crudely converted, they served as hay sweeps and pig carriers on farms; as breakdown trucks, taxis and hire cars; and of course, those ageless, vast limousine bodies had given many people their first and last ride in a Rolls-Royce – to their nuptials and to the grave.

These wonderful Royces, however, refused to die. Eric records: 'Fortunately many have been recovered from scrapyards, haystacks, barns and from the debris of years behind old garages and have been lovingly restored to pristine condition by dedicated enthusiasts all over the world.'

The Silver Cloud can also double as stylish pig transportation.

Of quirky owners, he chronicles the adventures of a Mrs Bower Ismay in the early 1930s, who instructed her chauffeur to drive her across the Sahara in her Phantom limousine, together with her maid, to Timbuktu. As she feared only the dark, she purchased twelve-dozen candles from Fortnum and Mason, the Piccadilly store also known as the Queen's grocers.

According to Eric Barrass, a Texan had the body removed from his Silver Ghost, substituted a full-sized model of his horse, with the steering wheel through its head and the controls adapted so – complete with chaps, Stetson and a six-shooter – he drove as he rode. I haven't heard this story from any other source, but if Eric Barrass recounts it, it just has to be true!

Being a Yorkshireman, I have to tell you that in my beloved, beautiful Yorkshire Dales – which attract many tourists anxious to see where James Herriot, the famous vet, found inspiration for wonderful books like *All Creatures Great And Small* – those who work the land do not drive tractors or pickups all the time. A farmer with a pig-breeding business triggered considerable anguish in the Rolls-Royce boardroom when it was learned that he was ferrying pigs to market in the back of an old Rolls. An emissary was dispatched to ask him to please end this unthinkable practice to which the Rolls-Royce man was sent packing with this bit of homely agricultural logic: 'Pigs paid for it. Pigs'll ride in it.' They're independent and fairly dour people in James Herriot country and they do not take kindly to interfering strangers, even if they're wearing a smart suit and come from Rolls-Royce!

A pork butcher, perhaps one of the Yorkshire farmer's customers, caused further grief when he replaced the Flying Lady hood ornament with a phallic-like symbol fashioned out of silver to represent a sausage. He clearly was not a man to argue with.

In Australia, a farmer installed a divider in his Silver Cloud to stop the sheep from licking his neck as he drove to market. I cannot vouch for the reliability of the source, but this story has been told for years at the Rolls factory.

Texas, of course, is noted for bigger and better, and some spreads are larger than some English counties. A Silver Shadow owner, whose ranch was shaped like an elongated football field, installed a fuel pump half-way down the drive – 100 miles from his front door – so he could make the round-trip to pick up the mail without running out of gas. He lived near Midland, a community of about 80,000, west of Dallas, with a thriving economy, boasting the largest number of millionaires per capita than anywhere else in America and possibly the world. Their fortunes are generated by hundreds of metal 'nodding donkeys' dotting the landscape as far as you could see. This rather barren area, where George W. Bush lost his Yale accent and developed his folksy 'aw shucks' twang, did not seem the likeliest place for a Rolls-Royce showroom. However, one enterprising dealer from Chicago, John Schaler III, saw the possibilities, opened shop there and did well. Midland is more pick-up truck than luxury car territory, but, with so many oil people awash with money and not fazed in the slightest by the prospect of shelling out six figures for an imported car if it took their fancy, British and German manufacturers found this part of Texas a profitable marketplace.

The affable Schaler, who always wore a benevolent smile, claimed that his clientele over the years in Indianapolis, Chicago and Palm Beach, included Burt Reynolds, Bing Crosby, George Hamilton, Gary Cooper and even Princess Margaret. He converted an old beer warehouse into an automotive emporium with a gallery filled with antique furnishings and hung out an impressive shingle proclaiming: 'The John Schaler III Collection.' Palm trees and an oriental garden helped to create what John described as an exceptional Rolls-Royce buying experience.

One customer had a swimming pool of near Olympic proportions and to celebrate the addition of another expensive British car to his stable, invited a crowd to a pool-side cookout. Among the guests was an auto-executive from New York who happened to be in town that day to discuss sales development plans and he was pop-eyed when the host announced laughingly through a bull-horn: 'Listen up, y'all. I'd like you to see my ayer-force.' A few moments later, he told me, a Boeing 707 roared over the ranch, followed by a Lear jet and a couple of helicopters.

Texas also lays claim to the only house with classic Rolls-Royce cars as centerpieces in the living area. Ed Swearingen, an aircraft manufacturer changed around his Spanish-style home on the outskirts of San Antonio, removing a three-ton pipe organ from the family room and putting in garage-sized doors to make room for the two favorite cars in his collection. One of them was a virtually wrecked Rolls-Royce Ghost he found in New England. Little more than the chassis and engine were left and using drawings and photographs, Ed spent five years restoring the car to its splendid original appearance. This tale has more than a few shades of Ian Fleming's *Chitty Chitty Bang Bang!*

When finished, copper and brass fittings gleamed in the engine compartment and the car was worth $150,000, but Ed wouldn't sell it. True to the principle that his cars were not kept around just as museum pieces, he drove the Ghost on two round trips, coast-to-coast, sometimes cruising along close to a comfortable 65mph, and covering more than 400 miles in a day. How many miles are on the clock? 'Don't know,' he said, 'but it is three-quarters-of-a-century old and I can tell you it has got a ton of miles on it.'

Behind the cars in the living room is a mural of one of the first air races to be held in France and through the big doors, there is a paneled garage and workshop where he overhauls engines, makes restorative metal body panels and, when necessary, fashions new parts of brass. There are many antique car lovers and restorers out there like Ed Swearingen, though I do not know of another who brings them into the house.

People have been known to become very attached to a Rolls. A Los Angeles couple handled the divorce arrangements quite amicably, but argued over custody of their 1972 Corniche convertible. The fight had to be settled by a judge who handed down a Solomon-like decision. He ordered that the couple would have alternate ownership of the car – one month at a time. They happily waltzed away and I do believe, lived contentedly ever after.

A London businessman in a hurry and quoting the slogan: 'Pride of Britain, Envy of the world,' set the world's speed record from London to New York using only Rolls-Royce power – Concorde, two helicopters and two cars. It took four hours twenty-three minutes, office to office.

Not all Rolls-Royce owners come from the ranks of the wealthy. In the 1980s a young British garbage man – they're called dustmen in England – worked six days a week for over five years, buying only necessities and saving every penny he could to buy a used Rolls-Royce. Around the same time, a coalminer in the north of England saved assiduously for more than thirty years, then spent the lot on a Rolls.

Rolls-Royce lovers can be astonishingly generous at times. Elvis Presley peered through the window of the Rolls-Royce showroom in Memphis, liked the cars he saw and bought several to give to friends.

Mike Tyson, when going through one of the more stressful periods of his life, was driving a Bentley through New York with his wife when they began to argue. He stopped the car, hailed a couple of cops and said, 'Take it!' They did, taking the car across the Hudson to a garage in New Jersey. When the story reached the NYPD top brass, they were not amused. Cops had been known to accept favors occasionally but a $200,000 Bentley was a trifle extreme.

Cartoonist Paul Rigby of the *New York Daily News* illustrated the scene in the Rolls-Royce boardroom, when they heard what Tyson had done. With directors in dark jackets and striped trousers collapsing in a dead faint, a florid Colonel Blimp-type, resting his head on the desk and pounding the top, shouted: 'Some beastly colonial pugilist is giving them away!'

The former heavyweight champion, known for a love of new cars, couldn't resist going to the showroom in Las Vegas where the new Bentley Azure, a glorious convertible and at $319,000 the most expensive car the Company had ever offered in the United States, was on show for one night on a hectic countrywide tour. He was smitten and told Chris Brown, the Rolls-Royce western states manager, that he would pay a $50,000 premium if he could drive the car away immediately.

The Azure was a prototype that had been admitted to the United States provided it was returned to Britain after the tour. Brown told him regretfully: 'I can't sell it, Mr Tyson. That would be illegal.' The promoter Don King, who was in the party, complete with bodyguards, shook with laughter and roared: 'Don't worry about that man. I've been doing illegal things for years.' Of course, he was joking.

Britain's legendary general, Field Marshall Bernard Montgomery – whose official title in later life was Montgomery of Alamein – believed that a leader must demonstrate style at all times and took his black and silver Rolls-Royce Park Ward Silver Wraith with him to war. The big limousine, with its famous grille sporting a union jack instead of the *Spirit of Ecstasy*, was shipped abroad to show the enemy that the Allies had arrived to stay. It was important also to Monty, whose nature was to intimidate the opposition, that he be seen commanding his men from a better car than the camouflaged Mercedes used by Field Marshall Rommel. The six-seat Wraith, built in 1939 and powered by a straight six 4.25-liter engine, had several unusual features. The driver's door could be unlocked only from the inside. The door and ignition locks turned counter-clockwise and when the ignition key was turned backwards, all the way round, a second switch had to be flicked to connect the circuit and make the starter button 'live'. How's that for an anti-theft device? Like China, Rolls-Royce made a specialty of confounding its enemies. Monty probably figured that the unorthodox ignition system would defeat any car thief drilled in logical mechanical training. This historic old motor car is living out her days as the prize exhibit in the Museum of Army Transport at Beverly in Yorkshire.

Some of the world's leading 'good-old-boy' communists did not permit political rhetoric to get in the way of comfort or a liking for the good life. Mao Tse Tung made the great leap forward from rickshaw to Rolls; Stalin had one and Lenin, the father of the Russian Revolution, who was selective in his egalitarian lifestyle, had nine Rolls-Royce cars, two of which are still in Moscow. One, in mint condition, is on show at the Lenin Central

Museum. Delivered in 1920, the five-seat Phaeton on a 1914 Eagle chassis weighs two tons and developed 75hp, with a top speed of about 125km/h. The other, a 1914 Ghost Continental with a torpedo body, is probably the only Rolls in history whose rear wheels were replaced by rubber caterpillar tracks.

Leonid Brezhnev, a former head of the Communist Party in the USSR, acquired several Rolls-Royce motor cars and the Company would send an engineer to Moscow, even at the height of the Cold War, to service them. The Kremlin acquisitions included four Shadow and Bentley models and a Silver Spirit. The top comrades, it seemed, knew how to protect a good capitalist investment.

A technician was also dispatched to Tehran to service the Shah's Rolls-Royce collection and to Morocco to give the King's cars a period tune-up. But the Company was not overly keen to see cars wind up where service was not available in the region.

Lawrence of Arabia took a fleet of nine armored Rolls-Royce 40/50hp into battle against the Turks. 'A Rolls in the desert,' he said, 'was above rubies. We drove them for eighteen months, not upon the polished roads of their makers' intentions, but across vile country at speed, day and night, carrying a ton of goods, and four or five men up.'

Built on a strengthened chassis, they were a combination of armored personnel carrier and pick-up truck, with a 5ft-wide tank turret up top that could swing around 360 degrees and out of which poked the menacing barrel of a huge machine gun. The outline of the famous radiator was still there, but thick steel doors substituted for the air-vanes. Just the ticket, I've often thought, for forcing your way through New York traffic where hordes of cabs could have been reduced to metal rubble in an instant.

The speed, reliability and strength of these demolition machines, and ability to absorb continuous punishment, gave them a terrific edge over the enemy. Despite carrying about four tons of armor plating, they would cruise over desert sands at up to 70mph, 'to destroy the enemy'.

One of the drivers who rejoiced in the name S.C. Rolls – some coincidence, but not related to the Honorable Charlie – described the mobility and great attributes of the cars in his book *Steel Chariots in the Desert*. On one occasion, he said, Lawrence took three of the armored cars and captured two Turkish posts, blew up a bridge, wiped out a Kurdish cavalry regiment, blew up another bridge and ripped up 600 pairs of rails – thereby throwing the whole Turkish supply system into chaos – all in one day! Nobody, to my knowledge, has cast doubt upon Mr Rolls's account.

Lowell Thomas, in his book *With Lawrence in Arabia*, recounts an interview with Colonel Lawrence after the armistice. Asked what he most would like to have, Lawrence recorded his admiration for Henry Royce's motor cars: 'I should like to have a Rolls-Royce with enough tires and petrol to last me all my life.'

Rolls-Royce designed and built fleets of armored cars for the British military in the First World War and some actually served in the Second World War. The MkII versions were fitted with double rear wheels to provide better traction on sand. A far cry, one might reflect, from the big luxurious royal Phantoms to come.

Henry Ford bought more than one Rolls and explained it away by pointing out that he was merely sampling the competition as any manufacturer would. He once said: 'Henry Royce was the only man to put heart into an automobile.' Ford purchased a Ghost in 1924 and when a bowler-hatted Rolls-Royce service engineer arrived at his door for a twelve-monthly check, the amazed Ford cabled Royce, saying: 'After I have sold one of my cars I do not want to see it or hear of it again.'

Only one American president, Woodrow Wilson, is on record as owning a Rolls-Royce. It is still running and we sought it out for the launch in Washington of the Silver Spirit and Silver Spur. To hype the launch and to do something a bit different, we rented Wilson's former home, just off Massachusetts Avenue, from the National Trust for an evening. We located Wilson's car, an Oxford tourer, in Maine, brought it to Washington and parked it in the driveway along with a new Spur. It came as something of a shock to journalists there that the former president owned a Rolls. The British ambassador, Sir Nicholas Henderson, who attended the event, bestowed posthumous congratulations on the late president for his fine judgment in acquiring a proper motor car.

Many aspire to the special feeling you experience when riding in a Rolls-Royce and Hong Kong provides the opportunity to depart the airport madhouse in style. Japanese tourists in particular happily pay a hefty premium to the Peninsula Hotel to be greeted by a liveried chauffeur and one of the hotel's fleet of ten Rolls-Royce cars.

People buy Rolls-Royce motor cars for many different reasons. Barry Sheen, the motorcycle-racing champion, asked by a journalist why somebody who piloted a two-wheel bike at suicidal speeds would drive a car so out of character with his lifestyle, said:

> I have a very noisy, stressful and quite dangerous job that makes big demands on me. At the end of the day, I want to leave it all behind and there's no better way to unwind than to cruise home quietly in a Rolls. It's the best thing Britain does.

Barry also had a wicked sense of humor. Invited to the factory to see how the cars were built and meet the people who made them, he complained to the engineering director that his Rolls got terrible mileage. 'I got only about eight to the gallon between the south of France and Calais.' Asked how fast he was driving, he said with a straight face: 'About 120mph most of the way.'

2

JUST WHAT IS A ROLLS-ROYCE?

We will have succeeded in our task if late on a winter's evening, in a dimly lit street, someone looks out of a window and catches a glimpse of a dark and travel-stained Silver Spirit and says 'A Rolls-Royce has just gone by'.

Those words by Fritz Fella, chief engineer for styling and new model projects, whose handiwork spanned more than forty years embracing Silver Clouds and Shadows and Spirits, give some idea of the values and commitment to getting it right, that imbued the Company and the many highly skilled people behind the name.

Fritz, a delightful gnome-like man, born in Austria, came to England as a boy, learned to speak impeccable Oxford English and loved Rolls-Royce more, possibly, than most of the British. He gave a *New York Times* journalist his take on the marque's position in the firmament. 'When you enter this car', he said:

You enter a different world. Many cars are faster than a Rolls-Royce and some are sportier to handle. But that's not what this car is about. This is for the man who's got just about everything. It's like entering a drawing room. It's this feeling of remoteness from the rest of the world, from everyday cares, that makes a Rolls-Royce different from all other cars.

Before delving into some of the remarkable attributes that combine to make 'An Empire on Four Wheels' as Fritz was fond of describing a Rolls-Royce, he told a German journalist how, as in any solid empire, change came slowly and only after considerable planning and testing:

We are not revolutionaries in motor car building. What interests us is not novelty, but the tried and true. We make changes in our cars only when we are absolutely certain that the novelty is better. We buy every car of outstanding caliber that is made anywhere in the world and take it apart to the very last screw. If there is a good idea in it, we test that idea for at least 50,000 miles. Then if we still like it, we begin to take an interest in it. The best example is the transmission we identified in a car made by General Motors. We had our own version, but the American one was better. Still, we are the people who built the first car with a heated rear window.

Before the Silver Spirit emerged, Fritz expounded on the rules of the game:

Our next must be a natural successor to our last car. We must aim to maintain product identity, not merely by using the distinctive grille and Flying Lady.

The 'Dobson-family Royce'. Derek Dobson, his son and five brothers, who between them served 211 years at Rolls-Royce Motor Cars.

Even without noticing those obvious features, anyone looking at the cars we have developed over the years should know that they are looking at a Rolls-Royce. Our designers must be bound by our traditions.

When the Silver Spirit and Spur were launched, the culmination of eight years' painstaking work by Fritz and his colleagues, *Road and Track* magazine noted that what they had done was to give the car a longer, lower and wider appearance than the Shadow and Wraith 'so that it now looks less like one of the stately homes of England proceeding down the road.'

. Fritz spent a lot of time talking to car stylists and studying their work to help him distinguish between trends that were transitory and those that would be longer lasting: 'The overriding consideration was that I had to make a motor car that was true to its heritage,' he said. By keeping a little distance from the rest of the industry, employing the best artisans to craft motor cars regarded the world-over as the finest, Rolls-Royce has marched quietly to its own drum and carved its own place at the top of the pyramid.

Certainly, as the American journalist Don Vorderman wrote:

> There are cars that go faster; will cling more tightly around corners and might be a tad quieter. But the Rolls-Royce, its leather and wood and Wilton carpeting setting the tone for an unsurpassed travel experience, represents an all-round package that sets it apart from mere mortals.

So, just what is a Rolls-Royce? What makes it so special that it is the most recognizable car in the world, and admired even by the millions of people who have never even ridden in one? There are many answers - a host of elements that come together in a sort of critical mass to create motor cars with a unique presence. Clearly, a major factor is distinctive, but generally understated styling, allied to good taste, not an easily definable quality but fitting the old saying: 'Not sure I can describe it, but I know it when I see it.'

An advertisement by C.S. Rolls, 1904.

Skillfully matched and cut Lombardian walnut veneers grace the completed instrument panel of a Corniche II.

Having turned wiring sphagetti into a perfectly organized loom, the craftsman then checks that each wire does what it should and is in the right place.

A Rolls-Royce is a magical blend of form and function, brought together by talented craftspeople and engineers, dedicated as was their mentor, Henry Royce, to producing the finest motor car human ingenuity could achieve. It is testament to their work that of the 130,000 or so built between Royce making the first one in 1904 and the Company hitting the wall as the century drew to a close, about three-quarters were still running, or in private collections and able to motor should the key be turned. I can't think of another company able to claim that seven out of ten of all the cars it had made are alive and purring.

One of the most important components of a Rolls-Royce was one an owner seldom saw and never got to own. It is a history book, a specification document that followed a car through each stage of production, listing the special features a customer had ordered and ensuring that each requirement had been met. It was also a record of how each car was built – the engineers and craftsmen and women who worked on it and in what sequence; which batches of steel, wood, veneer, leather, carpeting and mechanical components were used in its manufacture. All the materials and tests carried out were logged, so the origins of a problem, should one develop, could be traced.

And something else that amazed owners: the signature or initials of everyone who worked on the car also went into the book as tasks were completed, each taking responsibility for quality standards, finish and craftsmanship.

Quality has always been the key factor at every step. Each car would take between three and five months to build, coming off an assembly line that moved just a few feet each day and then only when each stage was completed and the craftsmen satisfied that the job had been done right. Each car was made up of 80,000 components, many of which were produced in the Rolls-Royce machine shop to be sure that the quality was absolutely right. The result was a motor car with several times the lifespan of an ordinary car.

At the Crewe factory, each engine was assembled by hand in bench areas with a history of engineering excellence – workshops where components for wartime Merlin aero-engines were precision machined. The same tolerances, to ten-thousandths of an inch, were stipulated for the car engines. One engineer took final responsibility for each one, which was run for two hours on test beds, with particular attention to quietness and vibration during which a specialist listened for unusual noises with the end of a dipstick. To his experienced ear, this was every bit as good as a stethoscope. One in every hundred was taken to the lab and put through a punishing twenty-hour test cycle, then stripped down to the last nut and bolt and every piece microscopically examined for signs of wear, the measurements of each component being computer-checked against original drawings. Then the engine was put back together and sent to the production line. A prototype of the legendary 6.75-liter engine that powered the motor cars for very many years was run at full throttle for the equivalent of 40,000 miles and found to be working well within accepted tolerances.

The company confidently, yet solemnly advised owners: 'Provided the engine is serviced and run on reputable fuel and oils with proper filtration and cooling, it will exceed 250,000 miles without the heads coming off for attention. Our engines regularly do just that.'

The turbos were subjected to extended full-power tests that I suspect would have made those of many other cars just blow up. At full throttle, the exhaust manifolds and down-pipes reached over 800 degrees centigrade and glowed red hot. Silver-plated nuts were used on the manifold to ensure the threads did not seize. Engineers were proud that every engine in the Bentley Turbo R and the Rolls-Royce Flying Spur was able to take full throttle acceleration from the moment it went on the road, though this was not recommended.

Even the exhaust system was acoustically tuned to suppress a wide range of sound frequencies. Should a technician on the 100 miles-plus test running by every car around the roads and lanes of Cheshire hear a sound that a roadside adjustment could not cure, he would send for a man with possibly the most acute hearing in the county. He would climb into the trunk, pull down the lid and lie with his ear to the carpeting, becoming a sort of human stethoscope, to identify the source. He had a sense of humor – you have to if you spend a few

From these sheets of rough-looking, paper–thin veneer, skilled craftsmen create the classic instrument panels and door cappings that set a Rolls-Royce apart from any other motor car.

An engineer takes his time handbuilding the engine.

Above and below: After rigorous bench-testing, one engine in every hundred is disassembled and checked for wear or imperfections.

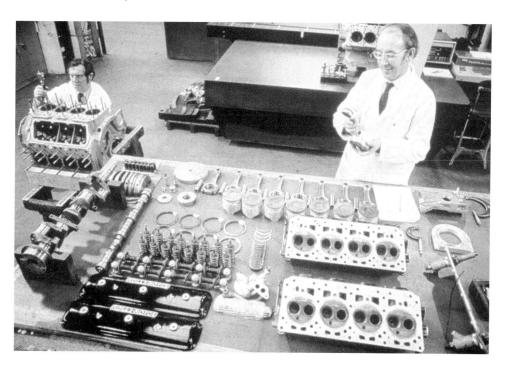

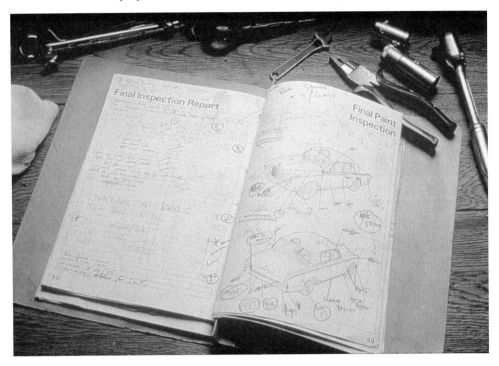

The History Book – The Rolls-Royce birth certificate and chronicle of a car's manufacture.

hours in a car trunk – and on occasion was known to lift the lid slightly and allow an arm to dangle out. The police would receive calls from alarmed citizens, reporting a body in the trunk of a passing Rolls, and an officer would wearily call the factory to remonstrate and threaten that next time, they would put the perpetrator in the slammer for the night.

The obsession with reliability was particularly reflected in the engine foundry. Forgings for crankshafts, machined to a tolerance of one ten-thousandth of an inch, rear axle and other key components were made extra long so that after heat-treating, a fillet could be cut off for metallurgical examination, checking tensile strength, durability and for any sign of a flaw that might lead to failure. All metals were given shock and stress tests. Henry Royce had a philosophy: 'Never use one bolt, if you can get two in' and he has always been taken at his word, regardless of the fact that additional built-in redundancy could be time-consuming and add cost.

Before other carmakers thought about it, Rolls-Royce was fitting two, and, for a time, three independent braking systems using discs and calipers of a size that would make you stare and not just one, but two massive calipers for each disc. If there were a failure, the car would still have four-wheel stopping power. The controller was a device that few owners ever heard of – 'the rat trap' as the engineers called it. One touch of the pedal triggered power circuits in the sophisticated braking system and would bring a car weighing more than two tons from 70mph to a halt within four seconds. Suspension and braking system fluids were kept at high pressure – about 2,000lb per square inch – for instant reaction and a valve ensured that braking had priority over the rear suspension. If pressure dropped, the valve would isolate the suspension, directing power to the brakes. Long before modern braking systems, the 1924 Ghost had an anti-lock servo-system not unlike one advertised by another manufacturer sixty-four years later as 'a major technological advance'. Rolls-Royce, sometimes, was way ahead of the engineering game.

Concern for safety has always been paramount. All braking and hydraulic system components, along with self-adjusting hydraulic tappets for the engine, were ultrasonically cleaned in a bath of paraffin to prevent contamination by airborne dust particles. Crown wheels and pinions

Few hides pass the test as experts check for blemishes or unacceptable markings.

were meticulously matched to ensure quietness in the rear axle and camshafts were driven by fine-pitch gears, a tradition going back to Henry Royce, who abhorred chains, and instructed that a new component had to bring value to the motor car, making it quieter or more reliable and efficient.

In the quest for quietness and smoothness, Rolls-Royce designed a unique electric gear selector. No push or pull was needed to engage drive or an intermediate gear. A slight pressure on the lever was sufficient for the transmission to respond without fuss or noise. A quiet interior has always been mandatory, even when accelerating to 100mph and beyond – including Bentley with a more lusty performance than a Rolls. Mulsanne Turbo customers were advised with quiet satisfaction that they could go from rest to 60mph in 7 seconds and 60 to 90mph in 7.4 seconds – 'and you can still hear every word at 120mph'.

When other manufacturers were relying on thermal switches, Rolls-Royce was using electronics, even in the speedometer to avoid any possibility of a noisy drive cable, and, because the occupants were pretty well insulated from the outside world, a light warning of ice outside was included in the instrument panel. Sensors inside and outside the vehicle, feeding temperatures to the air-conditioning control center, even took into account the heat of the sun coming through the windshield – a factor known as solar gain.

The suspension, with gas and coil springs sensitive to load, had a hydraulic self-leveling system to keep the car on an even keel and even took into account the emptying of the fuel tank. It was strong, and engineers claimed it would take the weight of a fully grown African elephant on the trunk without giving more than an inch. However, this test was not encouraged by the Company.

Another convenient touch saved the driver from fiddling about with a dipstick. With the push of a button, the fuel gauge switched instantly to an engine oil reading. A splendid sop to gentlemen in tuxedos who recoiled from the possibility of getting grime on their cuffs while checking the oil.

After three months of painstaking work the craftsmen's job is finished and it is time for the all-important female touch to ensure that the car gleams as a Rolls-Royce should.

Though the collision was severe, the tank-like front structure of a Silver Shadow absorbed the impact so well that all the doors would still open and the driver was able to walk away.

There are hundreds of features and processes that from the early days have set Rolls-Royce apart from others – their existence driven by an absolute commitment to 'get it right first time' and make it of the highest quality.

You get what you pay for, as the saying goes, and this certainly applied to the body, its anti-corrosive treatment and coats of paint. The body shell would be worked on for a couple of weeks before it even saw a mechanic. After steam-cleaning to remove a coat of protective oil, four days would be spent on detailed examination, correcting blemishes in the metal or deviations from specification. Then a zinc coating would go onto all areas likely to be exposed to corrosion. The huge sub-frames were also protected, inside as well as out, inhibiting oil being sprayed through access holes which were then sealed. At the end of week one, if the work passed a rigorous inspection, the shell went to the paint shop where, after further cleaning, it was submerged in primer to form a barrier almost impervious to water, and several coats of weather-resistant epoxy-primers. Two coats of black bituminous material were applied to protect the underside and also help to deaden sound. The body shell was rubbed down several times between more coats of primer, as the prelude to the real paintwork – between ten and fourteen coats. If the paint was chipped during road testing, another coat was applied if necessary – another expensive commitment to a beautiful final paint finish that would last for very many years.

Rolls-Royce has long been noted for the quality and richness of its color schemes. Each coat was hand sprayed, then hand rubbed before the next application and the final protective coating was 1½ times thicker than that on most cars. To check durability, painted panels were taken to Australia to bake for days in the blistering sun of the outback and to Northern Scandinavia to see how they stood up to extended winter exposure.

The beautiful double line running from the front to the back of the coachwork was hand applied with a brush. It was fascinating to see a craftsman carefully dip a fine brush into the paint until he had just the right amount, squint along the car's waistline and without pausing, apply two

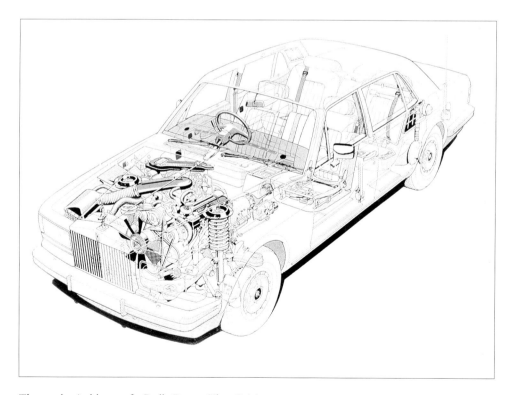

The mechanical heart of a Rolls-Royce Silver Spirit.

The Silver Spirit emerged from the shadows.

remarkably straight lines. His hand would appear to shake, akin perhaps to an athlete limbering up with energetic arm and leg movements before getting down to the mark, then suddenly become calm and focused. It is personal handiwork by such craftsmen and meticulous attention to other details that make up the kaleidoscope that gives the motor car its special character.

A Rolls-Royce is a beautifully designed and crafted mechanical device, but its heart and soul are its people – the engineers and artisans who pour their talents into it and pass those skills on to their children. One third of the workforce proudly point to more than twenty-five years with the Company, and seven members of one family, the Dobsons, had clocked 211 years of service when the Crewe factory celebrated its fiftieth anniversary in 1988. Derek Dobson, who began a seven-year apprenticeship in 1946, had more than forty years' service and his five brothers, 'mere youngsters', had twenty-five to thirty-seven years in tool-making, prototypes, leather coach trimming and road-testing. Derek's son, Andrew, also worked there as a coachbuilder.

While looking to the future, Rolls-Royce always acknowledged the past. In the early 1970s, Charles W. Ward, director of the Mulliner Park Ward division where the magnificent Corniche convertibles, coupés and Phantoms were meticulously coach-built, said: 'We are moving today toward light alloy aircraft-type construction although the craftsmanship of our men is inherited directly from the days of coaches drawn by six horses with postillions in knee breeches.'

Rolls-Royce motor cars are what they are because the Company has always believed in uncompromising quality in everything it has ever done – engineering, design, materials and skilled people. From the outset, easier and cheaper ways of doing things have never been an option.

What is a Rolls-Royce? It means tradition – the finest example of its kind – and some of its attributes are ethereal and difficult to pinpoint. But, as has been said, you'll know it when you see it and that certainly applies to a Rolls-Royce, no matter how old. A colleague, Melvyn Reynolds, once observed: 'Had Henry Royce been on the global stage at the appropriate moment in history, he would probably not have invented the wheel. But almost certainly, he would have been the first to make it perfectly round.'

I have no doubt that the great mechanic smiled, and agreed absolutely.

3

IT'S SERIOUS MONEY, BUT YOU CAN GET A LAUGH OUT OF IT

Trying to separate the well-heeled from a chunk of their wealth – like up to $500,000 for a motor car groaning under the weight of a couple of tons of machinery and wood and floating the magic to persuade them that this is an irresistible purchase, can be challenging, and at times very funny. Now and again, one is privileged to observe a scene so comical, it continues to elicit a chuckle years later. Such a memorable episode occurred at a formal company luncheon in New Jersey's Meadowlands – home of the New York Giants and later the stomping ground of the Sopranos.

It was a ground-breaking day for the new Rolls-Royce Motors North American headquarters, a miserable winter's morning, a cold mist enveloping the desolate marshes that would have given the surface of the moon a good run for a prize as the most unattractive landscape in the universe. For half a century the Meadowlands had been a massive rubbish dump, its only redeeming features being perhaps a distant view of the New York skyline and quick access to Manhattan through the Lincoln Tunnel, when there was not a traffic back-up, that is.

Brushing aside a widely held suspicion that Jimmy Hoffa's final resting place lay within the end zone at the stadium and historical allegations that many nefarious activities had been conducted around the swamplands, the development authority dreamed of building a huge corporate center. It held out low-cost loans to entice blue-chip companies to set up shop there and celebrated as a coup a decision by Rolls-Royce to come to the party.

It needed more than a press release to get journalists out for the ground-breaking ceremony – the Company's directors earnestly poring over blueprints spread over the hoods of three Rolls-Royce cars. It was a curious scene, the mists swirling around expensive motor cars as hard-hatted, suit-wearing executives tried to look interested in the sodden paper, while distastefully eyeing mud clinging to their Gucci's. A couple of spades of sodden earth were dutifully dug up and everybody fled to the Holiday Inn, the only place in the area where a corporate lunch could be held. It was that, or a diner on the truck-laden Route 3.

You will appreciate we are not talking about the type of hotel that is *de rigueur* for a Rolls-Royce event involving guests, media or new models. The windowless banqueting room could only be described as depressing and it sported dark wallpaper that could have figured in the hallucinations that spooked Ray Milland in *The Lost Weekend*. Already on the tables were tired-looking prawn cocktails that appeared to have been there for an hour or two.

Among the guests were two non-executive directors of the North American Rolls-Royce subsidiary – bankers accustomed to the opulent dining rooms of Wall Street where discreet waitresses smoothly serve and a gentleman's gentleman, usually a butler recruited from England, in black jacket and striped trousers, skillfully pours a fine Bordeaux.

Not today. As a leathery piece of New York strip was banged down in front of the reporters and other guests, there was a wondrous scene that made the whole miserable morning gloriously

A Silver Wraith owner
indicated dire consequences
if the Company did not give
him a new engine.

worthwhile. New Jersey is well blessed with larger-than-life characters, and we had one here – an ample, motherly waitress under the gun and with no time to waste on Manhattan niceties. The kitchen doors bounced open and out she came apace, each large fist clutching a gallon jug of Californian wine of indeterminate origin and vintage. Globules of condensation ran down the flagons of near frozen white and red as she steamed up to the top table and addressed the most senior Rolls-Royce banker: 'What'll it be, Mac?' It was a moment to savor.

The startled Wall Street heavy and his fellow Rolls directors – American and British – meekly muttered or pointed to the red or the white jug, metaphorically reeling from a merry vignette that might have been devised by Woody Allen. Martha Stewart, America's guru of stylish entertaining, who grew up in Nutley a mile or two away, would surely have dropped in a dead faint. The endearing, no-nonsense Jersey lady, with a lot of work to get through and not much support, ploughed around the tables, sloshing wine into each glass and exhorting the guests to enjoy. All that was needed to complete this glorious scene was Jackie Gleason as a *maitre'd* at his lugubrious best. Though the Rolls-Royce man within me probably should have tut-tutted, it did not. I have always enjoyed pricking the bubble of pomposity and contrived correctness (the sort you see when the cameras home in on a selection of ' terribly correct' establishment spectators at Wimbledon) and I could feel myself losing my composure. Fleeing to the corridor, I bit my knuckles to hold back the hysteria that threatened to explode and disgrace me.

A manager, sensing that the event was fraying a bit at the edges, whispered that new management had come in only a couple of days before and was still assessing adjustments that might have to be made. I wished him well, the staff he had inherited had enlivened a dull corporate day and brought home to the bankers that there is indeed a whole, different world west of the Hudson.

MESSAGE FROM A MAFIA HEAVYWEIGHT

Rolls-Royce motor cars occasionally run into problems triggered by owner neglect. Whatever the reason, it is academic when you get a sinister phone call such as the one the regional manager received from the owner of a Silver Wraith. He came in looking a little pale and said:

> I've just had a call from a guy with a gravelly voice who said he knows that I live on the 27th floor of my building, and that we take the dog out every night at about nine. He said he needs a new engine – the dealer says no, it is his fault. He is as mad as hell, and if he doesn't get one, he says, two of his associates will be round to see me.

I laughed. 'I'd give him a bloody engine.'

'But they cost $20,000,' the manager replied.

'It can't cost the Company anything like that,' I said, reflecting that I'd heard there was a tariff around there for having things done to people – a couple of thousand for a roughing-up and broken bones and a bit more for a real job – like people could be made to disappear for $5,000? 'If I lived 200ft up in a high rise, and some guy called up from Long Island threatening a visit by his friends, I'd ask "How soon do you want the engine?"'

They were all getting their knickers in a twist, as the English say, and the threat was reported to the FBI. Further calls discussing the problem were monitored, but the owner, having made his point, took care not to suggest that any harm would befall Rolls-Royce personnel if they rejected his entreaties.

It turned out he had been somewhat neglectful about servicing or checking the oil level and, after many months, not surprisingly, it ran low, causing even a Rolls-Royce engine to protest by shutting down. Eventually, an accommodation was reached, as they say, and the owner came to the party with a contribution toward the cost of a new engine. Result – a mollified owner and a relieved Rolls executive.

THE KEYS... THE KEYS...

We had our funny moments at Rolls-Royce. There was a delightful episode of near farce, worthy of the BBC comedy *Fawlty Towers* at the media introduction in southern Spain of the Silver Shadow II and Silver Wraith II. A dozen cars were driven by a factory team to a posh hotel near Malaga and small groups of journalists were flown from London for test drives.

The BBC needed a car for the better part of two days to prepare pieces for both news and the *Top Gear* motoring program. They got a lot done on day one. The sun shone and the crew was able to stop at will to film its comings and goings through the hills and on what pass for expressways in Spain. On day two, with just a few hours remaining before the BBC had to leave, a catastrophe! The ignition key of the light blue Shadow they had been using and which continuity required they stay with, could not be found. Normally a spare key was taped behind the front bumper as a precaution against such mishaps. Not on this car – Murphy and his laws were at work.

Rolls-Royce executives' blood pressure began to rise – always an interesting happening to observe – and the distress-factor on the Richter scale was demonstrated by David Roscoe, the normally jovial PR director, noted for a scintillating wit and skillful massaging of journalistic egos. In party mood, David could do a marvelous impersonation of John Cleese, immortalized by *Monty Python* and his wonderfully ludicrous 'Ministry of Funny Walks' act where in civil service uniform of black jacket, striped trousers and bowler, he covered the Whitehall sidewalk in exaggerated strides and lunges, plunging British viewers into hysterics.

'The keys, the keys,' Roscoe kept exhorting as he frantically circled the car, peering underneath, on top, in the trunk and under the hood. Fingers were stabbed into lambs' wool

Great drives and refreshments at great houses – a great way to sell cars.

carpeting seeking the means to extricate the Company from what was becoming a worrying situation.

David Plastow, Rolls chief executive was mightily concerned and as the search for the key turned up nothing, asked John Hollings, the director of engineering, if he could hot-wire the ignition or something to get the car started.

Hollings, a towering, bespectacled and mustachioed figure, six foot three, and not noted for excitable projections of his views, growled: 'No, most definitely, no.'

'Come on there has to be a way of by-passing the switch and getting the thing started,' said an exasperated Plastow, who saw the goodwill and value of the interviews he had given diminishing in proportion to the increasing impatience of the BBC crew. Hollings produced the Mohammad Ali rope-a-dope punch. 'Hot-wiring the ignition would be dangerous. As the publicity people are always telling the Press, you can't steal a Rolls-Royce without the key. (a steel pawl locked the transmission until the ignition key was turned). If we try to wire the starter, the car could come to a sudden halt in the middle of Malaga as the transmission lock kicks in.'

This, with a BBC crew aboard, taping as the car cruised through the busy town center, was a prospect not to be contemplated. With time pressing, the BBC reluctantly took off with another car, hoping the difference in color would not be too apparent and that the audience would accept that Rolls-Royce made cars in more than one color!

A few minutes later the key was found – in the trunk. It had slipped out of a driver's shirt pocket as he stacked packages. A Rolls-Royce test driver, doing a creditable impersonation of an Andretti, jumped into the car and went after the BBC crew, slaloming the Rolls around bends at speeds and angles that would have horrified Mr Engineer Hollings. He caught up with them before they had done much shooting, and called out 'I think this is the one you need'.

'WHERE'S THE CHAMPERS AND DO HAVE ANOTHER TROUT, TOMMY?'

Rolls-Royce has for many years operated a marketing technique known as 'Great Drives'. The objective is to get the right rumps onto the Connolly leather. The targets are old money, perhaps ready for another car, or the *nouveau riche* who believed a Rolls to be the instrument of instant social acceptance.

So long as they had the loot, they would receive a beautifully inscribed invitation outlining 'The Rolls-Royce experience'. They would assemble at some aristocrat's country house at a decent hour, perhaps 10a.m., where they would be introduced to a small fleet of proper motor cars.

After coffee they would set off through the countryside, stopping to change drivers now and again and winding up at another stately home for lunch. Then off again with somebody else behind the wheel to another castle or sprawling estate, where tea would be served and probably a glass or two of bubbly.

Sometimes sales resulted depending occasionally on how well the guests had imbibed. It was not an inexpensive enterprise, but the Company usually came out ahead. These events were organized by the Crewe marketing people, one of whom, I recall, could be a little pompous but excellent at fussing over the guests, especially if they had a title. This contrived bonhomie extended to the ability to make them feel special with the delivery of such appealing phrases as 'Do have another trout, Tommy, or perhaps another glass of champers?'

The alternative day out would be a visit to the factory, starting in London's Berkeley Square, where the guests would board a luxury coach fitted with videos and refreshments. Some of the aristocratic owners and potential owners aboard would be old boys who were dead ringers for an avuncular Alistair Sim or the lovable old buffer, A.E. Matthews, who specialized in playing benevolent absent-minded peers in Ealing comedies. Some, looking as though they had just staggered out of the Tory Carlton Club after a fine dinner followed by fine port, were the sort who were known to say: 'First thing I do in the morning is look at *The Times* obituary column. If I'm not in there I get up and go to the office or enjoy a little pigeon shooting.'

'BY JOVE, THAT WAS A NEAR ONE, BERTIE'

With the resurgence of the Bentley range, a meander through the countryside, while ideal for a Rolls, wouldn't cut it for the sportier cars with the Flying B. A potential Bentley buyer needed to experience the scalding performance of these amazing two-ton projectiles and the only place to demonstrate this was at MIRA – Britain's Motor Industry Research Association's high-speed test track.

One owner-participation Turbo R day out backfired. The elderly owners loved it, imagining they were the Bentley boys of yore, thrilled to be whizzed around the banked circuit at something approaching 120mph. That was until a tire burst. The car, traveling at a speed that would cover a football field in about 1½ seconds, lurched against the top steel guard rail and slewed all over the banking. Fortunately the skill of the test driver brought it to rest safely in the infield. Following the altercation with the guard rail that had happily prevented it being launched into space, the car was in less than showroom condition, 'pretty roughed up' was a more accurate description, but the passengers were safe.

One witness observed: 'They staggered out of the half-wrecked Bentley muttering "By jove I think I'm alive because I was in a Roller."'

The reason for the tire blowout led to a vigorous debate between the Company, the MIRA people and the tire manufacturer, each disclaiming responsibility. One faction said it must have been a nail on the track; another a tire defect. I'm not sure they ever nailed it down.

Most importantly, the tremendous strength of the Bentley body shell and the car's impressive stability protected the occupants from injury and the delightful old boys who wobbled away, survived to drink a Mayfair-club toast to 'those splendid chaps at Rolls-Royce who make such a jolly strong motor car'.

PEER BENEATH THE CARPET? GOOD IDEA

We also had a near disaster in Chicago, the great town known proudly as 'The City with the Big Shoulders'. We were introducing the Silver Spur limousine, a substantial, gleaming vehicle bearing an eye-popping sticker eight times the price of the nearest American limousine. It was a great media attraction. It was wintertime and those who have experienced a Chicago winter will appreciate the impractability of demonstrating the car outside.

So, we rented the ballroom of large hotel and by taking off the doors could just squeeze the big limousine through. Our engineer delicately eased the limousine back and forth to get it into the best position for photography. Suddenly a hotel manager galloped across the carpet shouting, 'Stop, for God's sake stop'.

The center of the ballroom floor, it seemed, was made up of glass blocks which, though thick, were not designed to take nearly three tons of Rolls-Royce motor car. Nobody had thought to ask how much the car weighed, or tell us that a glass floor lay beneath the carpeting. I still dare hardly think of the mayhem that nearly befell us. The hotel was a moment away from being the only place in town to boast a basement with a built-in Rolls-Royce limousine.

The Press and television would have had a great picture and the insurance claims would have been horrendous. That is to say nothing of a wrecked limousine. Upon reflection, the publicity might have been worth the loss of the car. Rolls-Royce people do not subscribe to provocative suggestions like that.

WHAT THE HELL HAPPENED TO THE FLYING LADY?

New York City was the setting for a funny, if slightly embarrassing Rolls-Royce event in June 1998 when the Silver Seraph was unveiled to an audience of journalists and wealthy owners at a pricey reception at the upscale Four Seasons restaurant, the only place I know where you are supposed to enjoy the austere ambience of a bank lobby as you savor your caviar.

The principal ballerina of the Royal Ballet was flown from London and donned flowing robes to depict a life-size *Spirit of Ecstasy*. In a humorous piece, Jean Jennings, editor of *Automobile Magazine*, described the scene as the Duke of Edinburgh and guests gathered for the dramatic car reveal. She wrote:

> As famed soprano Joanne Lunn belted out a stirring rendition of Handel's *Let the Bright Seraphim*, Ms Bull (the ballerina) did a few dazzling interpretations of the Flying Lady. Our tiny dancer with the massive and angular calves slid the brocade shroud forward, hooked the Flying Lady, and tugged. The hood ornament she had been hired to impersonate slid gracefully out of harm's way and into the grille, just as it was engineered to do. Now we had a ballerina *en pointe*, breast jutting forward, impersonating nothing behind her until the last seconds of her program when the real thing majestically reappeared.

This is the stuff of media hilarity and PR nightmares. Rolls-Royce had spent much time and expense to meet European safety regulations that outlawed frontal protuberances that might damage a pedestrian in the unfortunate event of violent contact with the car. The *Spirit of Ecstasy* had been designed to sink elegantly into the radiator shell should she be subjected to impact. No one had foreseen the effects of a strong tug on the little figure at an unveiling ceremony. The Rolls executives were paralyzed. It was like something out of a Leslie Nielsen comedy.

This new Silver Spur limousine came within a whisker of crashing through a ballroom floor in Chicago.

WHAT'S WITH THE ICE FOG?

A few years earlier we were a whisker away from a model's unveiling turning into farce by crashing the star of the show. I believe I was the only person who saw the funny side of it. Western States dealers gathered for their first glimpse of the Turbo R at the Plaza hotel in Montery, California. Chief executive, Peter Ward, with the editor of a leading automotive magazine in the passenger seat of a bright-red Turbo, was to sail in from the street through clouds of dry ice around the courtyard gates.

Inspired, perhaps by the majestic shots swooping through the mists atop the mountains near Salzburg and, zooming in on Julie Andrews trilling 'The hills are alive…', an attempt was made to give the car a similarly dramatic reveal but found it was not quite to be. The fog billowing off the dry ice was so thick, the Turbo nearly collided with the stone pillars, which would have been an interesting and expensive first for a Bentley introduction. The car more or less groped its way hesitantly into sight, somewhat losing the spectacular effect the planners had promised.

Further deflation occurred when the two got out and Ward introduced the journalist-guru who seemed to be quite miffed when he realized that his words were drowned out by background noise from nearby waterfront activity and that most of the guests and their spouses did not seem to know who he was or indeed show any interest in his opinion of the car.

A more effective and certainly simpler strategy would have been to place the car in the courtyard and unveil it when they all had a drink in their hands and were receptive to a few upbeat words from Ward.

WHAT'S IN A NAME?

Finding the perfect name for a car is serious business. It's got to a point where the potential for attention-grabbing names for new cars seems to be just about exhausted. Mustang/ Thunderbird/Grand Prix/Explorer/Expedition and so many more that conjure up automotive excitement have been taken. Computers now spew out suggestions. Lexus and Acura were the product of electronics rather than the brainchild of humans.

But, earnest creative people still pound away, dreaming up advertising copy, slogans or new car names, and sometimes their desperate searches produce a real boner. General Motors had a red face when preparing to market the Chevy Nova in Central and South America. 'No va' in Spanish, it discovered, meant 'won't go'.

In 2004, a new Buick, the *La Crosse*, named to suggest a touch of Gallic sophistication, was set to debut in Toronto when somebody discovered that this phrase referred to an act of self-gratification in French-Canadian slang. A Canadian journalist laughed: 'In the States, *La Crosse* is a sport. Here, it is a sin!' The name was changed to *Allure* in Canada. Ford had to do a back-pedal in South America with the *Caliente* – a word, it discovered, being a Brazilian term for a hooker.

The car industry is not alone. The slogan made famous by Frank Purdue: 'It takes a tough man to make a tender chicken' translated into Spanish: 'It takes an aroused man to make a chicken affectionate.'

Rolls-Royce, too, has had its moments. The prefix Silver has formed part of the name of many classic models. The name favored for the car that eventually became the Silver Shadow was Silver Mist. It sounded mysterious and classical until someone heard that in German, 'mist' is slang for manure.

The Camargue almost wound up being called Lagata – until it was pointed out that Lagata is a musical term meaning 'slowly, without breaks'. Eventually, Rolls-Royce turned again to France, which has provided the Corniche, Azure and Mulsanne with their splendid titles and decided that the wild horses region, the Camargue, was just the ticket.

HOW DO YOU ANSWER THIS?

It helps to have a wicked sense of humor in the PR business and David Roscoe, my public relations colleague at Crewe, certainly had that. He was asked by a journalist about a wire story reporting that the safety-obsessed Volvo was using cadavers in crash testing.

'Does Rolls-Royce use real bodies in its crash tests?' he enquired. 'I do not believe we do,' said Roscoe, 'but if we did, I'm sure they would have to be titled.'

PROUD HARVEST

The town of Crewe is very proud of Rolls-Royce and for decades has had a tagline on the boundary signs proclaiming: 'Home of the Best Car in the World'. The factory has played a major role in the area's economy for well over half a century, so it was not surprising that a trendy vicar who ministered near the plant decided to feature the fruits of industry at his harvest festival.

He asked Rolls-Royce to bring along a Silver Spirit and by opening both doors of the church found they could just squeeze the car into the aisle. While they were doing this, a journalist from a local paper asked what was going on. The vicar said: 'This is the new Rolls-Royce Silver Spirit and it is just coming in for its first service.'

LOOKING FOR A SENSE OF HUMOR AT MERCEDES

The Germans, as many Englishmen will tell you, are not reckoned to figure much in the humour league, having a serious approach to life and, along with the French (whom the British have fought for a thousand years and probably will continue so to do – in or out of the European Community), qualify as the people they would least like to be stranded with on an island without CNN.

Over the years, I've enjoyed gently pulling the legs of Brits and Americans working for German companies and have been intrigued by how Teutonic even the English become when they have had a few years under the influence of Mercedes or other strongly nationalistic employers.

A little straight-faced tugging of their uptight string can get them twitching and a calm suggestion such as 'relax, do not be so tense' can drive them over the edge. There are continentals of course, who do not care for the sometimes weird British sense of humor. And it doesn't do much for *entente cordiale* when *The Times* of London comes up with headlines virtually designed to antagonize the French. Years ago, a story about a fog blanketing hundreds of square miles, was headlined: 'Massive fog brings Britain to a standstill. Europe cut off.'

There was a merry moment for me in New York when Bruce Wennerstrom, founder of the Madison Avenue Sports Car & Chowder Society, which holds what might loosely be called a 'car enthusiasts' monthly commune' at Sardi's in Manhattan, asked me to talk about Rolls-Royce and its mystique to the motley collection of members. These included journalists and a large number of networking automotive advertising salesmen and 'PR practitioners', as they choose to describe themselves in these days of self-aggrandizing nomenclature.

Wennerstrom cautioned that when they did not like what the speaker said, they'd been known to throw bread rolls. I told him with a grin: 'If they chuck anything at me, they'll get it right back.' With a contingent from the Mercedes PR department right at the front of the crowded room, I couldn't resist a bit of the agent provocateur. 'About European cars,' I began. 'Some of you might have seen the interview Bill Mitchell (the General Motors design chief) gave recently on his retirement.'

Mitchell, who was responsible for a range of notable cars, was asked if he was influenced by European styling, particularly Mercedes-Benz, when he designed the distinctive lines of the Seville. 'Sure I was influenced by the Europeans,' he replied. 'But not by Mercedes. When I was a boy, my father told me "if you are going to steal, rob a bank, not a grocery store". I stole from Rolls-Royce.'

The assembled throng roared, and sadly, the only group that did not seem to appreciate the story was the Benz team. A journalist friend of mine told me later: 'I wish I'd taken a picture of the Mercedes guys. The caption could have read "Ever heard Auld Lang Syne sung through clenched teeth?"'

A while later, another opportunity presented itself for an impish sideswipe at Mercedes – who I have always acknowledged, make a very good car – a luxurious Panzer maybe – but a solid metal brick that gives you a better chance than most of walking away from an accident. Mercedes announced a first. It would offer free roadside assistance to any owner who broke down between 10a.m. and 10p.m. The *Associated Press* called and asked if Rolls-Royce had a similar scheme to come to the aid of stranded owners. I was floored. We had not even thought about it. Towing and other services could run into serious money when you had hundreds of miles between a small number of dealers spread over many states.

What could I possibly say to a wire service whose story would go worldwide within the hour, without giving the impression that the Germans had stolen a march on us?

'No,' I said. 'Rolls-Royce doesn't have a breakdown service. We've never found one to be necessary.' That was chutzpa on an Olympic scale, but what was the alternative with but a moment to react?

Mischievously, I added in the form of a question to the *Associated Press* reporter: 'The Mercedes program appears to be somewhat restrictive. What happens if the Benz conks out between 10:01p.m. and breakfast time?'

He said: 'I think I'll get back to them on that.'

4

BEVERLEY HILLS NIGHTMARE AND OTHER BUMPS IN THE ROAD

Imagine the scene that belongs in a luxury car dealer's darkest nightmare – Wilshire Boulevard, Beverly Hills, at the height of midday traffic and a media circus outside your chic Rolls-Royce showroom as an owner parades a graffiti-daubed Silver Shadow with a lemon tree sticking out of the roof. The slogan proclaims: 'This Lemon was sold to me by Rolls-Royce.' The troublesome car has driven its owner to breaking point. He has hacked a hole in the roof, planted the lemon tree in it and it waves in the wind like the flags fluttering on a cruise ship. He hauled the car on to a trailer, put on a tuxedo and accompanied by a couple of shapely and scantily attired California blondes riding shotgun has journeyed from the Newport Beach area, up Interstate 405 – one of the most heavily trafficked freeways in the country – to Beverly Hills, the spiritual American home of Rolls-Royce.

Even here in the Hollywood hinterland where many of the people are, shall we say, unusual, and the bizarre is taken in stride, this procession stopped the traffic. The colorful wagon train is something new even for Wilshire Boulevard, the elegant thoroughfare that winds from downtown Los Angeles all the way to the ocean at Santa Monica, intersecting with Rodeo Drive at Beverly Hills, the ultimate monument to extravagance and excess where movie stars, producers and the like will splash $10,000 or more on a couple of suits.

Even for these cool movers, the sight of an angry Rolls owner in black tie out in the noonday sun, waving his arms, shaking the lemon tree and bawling attention to the decimated luxury car and a couple of pirouetting blondes cavorting on the sidewalk, is not normal behavior. Quite startling, in fact, when you are en route to your designer water, shredded carrot and lettuce entrée and double-decaf cappuccino at the Four Seasons or the Beverly Wilshire.

P.T. Barnum is nowhere in sight, but the street carnival could be his handiwork. The not-so-subtle artistic graffiti proclaiming its unhappy message hits home with the onlookers. The trailer, with its colorful Rolls-Royce cargo, stops right outside Rolls-Royce of Beverly Hills – a swish cathedral of commerce dedicated to answering the prayers and aspirations of the *nouveau riche*, as well as the traditional hedonistic heavy hitters of the show business community, for whom the latest Rolls or Bentley is *de rigueur*.

The owner shouted the odds about his Rolls-lemon to an expanding crowd. Television crews and a reporter from the *Los Angeles Times* turn up. The show was on the road. This was an almost heart-stopping experience for anyone in the business of selling very expensive products and relying upon sophistication, stylish presentation, polish and discretion to persuade a prospect to part with a lot of serious money. For the Rolls-Royce dealer here, image is everything. More than anywhere else, he's selling the sizzle as much as the steak.

The president of Rolls-Royce of Beverly Hills, Tony Thompson, not your typical car dealer, being a beautifully spoken, immaculately suited English gentleman, always looking as though he'd just stepped out of a Mayfair club, just about threw a fit when he saw the pandemonium outside his showroom. 'Get that fellow out of here!' he shouted, shaking with a fury fuelled by the awful realization that in the town where media-hype was invented, his business was taking an Exocet missile. The only soothing statement I could dream up to try to explain it away would be: 'Rolls-Royce enjoys the patronage of a diverse range of entrepreneurial and self-expressing individuals who add color and character to our world.'

The rubber-neckers, en route to Van Cleef and Arpels or Spago, drove by at a crawl, gaping at the spectacle. The Mercedes and BMW dealers farther along Wilshire came out to stare at the commotion; shuddered and ducked back inside, breathing 'there but for the grace of...'.

With the horror story unfolding like a black comedy, Thompson jumped on the phone to the Rolls-Royce headquarters. I had never heard the normally urbane Tony so hyper. Usually he projected the charm and soothing demeanor of Sir Humphrey Appleby of the BBC's *Yes Prime Minister*. But his fuse was lit. In a state of semi-controlled hysteria, he attempted to describe what was happening, shouting: 'This bloody lunatic out here is destroying my business and torpedoing Rolls-Royce – and I did not even sell him the ****ing car!' I had never heard him use an expletive. Clearly, he was upset.

I was nearly 3,000 miles away, trying to picture a scene that though comical to onlookers, and making me chuckle, was potentially serious for the Company's image in the epicenter of its most important market, the lucrative gravy train known as southern California. 'This could happen only in California,' I mused. In New Jersey the owner might have just looked for a Tony Soprano-like mediator to persuade a dealer to buy the car back.

But this one was having his day in the sun and condemning Rolls-Royce with evangelical zeal. I said to Tony: 'Whatever you do, do not go outside. It's not an interview you can win.' I suggested he call the splendid Beverly Hills police department whose iron-fist commitment to a quiet law-abiding atmosphere extends even to stopping anybody strolling in an area of expensive real estate and asking: 'What are you doing here and why are you not in a car?'

The squad cars added to the gridlock and the swelling crowd turned Wilshire Boulevard into something like the approaches to Dodger Stadium on game night. The officers looked at the loader and apparently found a defective rear light that required the vehicle's removal from the street. Later that day, I got a call from a reporter in Los Angeles. What did Rolls-Royce think about the Wilshire Boulevard circus? It was a delicate moment. How could I defuse a damaging and weird event that might make some people think twice about buying a Rolls-Royce once that stuff got on the evening news? And even more alarming, if the story hit the wires, we'd have national publicity. 'What about this guy in the tux and his lemon Rolls?' the reporter asked.

'Well,' I proffered. 'To cut a hole in the roof and plant a tree in there strikes me as being a most unusual way to treat an expensive motor car. Rolls-Royce owners are extremely demanding, expecting perfection and understandably so. But occasionally they can become emotional if the car doesn't perform as well as they expect.'

Even a Rolls could have off days, I went on and being a complicated piece of machinery could require attention. However, this gentleman had given vent to his feelings in a way that was not characteristic of Rolls-Royce owners. Colleagues, hearing me putting the spin on an awkward situation, would back out of the office to put distance between themselves and the bolt of lightning they were certain the Almighty would unleash in my direction at any time.

I told the journalist that the Company would be happy to begin a dialogue with the aggrieved owner when he had calmed down and would do everything it could to restore his faith in Rolls-Royce. Much as we sympathized with his distress, we had to focus on any shortcomings the motor car might have had before he took the axe to it and given it a unique paint job. We could not entertain a request for payment for a new roof or a respray.

That is called 'Rolls-speak', developed over many years by disciples who raised semantics to new levels and reveled in playing the strings of the English language like an Itzhak Perlman. It involved stepping back from the situation, murmuring understanding and suggesting that all will come right in the fullness of time.

The car was taken to the Rolls California office while discussions went on about how best to fix it up and who would pay for it. Eventually 'an accommodation was reached' with the Company, the selling dealer and the owner chipping in. The excitement abated, along with Tony Thompson's blood pressure and as far as I can recall, fears that business would drop-off did not materialize. That's Los Angeles, as they say.

Rolls-Royce has always had an absolute commitment to owner satisfaction, going all the way back to Henry Royce himself. In 1906, the year the partnership with Charles Rolls was sealed and the Rolls-Royce company came into being, Royce issued what today would be called a mission statement: 'Our interest in the Rolls-Royce car does not end when the owner takes delivery. Our interest in the car never wanes. Our ambition is that every purchaser of a Rolls-Royce shall continue to be more than satisfied.'

He also said: 'The quality will remain long after the price is forgotten' and, in most instances, the great engineer was proven to be right. Many owners adopt a loving, forgiving feeling toward their cherished Rolls and lean over backward to avoid criticism. But there is a limit, and when that point is reached, they snap.

When lawyers feel aggrieved, they can invoke colorful rhetoric. One, whose front number plate proclaimed: 'I'm spending my kids' inheritance,' bombarded the Company with complaints that his car refused to select reverse. This reminded me of a story, possibly apocryphal, that quoted Henry Royce saying that he would not fit a reverse gear on his motor cars because it was not dignified to see a Royce going backwards.

When high-profile owners in a position to bad-mouth the Company had Rolls-Royce trouble, the effort to put the car right as quickly as possible took on additional urgency. Occasionally, however, if the aggravation persisted, the mechanical problem being particularly difficult to fix, the irritation factor triggered irate calls. The famed San Francisco lawyer, Melvin Belli – a large, flamboyant man with a mane of white hair, commanding presence and voice and an intimidating advocate – had a convertible that had been more troublesome than he felt was reasonable.

He called the Rolls-Royce office and the engineer who answered dined out for months on the conversation – well it was hardly a conversation – more a one-way communication. The voice, rich in timbre and depth, a courtroom weapon for which Belli was noted, and honed over many years of addressing juries, boomed: 'This is Melvyn Belli. I am going to say this once – so listen good.'

Moving in the influential circles of Bay area society, Melvyn Belli was in a position to do Rolls-Royce considerable harm with disparaging comments about his car, the most expensive Rolls-Royce model. In his terse phone call, he outlined the problems in a few sentences, then rang off. The car was fixed, pronto, as I recall.

Another famous owner also had a problem, his car being one of the first to have mineral oil in the braking system. Mineral oil was more efficacious than ordinary brake fluid and Rolls-Royce became the first car to have the space-age fluid used by Boeing to bring jetliners to a stop. But there was a downside. Adding normal brake fluid to the reservoir was tantamount to pouring disinfectant into a Bombay Sapphire martini. The seals would be destroyed, requiring major remedial work to replace all the critically important tubing serving the braking and suspension systems. To prevent contamination and recognizing that mineral oil might not be readily available everywhere, the factory placed two plastic bottles of the precious liquid in the trunk.

Despite the warnings, however, some early models were contaminated and one of them belonged to the actor, Walter Matthau. When the dealer pointed out that the hydraulic system would have to be dismantled with the bill running not much short of $10,000, the famous look of quizzical puzzlement – the Matthau trademark – crept across his lined features. 'I do not understand how that could be,' he growled. 'Well Mr Matthau, you contaminated your mineral oil reservoir with brake fluid.'

'I did WHAT? I do not even know how to pop the hood!' came the startled reply. The mineral oil mix-up had to have happened at a service station. In went the brake fluid and hey presto, another intricate reparation job that helps sends mechanics' kids to college. I was concerned when I heard that the California office was standing on a technicality and sticking the owner with the bill for putting the car right, especially as Rolls-Royce was alone in using mineral oil at that time. The public and customer relations consequences could be far more expensive for us than the cost involved.

Apart from being a good customer, Walter Matthau was in a position to make critical remarks about Rolls-Royce dodging responsibilities for a nearly new car all over Hollywood and the entertainment industry, the most important wellspring of our revenues in the United States. More than one third of North American sales were in southern California and the bulk to the show business community.

The work was done without charge and Matthau was reported to have told friends that he had to hand it to those guys at Rolls-Royce. They had stepped up and put things right. It was a good return from a modest investment of a few thousand dollars. For many decades, Rolls-Royce has enjoyed a brand image that marketers dream of, a reputation for being the perfect car, engineered never to go wrong and, mythology has it, sure to motor along silently and luxuriously until the end of time. But, it is a machine built by humans and, like a hand-crafted watch, if the pieces do not perform in unison, the machine can go wrong. Now and again, Rolls-Royce motor cars have been known to do that.

The occasional car might have had a citrus aura to it, but it also has to be said that some owners, expecting nothing short of perfection in a mechanical device, can demonstrate a degree of neurosis, even paranoia, that would intrigue even the highly priced shrinks of Wilshire Boulevard or Park Avenue. To the purists who believe in the mythology, any criticism of a Rolls or Bentley is irreverent and comparable to calling into question the Pope's commitment to Christianity. Few appreciate the humor of quizzical comments that pull the Company's leg, or suggesting that the motor cars are less than flawless.

CNN learned that several unhappy Rolls-Royce owners were suing the Company. Five were interviewed and outlined stories of breakdowns and repairs that led the network to question whether the world's finest motor car fell somewhere short of the public's perception. One lady of mature years from the Dallas area told investigative reporter Larry Woods of the litany of troubles she had had with her Silver Spirit, saying it had spent more time in the shop than on the road. 'Do you think you have a lemon?' he asked. 'I'll say,' she cracked, rolling with laughter. 'I think Rolls-Royce sold me a lemon, the tree and the whole God-damned orchard.'

It was a classic observation. The company should perhaps have presented this endearing Texas grandmother with a new car, wrapped in satin ribbon. That would have been great public relations, but it might have opened Pandora's box and Hell would have frozen over before that happened.

The Corniche convertible was for many years the quintessential Beverly Hills dream machine; almost as important to the beautiful people as their plastic surgeons. More than one young man, eager to impress a girl with a stylish weekend in Las Vegas, bought one from Rolls-Royce of Beverly Hills on a Friday, then rushed back on Monday complaining that the color was not right and the car not really 'him' and he'd like his money back. Tony Thompson, survivor of the hole-in-the-roof debacle, was not soft in the head and would amiably, but firmly lay out the facts of ownership life to the young buck. Rolls-Royce was particularly sensitive to unfavorable publicity about this high profile and profitable car and in 2001 was appalled when one exploded just after being refueled. Vapor underneath ignited when a technician pressed the master switch to raise the windows which blew out. The convertible top and interior also were damaged. The dazed driver suffered temporary hearing loss and a pedestrian was injured by flying glass. The factory moved quickly on a recall to fix the problem.

The Times of London ran a piece headlined: 'Rolls-Royce Recall Not Likely to Go Smoothly.'

The story started:

For Rolls-Royce and Bentley there is bad news, and there is terrifying news. The bad news is that the Company had to recall nearly 500 cars because of a design fault. The terrifying news – two of the owners are Saddam Hussein and Mike Tyson. Trying to part former heavyweight champion Tyson from the Corniche he bought during a visit to the factory may be more of a problem than the repair. One boxing promoter said, 'Mike loves his cars. He will not be happy.'

The Times added that in January 2001, a new Bentley convertible was transported to Iraq for either Saddam Hussein or his son Uday who was 'fond of killing opponents and driving expensive cars in equal measure'.

The London *Sunday Telegraph*, demonstrating uncharacteristic humor, wondered if some Machiavellian plot by British Intelligence to assassinate Saddam had backfired. Noting the delivery of a gleaming convertible to Baghdad, the paper observed:

> Aficionados of James Bond and Q will reflect on what a coup it would be for British Intelligence, were the Iraqi dictator to perish in an exploding car which he had himself procured at great expense. Of course, such things do not happen in the real world – or could it be that some terrible mix-up has occurred, and Mr Hussein is driving around in a car really intended for a distant American showroom?

Though built to the same technical specification, each Corniche seemed to have its own personality and a different feel to it. One quirk in the driver's seat mechanism triggered complaints about owners becoming prisoners in their own Rolls-Royce. It sounds funny but it was no joke for the driver. When the ignition was turned on, the maverick seat would sometimes motor inexorably forward, until the occupant's knees were scrunched up against the instrument panel. He would wind up looking something like the Hunchback of Notre Dame, imprisoned in a very expensive straitjacket. Desperately punching the seat switch achieved nothing. The seat seemed to develop a mind of its own. The engineers found the problem, but there was no way to placate a Florida owner with a bruised ego who felt humiliated by having to be rescued from his $250,000 convertible on, of all embarrassing places, Palm Beach's Worth Avenue.

Rolls-Royce motor cars usually deliver on their promise and, apart perhaps from piloting a Ferrari at insane speeds on the *autostrade*, the joy of driving and riding in one is an experience unsurpassed. Ambience, smoothness, a feeling of well being, luxury and absolute safety all come together to set these motor cars apart. When you open the door of one of these magnificent carriages and savor the beautifully stitched Connolly leather; the exquisitely crafted veneers and the soft Wilton carpeting and lambswool rugs – the sight is unmatched by any other manufacturer be it British, German, American or Japanese.

There are luxury cars boasting leading-edge technology, with dazzling space shuttle-like electronics that require hours of study and they are fine value. But none measures up to the unique package that is a Rolls-Royce. That is why people buy them and why so many love them. The New York advertising man Jerry Della Femina once said of advertising: 'It's the most fun you can have with your clothes on.' He could well have been referring also to a Rolls-Royce or Bentley.

5

WHAT'S THAT CHAP DOING WITH A Q-TIP UNDER THE ROLLS?

Few of the earth's billions get to experience traveling in a Rolls-Royce. For those who do it is usually to their wedding or the stately journey to a final resting place. Even fewer have ever had the pleasure of owning one. Yet there are many who are fascinated by the mystique of these legendary motor cars and it is probably true that Rolls-Royce has the largest number of appreciative non-owners of any company on earth. It owes an enormous debt to them for doing far more than advertising could ever achieve.

One reason some have for buying a Rolls is to savor the acknowledgement of non-owners, the metaphorical tugging of the forelock, denoting that the car is something special and by implication the owner, too.

The enthusiasts and their clubs constitute the greatest unpaid public relations army a company has ever enjoyed. When they show their cars off, as they love to do, on tours or parade them at county fairs, they feel proud, as well they should, because their motor cars are unique. They will speak at length about the beautiful leather and woodwork and lift the hood to reveal an engine burnished like a cavalry officer's boots; not a speck of dirt to be seen.

The highlight of the enthusiasts' year is the annual meet, the Super Bowl of Rolls-Royce events, which is held at a different North American watering hole each year at appealing places like the Monterey Peninsula or Rhode Island's Newport. Here, the mansions or 'summer cottages' as the Vanderbilts and friends coyly described their monuments to wealth, provide a rich backdrop to the splendid gathering of Rolls-Royce motor cars. The faithful make the pilgrimage, some from as far away as England and Australia, to enjoy the Woodstock of the hobby, though you would be hard-pressed to find anybody smoking pot or gray hair encased in a bandana.

What you will see is feet sticking out from beneath classic Ghosts or Phantoms or Silver Clouds as the owner cleans and polishes the underside. From as early as 6a.m. on judging day, owners will wriggle under the car – the chairman of a corporation in New York, the CEO of a supermarket-chain in Arizona, or a young orthopedic surgeon from Chicago. Every cranny of the chassis, engine, wheel wells and spokes will be thoroughly cleaned with Q-Tips, toothpicks and other tiny implements in the hope that the car will be as pristine as any Rolls in any showroom and that the judges will award it a best-in-class trophy.

The mega-rich see a car that takes their fancy, sign a check and acquire instant membership of an exclusive club that is important to their psyche. The car is a not-so-subtle flag to announce they have made it. Others, with more enthusiasm than cash, cherish their cars with depth and passion. These aficionados perhaps inherited an old Rolls or Bentley, or bought one for a reasonable price because it needed doing up, something a really wealthy owner might not have the inclination to do, or indeed would wish to devote time to.

Rolls-Royce company people have observed wryly, that they can spot the difference between a member of the Rolls-Royce Enthusiasts' Club in England, and his counterpart in

Above and opposite: The annual rally of Rolls-Royce and Bentley aficionados in England is the largest in the world, more than 1,000 motor cars often making the pilgrimage. This one, at Castle Ashby attracted a record 1,200 owners.

the Rolls-Royce Owners' Club of the United States. The American (not true in most cases, I emphasize) will say to you: 'Look at my Silver Cloud. I got it for a song, had some work done, and now it is worth at least fifty thousand.' The British enthusiast will likely say, if you stop to admire his car as you stroll around the annual rally at Castle Ashby or Princess Diana's family seat, the Spencers' Althorp Hall:

> This car has an interesting history. It's a Thrupp and Maberly Cabriolet de Ville on a Phantom chassis. Found it on a farm in Northumberland where it had been in a barn for donkeys' years and the moths had really got at the old girl. I spent a lot of nights and weekends on her but now the work's finished and I like to think she looks something like she did in her glory days back in the thirties.

No mention of cost or value and only a passing reference to the long, arduous labor of love that restored the car to what you might call Rolls-Royce condition.

There are American owners who do the same thing, toil in a garage on nights and weekends, rebuilding the engine of an old Rolls or Bentley – no mean achievement – interminably rubbing down the bodywork to prepare for repainting and finally driving the restored car to display with great pride at the annual meet. They are the soul brothers of the British enthusiasts. Their philosophy is summarized by Eric Barrass, the eloquent and distinguished chairman of the Enthusiasts' Club and the Sir Henry Royce Memorial Foundation in England: 'We do not own these wonderful motor cars. We are merely the custodians, entrusted with their care, charged with a duty to nurture and cherish, and preserve, to ensure that they will be safely passed down through generations.'

If Eric Barrass, a retired Lieutenant Colonel of the British Army, did not exist, you would have to invent him. Right out of central casting, with a warm smile, mane of white hair, stentorian voice and military bearing, he is the Englishman, who probably more than any other, empathizes with the soul of Henry Royce. He regards Royce's standards as benchmarks of honesty, integrity and commitment that behooves everybody to try to emulate.

The Enthusiasts' annual summer rally was held for many years on the rolling grounds of Castle Ashby, the ancestral home of the Earl of Northampton, attracting the largest gathering of Rolls-Royce and Bentley motor cars in the world – often 1,200 or more.

Eric, impeccably turned out in tweed sports jacket and flannels with a cravat neatly tucked around his shirt collar, would walk the rows of neatly parked cars, barking benevolently at a

Above and opposite: Proud owners lists their cars' attributes.

Shadow owner to kindly move his motor car from the line of Silver Wraiths and have it join its brothers over there with the other proper motor cars of the post–1965 era.

With an unrivaled knowledge of all things Rolls-Royce, he would do the commentary as the best in class were driven up to be given their awards. His expert observations, drawn from an encyclopedic memory and highlighting the outstanding features of each motor car, were colorful as well as educational and he would toast the magnificent machines with a glass of wine as they purred by. On one beautiful Sunday afternoon in June, as hundreds of enthusiasts strolled the greensward of Castle Ashby, a Spitfire flew over to mark the anniversary of the Battle of Britain in which Henry Royce's legendary Merlin engine played such a critical role. Eric's voice boomed through the speaker system: 'What a wonderful and glorious sound. Savor it ladies and gentlemen. But for the Spitfire and its magnificent engine, who knows what would have happened to our great country? What a sight. What a sound and there probably should not be a dry eye in the house.'

I am not alone in thinking that Eric missed his calling. He should have been doing *King Lear* at Stratford. He was the driving force in the creation of a unique organization, the Sir

Henry Royce Memorial Foundation, which is headquartered at the Hunt House, a handsome Georgian mansion nestling in a village not far from the Silverstone motor-racing circuit. The Foundation treasures the world's finest collection of Rolls-Royce records, chassis files and historic company documents. Also there, in the Henry Royce room, are some of the great mechanic's tools and artifacts. It was in the library that Eric showed me an early Rolls-Royce ledger chronicling the motor cars. One copperplate entry, noting the chassis number of a Ghost, stated of its owner: 'Alas, perished on the *Titanic.*'

I recall an annual meeting of the Foundation when a delegate from the Rolls-Royce Owners' Club, a gentleman from California, proposed that some of the historical documents at the Hunt House be transferred to the Owners' Club in the United States. The very suggestion, bordering on heresy, went down like a lead weight, astounding the board, whose sentiments were expressed by the articulate Colonel Barrass, bristling at the very idea of permitting such valuable and irreplaceable papers to leave the shores of the sceptered isle. As a concession to the colonies, however, he indicated in his rich baritone, there would be no objection to photocopying some of the documentation, but the idea that any of the records should leave their spiritual home was out of the question.

Business dealt with, the members and guests adjourned to the bar to prepare for an English roast beef dinner accompanied by a copious supply of good claret, treacle pudding, Stilton and

very old port. The enthusiastic and energetic way in which the English tuck into 'cholesterol festivals' can unnerve the American visitor. Abstemious Rodeo Drive joggers who get their highs on mineral water, light salad and a sorbet should go nowhere near such indulgent events. Dinners like these, enjoyed by Rolls-Royce lovers at the Hunt House, have been happening in England since the outlaws of Sherwood Forest hunted wild boar and brewed olde dark English ales of strength that made Tennessee whisky taste like a modern cola.

Meanwhile, back in the United States, there are very rich members of the Rolls-Royce Owners' Club who pay a fortune for a rare Rolls and spend another fortune – $100,000 and upwards – having it professionally restored to the point where they claim it has more coats of lacquer than Rolls-Royce gave it in the first place. The car, now akin to a Beverly Hills socialite fresh from the umpteenth face-lift, body-tuck and collagen, is transported to the meet in a large container with padded interior to avoid scratches. At the show field it is polished by aides specially employed to cosset the car and possibly takes first prize as 'a hundred point Rolls-Royce' – a perfect score! The owner basks in the glory of his outstanding possession and beams as he accepts his trophy to add to others on his mantle that also were acquired with the check book rather than by getting grease under one's fingernails.

There is a slightly regrettable side to this pedestal placing. The car is now like a prize bull confined to a small pasture and seldom getting to do what it was built for – be taken out on the open road to give enjoyment to driver and passengers and show the world what peerless carriages Henry Royce and his faithful workpeople created over the years.

The pristine 'Best in Show' Rolls, gleaming like a Hollywood spaceship and carrying so many hand-sprayed and hand-rubbed coats of paint as to increase the original weight, is destined to sit in a climate-controlled garage or specially built showroom on the grounds for visitors to admire, but never touch. This brings to mind people who put fences around animals that should be roaming the wilderness where they truly belong.

Though they apply different values to ownership, one common denominator is evident. Owners share a reverential appreciation of Rolls-Royce craftsmanship and engineering and a desire to preserve these magnificent examples of artisan skills. In the world of Rolls-Royce you encounter owners who are steeped in their love for the marques and care for them like children. Just as they will not permit smoking in their beautiful cars, so rain, acid or otherwise, must not be permitted to fall on the paintwork. Those not belonging to the mega-rich circles, will still lavish a fair chunk of disposable income on their Rolls.

Some use their motor cars as daily transport. Allen Swift, a gentleman in West Hartford, Connecticut, was a good example. He drove his American-built Rolls-Royce, a 1928 Phantom I Piccadilly Roadster, almost every day for nigh on seventy-five years, including a trip to the 1994 Owners' Club meet in Philadelphia where I arranged a special Rolls-Royce award to mark his long ownership – a beautiful porcelain *Spirit of Ecstasy*. Allen, who had started work while his brothers went to college, was given the car by his father as compensation. Like a good workhorse, it was fed and watered and repaid with loyal and sterling service.

The car was sixty-six years old when he drove it to Philadelphia and it could perhaps have done with a little paintwork, hardly surprising after daily use for well over half a century. But a little later, Allen decided it was time for a repaint in the original two-tone green and here he demonstrated a Henry Royce-type commitment to getting it right. To be sure that the colors were exactly like the original, he had the body removed so the new paint could be matched with an area of the chassis that had not faded or been weathered by the elements.

Apart from a set of pistons, the car has needed little mechanical work. It faithfully carried Allen about his daily business – in his mid-nineties he was still putting in an eight-hour day as a goldbeater making gold-leaf and he always drove the Rolls to church every Sunday, come rain, snow or shine. Essentially it represents what a Rolls-Royce has always been meant to do – get out there, work, be driven hard and enjoyed. Allen Swift's ownership of his wonderful old New York Brewster-bodied car, in which he covered more than 172,000 miles, epitomizes something I often said to journalists: 'Once you acquire one, it is possibly the last car you'll ever need to buy.'

Some classic Rolls-Royce have specifically fitted picnic basket compartments to add convenience and style to a rally lunch.

Two delightful ladies in Ireland would agree. Miss Letitia Overend drove her 1926 Rolls-Royce 20 Tourer every day for fifty-one years. After her death in 1978 at the age of ninety-one, her sister, Naomi, continued the family tradition of a daily outing for Mr Royce's splendid horseless carriage for a further fifteen years until she passed away in 1993 aged ninety-three. The sisters doted on the car, a convertible, and maintained it themselves on their 40-acre estate at Airfield Dundrum, County Dublin. Letitia actually went to England to take the driving and maintenance course at the Rolls-Royce School of Instruction.

Still in near original condition, the car was put on permanent display at the Overend home, an eighteenth-century farmhouse which the ladies bequeathed to the public through a trust. The house's antiques were auctioned to raise money to open the farm as a museum and education center. The sisters Overend were certainly a class act.

There are many other owners who do not believe in parking their classic cars in the garage to gently slumber the years away. Ken Karger and his wife Mermie, for many years editors of *The Flying Lady*, the Owners' Club magazine in the United States, drove their 1913 Ghost

Delving into engine mysteries – even on a day out.

on long journeys all over the country. Other enthusiasts joined them, usually in younger Royces, as they are often referred to, opting for the comfort of air-conditioning and a modern suspension rather than the rigors presented by a car made before the First World War. But the point is, they enjoyed their cars and never passed up an opportunity to hit the road.

The older cars have heavy steering and can take some handling. An unforgiving crash-gearbox screeches your incompetence to the world should you mess up the gear change and a firm ride tells your tailbone, better than any odometer, how far you've driven. But all these tribulations tend to be submerged by the sheer exhilaration of sitting high up, bowling along in grand style, listening to the sweet, deep rumble of Henry Royce's magnificent engine, savoring the whiff of oil, pumping the handle to make sure the car receives its correct lubrication – simply enjoying the experience of riding in the finest motor car of its era.

There are many judging categories at the annual meet, for which owners prepare for months. You'll find a group of elderly gentlemen studying the engine of a very old Rolls-Royce in immaculate condition like surgeons peering into the chest prior to starting a quadruple bypass. They are judging the 'Most Silent Ghost' class and will shout for absolute quiet from chattering onlookers as they study the audiometer, which registers how quiet the engine is and solemnly mark their clipboards. They frown in disappointment if the car comes up short anywhere on the score sheet, but the respect in which they hold the old Ghosts is lovingly displayed. They gaze at the beautiful machinery like fathers welcoming home the prodigal son. The judges are sticklers for authenticity. Woe betide the owner who puts a cell phone into a car made before 1946. Points are deducted for such a non-standard modern contrivance. Conversely, a phone and aerial may be fitted to a post-Second World War car 'provided it is unobtrusively installed in keeping with Rolls-Royce workmanship standards'.

The board of the Owners' Club, responding to the inequity of the expensively restored car that hasn't seen the open road in years enjoying a virtual walkover in the judging, decided to introduce two categories – 'Concours' for those cars, and 'Touring' for 'real world' cars that actually were driven to the event. This righted a wrong that applied for many years. In the egalitarian segment, the car has to be driven to the meet from home or wherever it is normally garaged, which calls for quite a trip if you live in Boston and the Owners' Club gathering that year is in San Diego. But the real enthusiasts willingly do it in an open-top Ghost or Phantom that makes great demands on stamina and the driver's skills. A 6,000-mile round trip in an antique car with a seventy-year-old braking system can also challenge the nerves as drivers negotiate precipitous mountain roads and other challenging terrain. But do it they do, despite mechanical glitches causing delays and frustration. These devout disciples of Henry Royce and his wondrous machines are the sinews of the Rolls-Royce faith.

They arrive flushed and triumphant, ready to share their experiences and technical knowledge – the funny little idiosyncrasies of a 1914 Ghost or a 1929 Phantom with fellow Rolls-Royce nuts. Owners go to inordinate lengths to make the cars an integral part of their lives and behave in ways that are perhaps inconsistent with the tightly focused manner in which they conduct business.

One collector in the Midwest celebrated the sixtieth birthday of his Phantom II by having blocks of chocolate cast in the shape of the car. Along with a happy note, they were sent to all his friends. He houses several classic cars housed in pristine garages clean and neat enough to live in. A huge cocktail cabinet shaped like a Rolls-Royce grille dominates one garage and when guests come to view the collection, a lady harpist creates a soothing ambience. When he ordered a Silver Spur limousine, he went to Crewe to discuss additional special features for the passenger compartment. The crystal in the cocktail cabinet was, in his view, inferior and not befitting a car of this quality so he ordered a set from the glassblowers of Eastern Europe. The same went for the *hors-d'oeuvre* dishes. Shrimp would tarnish the sterling silver, so he ordered the bowls to be gold-plated to ensure that a presentation of seafood tidbits would be as it should be.

A multi-millionaire from New England, Prestley Blake, a likeable and popular old boy with a wrinkled grin and a friendliness belying his enormous wealth, has a large and much-envied collection – all Rolls-Royce. I asked him why he did not have any Bentleys. 'Imitation Rolls' he would growl, a statement that would cause fanatical members of the Bentley Drivers' Club to hyperventilate. Technically, that was true between the 1960s and the early 1980s when the only difference between a Rolls and a Bentley was the grille. Prestley Blake is a Rolls-Royce purist. He admires the coachwork and the engineering and is not interested in making statements about his wealth. He has always been adamant about the unparalleled quality of the cars that bear the RR badge. A Rolls-Royce, in his view, is the only motor car to have.

He puts his money where his mouth is. At one point, he had twenty-four Rolls. One was a Silver Shadow which he placed on blocks in the huge garage designed on similar lines to his house. Asked why the car never went out on the road he said: 'Somebody said in 1971 that Rolls-Royce was going out of business so I bought an extra one. Got to make sure I can get spares from somewhere.'

His love of Rolls-Royce fired up as a boy in Springfield, Massachusetts, where, in the 1920s, Rolls-Royce opened the only factory it ever established outside England, to build cars for a

Allen Swift and his American-built Phantom I that he drove almost daily for three-quarters of a century, setting a record for owning the same Rolls-Royce longer than anyone else in the world.

ten-year period for the developing North American market. I asked Prestley if it were true that when the escape siren sounded one night at a prison near his New England estate, he rushed from the house to the garage to protect his cars. He grinned and wouldn't confirm it. Nor did he deny it. He is an innovative thinker, a talent that helped him make a fortune. As teenagers, he and his brother rented a shop and began making ice cream. They built the business into one of America's largest family restaurant chains. Prestley also applied business acumen to his car collection.

In England, during the 1980s, he discovered a 1926 Rolls-Royce chassis and engine still wrapped in the heavy cladding applied at the factory for rust protection. He also had a body design that had been drawn by a Rolls-Royce engineer at about the same time. He engaged a British coachbuilder to make it and asked me to confirm that the 'warranty clock' on a Rolls-Royce traditionally did not start until the body was attached to the chassis.

'Will you give me a warranty?' he asked. 'Of course,' I said, amused at the huffing and puffing this would cause at Crewe. The bean-counters wouldn't comprehend the wonderful publicity value to Rolls-Royce to offer without hesitation a warranty on a 60-year-old engine and chassis. There was no risk, of course. The car would be an instant classic and would never be driven more than a few miles a year. The gesture underscored Rolls-Royce confidence in its workmanship, no matter how old the machinery.

Prestley Blake also desired another one-off – an open-top Silver Spur – a car that did not exist. Again he called, asking me whether the Company would warranty the car. 'Prestley, if you cut the roof off, take out two doors and shorten the body by 2ft, you'll sure as hell invalidate the warranty.' He went ahead anyway and spent $120,000 on the car and a further

$100,000 on the extensive body surgery carried out by coachbuilders on Long Island. But not before buying three Spurs. When the first was delivered, he told me he thought the paintwork so attractive: 'I couldn't let them chop it up.'

He made the same mistake with the second, so he bought a third in brown, a color he did not much care for and this was the one that went under the coachbuilder's knife. He unveiled the car at the Owners' Club annual meet in California. It was stylish and a sensation. Prestley was as excited as a schoolboy who had leaned over and caught the home-run World Series winning ball at Fenway Park. He had a Rolls-Royce unlike any other in the world. I was delighted for him. It was a beautiful car. If you have the money, why not indulge yourself and create something nobody else has, not even another Rolls-Royce-loving millionaire!

Owners, for the most part, are sticklers for correctness and behave as they believe Sir Henry would have wished. An owner whose car distressingly failed to proceed one afternoon on a street in the north of England, dutifully awaited nightfall before having it removed in a plain van. He accepted, without question, the lore which forbade the lifting of a Rolls-Royce hood in the street, in case passers-by thought the car had developed a mechanical problem.

Taking the biscuit for correctness, however, was the decorum in stressful circumstances, demonstrated by a distinguished retired American banker whom I have known for many years. William M. Davis is a courtly gentleman whose collection of eight Rolls and Bentleys includes a brace of 1930s Phantoms, an H.J. Mulliner 1952 coupé, a magnificent 1965 James Young Phantom V touring limousine, a couple of 1960s vintage Silver Clouds and a 1973 Corniche drophead. But the real vice that brought the schoolboy out in him was a performance car, a Turbo R.

Bill, whose deep automotive knowledge qualifies him as a judge at the Pebble Beach Concours, has always been as meticulous about maintenance as about adding up the numbers at the banks he and his family happened to own. So insistent is he on mechanical rectitude

Would anybody slap a parking ticket on this beauty?

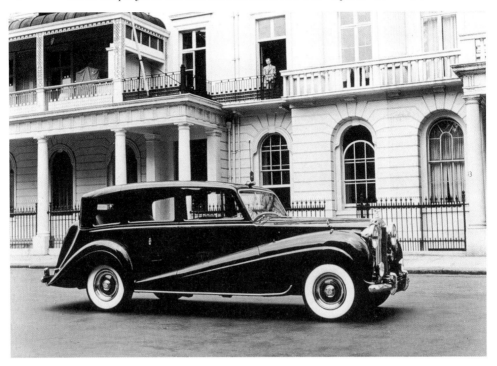

Phantom IV landaulette, (1950–56)

The sweeping lines of the 50hp Phantom III Sedanca (1936–39) inspired the styling of the Cadillac Seville forty years later.

he drives his motor cars in rotation 600 miles to the Albers Family Service Shop at Zionsville, near Indianapolis, where, journalists have written, the work areas are as clean and well organized as an operating room.

Herman Albers, the owner, was one of the great authorities on Bentley and Rolls-Royce models, being able to pluck complicated catalogue part numbers by the score from memory. Herman wove his love and knowledge of all things Rolls and Bentley into his servicing and sales business. Customer relationships and quality of service were paramount – attributes that more people in the car business would do well to emulate. He was a remarkable man who maintained service and customer standards that Henry Royce and W.O. Bentley would have admired.

That is why Bill Davis takes his cars such a long way for service. The system worked without incident until he bought the Turbo R. En route to Indiana, he hit a rough road surface, lurched through a guard rail and hurtled down steep banking. He survived the crash rather better than the car, whose tank-like construction undoubtedly saved him, but was in less than showroom condition when it came to rest. It gave its all for its owner and was later pronounced a write-off and Bill reluctantly took the record for being the first owner to destroy a Bentley Turbo.

He clambered out of the wreckage, a little dazed but in good shape considering the bouncing around and impact that had ripped off a door among other violent rearrangements of the car's styling. As he gathered his senses, he saw that his jacket had flown out; his glasses too. A motorist peered over the demolished guard rail. 'Are you okay?' he called. 'Yes, I'm fine' said Bill, 'but would you mind handing down my jacket?' A Bentley owner, he determined, could not possibly greet the tow-truck in a disheveled state.

In the absence of his regular spectacles, Bill found a pair of sunglasses in the center console. Wearing the shades and once again sartorially elegant, he confesses to looking sharp, but finds it difficult to accept that he resembled a hip, rather cool impersonator of an older Elvis at the conclusion of an energetic concert. Certainly, Bill Davis's emergence from the wreck was done in style. But, of course, nothing less would be expected of a Bentley owner!

He ordered another Turbo R with the new automatic ride-control suspension – fast wheels for a banker – and he loved it. When I talked to him at the Rolls-Royce Centennial meeting at Gettysburg in the spring of 2004, he noted that it had 143,000 briskly-driven miles on the odometer and was a joy to drive.

6

'HELLO DOOK'

Rolls-Royce has always courted, and been sensitive to royal patronage, having been the principal supplier of motorized carriages to the Queen and her family since the royals realized that a Rolls was a pretty good car to get around in. The Company has always enjoyed a special relationship with the first family, some of whom occasionally become involved in commerce while still sauntering through attendance duty at the Chelsea Flower Show and similar 'absolutely must be there ducky' social events where hangers-on have been observed performing the extraordinary feat of obsequiously bowing while walking backwards.

The Duke of Kent, a cousin of the Queen, was more into business than most of the family and Vickers, the parent company of Rolls-Royce Motor Cars, regarded it as a coup when he agreed to join the board as a non-executive director. The duties of non-executive directors in Britain have traditionally amounted to little more than turning up for the monthly board meeting, nodding assent to the actions proposed by the executive directors, then strolling into the dining room for a splendid traditional English city luncheon. This would be served by delightful elderly ladies in crisp black-and-white uniforms, supervised by a butler in black jacket, striped trousers, white shirt and gray-striped tie, looking rather like Sir John Gielgud in his Oscar-winning role as Hobson in the movie *Arthur*.

The character of non-executive directorships has changed. It is more pragmatic these days and is no longer predominantly the old boys' club, where a title almost guaranteed you a lucrative board membership, even though you perhaps did not follow too closely what the other directors were talking about. Appointments have had to be taken more seriously since corporate scandal and excessive emoluments and share option packages have come into public consciousness and have been known to oust the chief executive for failure to perform. They are there, after all, to represent the shareholders and make sure the executive managers of the Company are doing their jobs.

Vickers, run by former Rolls-Royce CEO David Plastow, a chairman with the gift of mixing charm and humor with a firmness committed to forcing through decisions he believed were absolutely right for the Company, enjoyed a generally urbane boardroom atmosphere. Except that is, for one famous occasion when Colin Chandler, the group chief executive, and Peter Ward, chief executive of Rolls-Royce Motor Cars, had a heavyweight shouting match that could be heard along the corridors. The frustrated Ward had reason to raise his voice more than once as his company, though contributing the lion's share of Vickers profits, was denied much of the investment needed for new models. With Rolls-Royce struggling to keep a foothold in the market and desperately needing group support, Vickers, for too long did a pretty good impression of the fiddling Nero. Such corporate verbal brawling seldom reached the ears of non-executive directors, who most days of the week had other things to do.

The Duke of Kent wore a multiplicity of public hats, among them the chairmanship of the British Overseas Trade Board, which required his being a sort of drum major at international trade shows where British industry would chase new business. Such an event was taking place in Texas and the Duke, noting that Rolls-Royce had a dealer not far from Houston, thought he should show the flag and drop in for a visit and a spot of tea after his luncheon speech.

The media-sensitive David Plastow called me, noting that I was supposed to know how the minds of the Americans worked and 'being a former BBC chap' would recognize and be attentive to the proprieties required of a royal visit in a state not generally regarded as being on the leading edge of cultural sophistication. The simple message was: 'make sure it goes right.' This meant curbing any excesses by the Texas media and ensuring that the Duke's tour of the showroom and chats with customers and staff would constitute a seemly pleasant interlude. The dealer, a delightful and bouncy self-made zillionaire, laid on his two personal Rolls-Royce limousines and packed the showroom and parking lot with cars from his own Rolls-Royce collection. Tea, cakes and biscuits from Harrods were laid on along with a stack of Danish pastries and doughnuts in case the Duke felt like a gastronomic depth-charge. The dealership staff put on suits and ties, and everything was spiffed up. One of the Silver Spur limousines was provided for the Duke, it being decreed that the Queen's cousin, ninth in line to the throne, should arrive and depart the Houston Chamber of Commerce event in a splendid royal chariot.

Before the royal arrival, I spent some time rehearsing the dealer in the appropriate protocol. Upon a heads-up from the Secret Service that the entourage was nearly there, the dealer and his wife would take up a position at the door to greet the Duke. I invested considerable time walking up and down outside with the dealer, coaching him about how to greet the royals. 'When he gets out of the limousine, you walk forward and say: "Good afternoon, your Royal Highness. Welcome to our Rolls-Royce showroom. May I present my wife," or something on those lines.' A wonderfully laid-back Texan, never fazed by anything and a very friendly man, he wanted to keep the whole thing as informal as possible and he was right. This was not a stiff English royal event where every move and greeting is carefully choreographed.

Everything was ready. The cars had been polished; the dealership staff, including a young driver from the parts department who had been told that he, too, would meet the royal visitor and had put on his best suit for the occasion, knew what to say if asked a question and there was half an hour to go. Well, there should have been half an hour to go. Suddenly a large Houston motorcycle cop, a dead ringer for Smokey and the Bandits, is Sheriff Buford T. Justice, festooned with guns and radios and wearing the inevitable intimidating shades even though it was a gloomy afternoon, zoomed to a halt outside the showroom.

'He's ahead of sked – he's here,' he shouted. And moments later, the motorcade swept on to the frontage. I hurried the dealer and his wife outside and as the Duke stepped out of the limousine, the dealer jumped forward, thrust out his hand and said, 'Hello Dook. Good to see ya.'

It was the natural thing to do, especially in Texas, and if the Duke was taken aback by this unorthodox greeting, he did not let on. He smiled warmly, shook everybody's hand and went inside. The official party of British diplomats was a bit gobsmacked for a moment. No one had ever heard His Royal Highness greeted as 'Dook' and then hauled inside to look at the engine in a Bentley. Right there was a photographer wearing a tuxedo, seen more often perhaps in Las Vegas or Beverly Hills than Houston at 2.30p.m., but this was a royal occasion and real life 'Dooks' do not happen by every day.

He clicked away with a battery of Nikons and Hasselblads hanging around his neck like a man with a major shareholding in Kodak and when the Duke paused to inspect a convertible, the dealer called for a souvenir group picture. He stood on one side, his wife on the other, she linking her arm in the Duke's and the dealer putting his arm around the Duke's shoulder. It was a great shot – much more informal than royalty is accustomed to. Normally, it is decreed, one does not dare touch the royal personage but this was a town inhabited by people who follow instincts and where unusual things happen.

There's no doubt the Duke enjoyed it – the enthusiasm and pride with which the dealer took him around the extensive showroom, talking about the cars and cracking jokes came through. He was relaxed; he grinned, made a few humorous remarks, talked to everybody, including the mechanics in the service bays and was plied with the Texas/English style afternoon tea. Then came the hijacking, the Duke being whisked away from under the noses of the security people. The final stop on the program was a classic car museum – also owned by the dealer – where he had on show millions of dollars worth of cars from the Duesenberg, Pierce Arrow era and also his Ferrari collection. This included about thirty 'impossible to get' black, yellow and bright red Testarossas jammed into a back warehouse and still bearing their stickers. As the Duke, his private secretary, and the remainder of the party, including the British Consul General, moved toward the door, the dealer exclaimed enthusiastically: 'Come and ride with us, Dook.' Before the entourage realized what was happening, the Duke was bundled into the dealer's limousine and off they sped with the security detail and the rest of the party playing catch-up. It was a merry and spontaneous end to an unusual afternoon.

David Plastow called me from London the following week. 'The Duke tells me it was a fascinating afternoon. They all had a terrific time and he said he'd never experienced anything quite like it. What happened?' Plastow had met the dealer a few weeks earlier. 'Well, you know him,' I replied:

> He was just being himself. He kept calling him 'Dook' as though he were a favorite son, and maneuvered him into place for the family picture taken by a guy dressed like he was covering the Oscars and they put their arms around him. Everybody was polite, with a bit of backslapping thrown in, and even his secretary seemed to be delighted that protocol went out the window. And they got everything right – a choice of lemon or milk with the tea and solid gold teaspoons about the size of soup spoons. The Duke seemed to have a good time. It was very different from the norm and sure as hell was a long way from a Cheltenham Ladies' College speech day reception.

A few days later, as he wound up his United States trip, I met the Duke again when we invited the media to cover his visit to Carriage House, the Rolls-Royce dealership in New York City. 'You know' he said. 'I really enjoyed Houston. They are very hospitable people.' I simply observed: 'Larger than life and that's Texas'.

Dealers can sometimes give the Company minders some anxious moments when they are away from their home turf. Rolls-Royce, like other carmakers, takes the most successful dealers and their top sales people on trips to exotic places or interesting events like Wimbledon or the Henley regatta. If the itinerary is Europe, there's a mandatory visit to Crewe, the gritty northern industrial town famous for its railway station which, as they say about Atlanta, everyone passes through at least once in their life.

Dealers from sunbelt states like Florida, California and Texas are outgoing people, with a fondness for colorful jackets, Hawaiian-style sports shirts that can look from a distance like a mobile migraine attack, heavy gold necklaces and bracelets and big Rolexes. You can imagine the reaction of the factory workers on a wet Monday morning, after hauling themselves through cold, drizzling streets at half-past seven – some to put on waterproof gear and spend eight hours using wet/dry sandpaper to rub down body-shells prior to painting – to see their workplace invaded by a jolly band of wealthy brothers from the colonies. Some, as if ready for the links at Pebble Beach, would be wearing tartan or orange jackets, and maybe a porkpie hat, that added up to a startling sartorial accident. In general the craftsmen in the engineering, wood and leather shops welcomed the questions and the jokes of visiting dealers, while never understanding their extraordinary taste in outfits.

Such visits usually took in a trip to the English countryside and famous watering holes like the beautiful Lygon Arms in the Cotswolds or the Compleat Angler at Marlow, an internationally famous hotel noted for its cuisine. It was here on one celebrated occasion, still recalled with a shudder by Rolls-Royce executives, that a young Texas salesman and his wife called over a waiter and sent back the vichyssoise, complaining that it was cold. Also at gourmet restaurants where the party of dealer salespeople were invited to partake of the finest European delicacies, the Texan and his wife could be heard asking: 'Ain't yer got any beef?' Before a visit to the theater and dinner at the Savoy Grill, the Rolls managers had to diplomatically dance around the delicate task of shepherding the guests away from colorful jackets and sports shirts and into something a little more formal with a tie.

But it was important to keep in mind that the colorful, outgoing guests were successful salespeople being rewarded for doing their jobs well and making profits for Rolls-Royce. After all, despite all the hammering, and stitching, and smoothing, and piston fitting and planning and marketing, nothing really happened until the tail lights disappeared out the showroom door and these good folks who did not like chilled soup and preferred beef to coronets of sole were the people who did it for us in the most competitive market in the world. As one of my colleagues once remarked: 'Good on ya, Charlie. You put the wine on our table.'

When a new car or model facelift was being introduced, we would often help the dealer run a media event with an English breakfast. We would shamelessly prime newspaper, radio and television newsrooms in the area with promises of an interesting photo opportunity with a $200,000 Rolls or Bentley along with a genuine English aristocratic sort of chap. To create a 'traditional English atmosphere', we would advise the hiring of an actor to dress up like a medieval town crier and do an 'Oyez, Oyez' act, ringing a handbell. My colleague Ian Kerr – a fellow Brit and the most effective communications operator I ever had the privilege to work with – would write the copy, proclaiming the arrival of the latest wondrous carriage from the Her Majesty's personal coachbuilders in Merrie Olde England. The television crews loved it – a gleaming Rolls and some nut in a wig and strange hat, swinging a bell and talking funny!

We had a very successful event in Cincinnati, despite a swerve from the norm by the local caterers, who were so carried away by the idea of serving a traditional English breakfast of bacon, eggs, black pudding, mushrooms and deviled kidneys, they threw in a sherry trifle as dessert – at 8.30 in the morning! For this unforgivable blunder, they would of course have been put to the sword back in the Old Country. To cap it all, instead of getting a town crier outfit, the dealer staff dressed the actor up as a Beefeater looking as though he'd just stepped off a gin bottle label. He also happened to stand about 6ft 5in, which made for a somewhat unusual royal protector. But the television reporters did not care about accuracy fudging. They had an American dressed as a transplanted refugee from the Tower of London, addressing the multitude like a sort of English lord in a strangulated English accent and it made for a colorful piece.

As I talked to a television interviewer about the new car, I could see the Beefeater, away to my left, diving into the trifle and talking to another reporter about English traditions of which he knew nothing. This, I decided, I did not want to know about. And just as well. The Queen, he confided, was elected by an English Congress and was required always to wear a crown and smile as she drove by the groveling, forelock-tugging populace. The amazed reporter nodded and made his notes. It was weird but it worked. The history lesson, as full of half-truths and inaccuracies as a political spin-session in Washington, thankfully did not reach England.

We got a lot of coverage on the evening newscasts and in the Ohio papers, and Rolls-Royce benefited from a wave of publicity not usually accorded car companies. We really should have been jailed at times for such naked publicity antics, blatantly capitalizing on reporters' and newsrooms' fascination with all things English. Back in England, the techniques we used in the United States often made them roll their eyes in disbelief, but the stunts were effective, and they brought people to the showroom for days afterward.

At a major launch in a large city like New York, we would engage Michael Sedgwick, an English actor with a ringing, stentorian voice. He made a great town crier, booming the message about Sir Henry Royce's latest masterpiece to every corner of the showroom for the benefit of the television cameras and reporters, delighting them with deliveries like: 'The meticulous builders and purveyors of excellent horseless carriages, the Honorable Charles Stewart Rolls and Sir Frederick Henry Royce will today reveal to you their wondrous new transports of delight.' In his olde English gear and wig, Michael looked like a European version of a slim, beaming Benjamin Franklin and his appearance and verbal presence were so compelling, a reporter interviewed him and asked about his background. 'I come from England, the land of green and yeomen and stout oak,' said Michael in his vibrant Shakespearian tones.

Somewhere in the translation, the reporter assumed he had come over specially, at the behest of the Sheriff of Nottingham who was too busy chasing the outlaws of Sherwood Forest to come to introduce the car himself. This was a major point in the news report – a genuine English town crier had crossed the ocean to break the news about a British royal carriage to the New World. It was true that Michael Sedgwick had come from England. What he was not asked, and did not volunteer, was when – which was about twenty years previously. He lived about thirty miles out of Manhattan, and when not acting, ran a direct mail business.

7

THE BHAGWAN, THE SULTAN AND OTHER UNUSUAL, VERY RICH PEOPLE

Let me tell you about the very rich.
They are different from you and me.
F. Scott Fitzgerald

How much is enough? Just as you can only eat so much caviar at one sitting or wear one Brioni suit, so you can drive only one car at a time. But it does not stop some from overindulgence bordering on the gross. No matter the size of your wallet, one hardly needs to own hundreds of Rolls-Royce and other exotic cars to tell the world 'I've got all the marbles'.

Acquisitiveness and heavy money have always been synonymous with Rolls-Royce, from Maharajas who enjoyed luxury beyond the dreams of the poor wretches sleeping on the steamy streets of Calcutta, to oil-rich princes with substantial collections of Rolls and Bentleys, along with a phalanx of wildly expensive sports cars to sweeten the mix. The saying 'You can't make this stuff up' applies to a couple of particularly heavy Rolls-Royce hitters, whose lifestyles could be taken from a combination of the *Arabian Nights* and the *Wizard of Oz*.

Firstly there is the Bhagwan, the cult leader whose followers vowed to present him with 365 Rolls-Royce motor cars – one for each day of the year. When the United States Government, rather unsportingly moved to deport him, with more than eighty cars purchased, a bolt of panic shot through Rolls-Royce. I told the parent company, tongue in cheek, that we were looking to hire the best immigration lawyer in the land to keep the Bhagwan here and enable his flock to continue adding to his collection.

Bhagwan Shree Rajneesh had come to the United States with a group of religious disciples from India, picking up more en route as they moved westward. Protected by gun-toting bodyguards on a 65,000-acre ranch, the bearded Bhagwan, aged about fifty, but looking quite a few years older, ran a sinister operation that took over an Oregonian valley and a town called Antelope, renaming it Rajneeshpuram. With 3,000 fervent followers, he created a mini-country, ruled with the help of an armed police force to help the faithful keep the faith. Yet his disciples adored him, the adulation extending to giving generously to the cause and in return receiving bunkhouse living and manual work in the fields.

There were strict rules and in the Rajneeshpuram hotel. Personal hygiene was encouraged with condoms and latex gloves placed in bathroom cabinets. Though local politicians in Portland, and later state authorities, expressed increasing unease about the weird set-up, an Orwellian concept with tightly controlled communications, its own airport, newspaper and radio station and border posts to keep out the uninvited, the authorities mounted no meaningful challenge for several years. Even when the Bhagwan bussed homeless and other indigents into Antelope to 'vote the right way' in council elections, protests were muted.

Above, opposite and overleaf: A few examples of the Bhagwan's Rolls-Royce psychedelic paint jobs.

Meanwhile, what was going on there? Many of the disciples were from California, long known as the land of flakes and nuts. Indeed, Senator Alan Cranston, a notable Golden State congressmen once commented on how it came into being. He remarked: 'The Almighty picked up North America and shook it, and all the loose, nutty bits rolled in one direction – right into a place they now call California.'

Perhaps it was not surprising that many of the Bhagwan's supporters came from this restless, out-of-the-box place. Ageing hippies who had accepted reality and settled down; lawyers and other professionals gave up steady jobs and homes in California to trek to Oregon to join the Rajneesh commune and throw their assets into the kitty. In return, they got a jumpsuit, tools, and an exhortation to till the fields for the cause. The principle one being to generate revenues to enable the Rajneesh Car Collection Trust to negotiate the purchase of several Rolls-Royce Silver Spurs each month.

They made some amazing alterations to the cars' appearance. They ripped off the Everflex roof covering, leaving a roughened surface to which adhesive was still clinging, and subjected beautiful Rolls-Royce paintwork to what amounted to psychedelic vandalism, the handiwork of brush-happy disciples gone berserk. Multiple hues and color schemes from purple to neon-green adorned most of the cars. There were oriental tapestries, strange patterns, waves and patchworks, birds in flight; sunrise and sunsets, flames, rich gold metal flake, ice crystals and other shapes and colors that were surely enough to make anybody with a propensity for illegal substances swear off forever. One disciple painted sixty-four white cranes on a black Spur, peacocks on another and an assortment of clouds and rainbows on others.

A Rajneesh spokesperson, Ma Prem Savita told the Associated Press the exterior treatments were a reflection of the Bhagwan's philosophy of trying to go beyond individual limits. She wouldn't discuss how many cars were in the Rajneesh fleet and she did not care if some considered it ostentatious for a guru to have such a luxury car collection: 'The Bhagwan enjoys driving the cars and that's perfectly in keeping with the Rajneesh outlook that life

should be enjoyed to its full. We do not worship poverty. We believe in living well and making money to do that.' And where did the money come from? Investments, was the response.

An aggressive lady, Ma Anand Sheela, whose outside-world name was Sheela Silverman, was the mailed-fist front-person for the Bhagwan. She would wax alternatively sweet and tough with Rolls-Royce dealers, hammering Tony Thompson, the English gentleman dealer at Rolls-Royce of Beverly Hills and play him off against Monte Shelton, a racecar driver who ran a successful Rolls-Royce and Jaguar dealership in Portland. Shelton's multiple sales to the guru propelled him into first place among Rolls-Royce dealers in North America. But envious eyes were cast on his lucrative relationship with people spending serious money. Beverly Hills, anxious to regain its crown as the number-one-selling dealer in the western United States, slashed prices to get more of the business.

Ma Sheela and a co-negotiator, vice president of the Rajneesh Investment Corporation, Swami Prem Jayananda (AKA John Shelfer), over the course of buying eighty-four cars, mainly from Beverly Hills and Portland, would write: 'Beloved Tony' or 'Beloved Mr Shelton – Love,' before demanding heavy discounts and even half the holdback, the several thousand dollars baked into the manufacturer's invoicing paperwork to give the dealer additional negotiating margin. The letter would end with the salutation: 'His Blessings'.

The cost-pinching demanded by the Rajneesh reached a point where the Portland dealer decided it was not worth the aggravation, and he stopped doing business with them. The guru's followers, apart from the inner-peace and feeling of self-fulfillment that commune membership was supposed to bestow, would also get an afternoon treat. Smiling benignly, Bhagwan would take a drive down the dusty valley roads in a Silver Spur, waving acknowledgement of adulation from the laborers in the fields. Just behind, a bunch of grim enforcers, toting automatic weapons, watching for any threat to the monarch.

Eventually, state and federal authorities took a serious interest in the hijacked town of Antelope and reacted to concerns about an attempted mass poisoning and a firebombing. Immigration irregularities enabled the Feds to oust the Bhagwan as an undesirable alien. They swooped, and he was soon on a jet back to India.

This left Rolls-Royce with two concerns. The loss of all those potential sales – 281 cars if the Rajneesh Collection aspirations were to be believed – and the worrying possibility of a flood of used cars surging on to the market, affecting second-hand values. Another issue was the bizarre decoration. Nobody wanted to see them on the street in that condition.

A posse of two executives, a dealer and two engineers flew out to examine the fleet and hopefully buy the collection. At Portland, they took a small plane to negotiate the difficult approach through mountainous terrain to the Rajneeshpuram airstrip. The delegation, pop-eyed, viewed the collection – seventy-seven Silver Spurs, three Camargues, two limousines, one Silver Spirit, and a Silver Wraith II. Mechanically, they were spot on. Appearance was the problem. The experts judged that it would cost $10,000 to bring each up to saleable condition.

The executives flew out before darkness stranded them in the valley for the night, leaving engineers Cal West and Joe Murtagh to arrange to bring the cars out if a deal were struck. It was a disturbing experience for them. Before getting rooms at the hotel they were interrogated separately and required to sign forms giving the Rajneesh community the right to search them and their possessions; also a waiver stating that the commune was not responsible for any harm that might befall them during their stay – including death. They were given a short orientation about the compound and its rules and a hospital-style wristband allowing them access to the commissary for meals. The wristband also was a means of tracking them and ensuring they did not wander into unauthorized areas. Phones were monitored and the only way to get a call out was through a Rajneesh operator. Concerned by the sinister atmosphere, the engineers got a call out to Monte Shelton in Portland. He went straight to the airport to prepare his Cessna. The winter morning was not the best day for flying.

Four inches of snow had fallen overnight and the approach to the airport at Antelope was not an easy one for a pilot to negotiate a path through the hills, eventually lining up sharply after rounding the base of a mountain. Cal and Joe had an anxious three-hour wait in a hut at the desolate airport before they heard the welcome voice of Monte Shelton asking permission to land. He came in skillfully and made a quick U-turn at the end of the strip. They grabbed their bags, pelted through the snow and jumped aboard. Monte gunned the power and roared

Java, the concept car that never went into production, except for a Sultan for whom two were built by hand.

back over the trenches that he had made when landing. The Rolls-Royce men were glad to be out.

Negotiations between Rolls-Royce and the Rajneesh lawyer failed. An offer of $4.3 million for the collection was rejected in favor of an offer of $5 million from a Texas car dealer, Bob Roethlisberger, who arrived with $2 million in cash and a bank credit line. Within a few days, Roethlisberger had trucked the cars to Carrollton, near Dallas, and set about making them presentable. He drummed up a lot of publicity, getting the bizarre collection and their story all over national television.

He approached Rolls-Royce with a sensible proposition. It was in everyone's interests to ensure they were repainted properly and to avoid a glut of Spurs hitting the market. It was agreed that Rolls-Royce dealers would do the necessary remedial work and the cars would then be filtered out gradually. Roethlisberger, a young man in his forties, tragically died of a heart attack. The bank moved to recover its money with a series of auctions. A steady number went under the hammer; some went abroad – about thirty to Arab countries. In recent years the odd one has come back onto the auction circuit, but they have never achieved the high-value collector-status the Texas buyer was hoping for.

The Bhagwan was not alone in having 'extensive customizing' done to a Rolls-Royce. An Arab Princess insisted that gold leaf be applied to the instrument panel and all the chrome and stainless steel in and on the car should be plated in 24-carat gold. Many cars have wound up in the collections of fabulously wealthy Indians. One, the Maharaja of Mysore, had his motor car blessed each year with a shower of rose petals. Equally flamboyant in his taste for the way out, the Maharaja of Patiala owned more than twenty cars, including a Ghost with solid silver fittings and a notable open tourer with coned wheel covers and swooping wings that looked rather like gaping nostrils. Another Maharajah had the interior of one of his carriages set on a Ghost chassis trimmed entirely in silk.

A Phantom VI – a Saudi favourite. This car was hand built by the Mulliner Park Ward Division of Rolls-Royce Motors and offered exceptional comfort for up to seven passengers.

THE HEAVIEST HITTER OF THEM ALL

But the heavyweight champion has to be His Majesty Sultan Haji Hassanal Bolkiah, head of the Brunei royal family, one of the world's richest men, with a 1,700-room palace and strong British connections. His small oil-rich country bordering Malaysia and on the north-east coast of Borneo, provides the family with about $2 billion a year and he reportedly gave his daughter an Airbus for her eighteenth birthday.

A friend of Queen Elizabeth and graduate of the military academy at Sandhurst, Britain's West Point, he has long been a Rolls-Royce fan, owning about 350 Rolls and Bentleys, along with Ferraris, racecars and other exotic metal cramming huge garages. *Car and Driver* magazine, in 1999, put the collection of the royal house of Brunei at a staggering 5,000 cars.

Many are unique, handcrafted Rolls-Royce and Bentleys fitted with an extraordinary range of luxurious special features. He insisted in 1991 on having the very first Bentley Continental R coupé and paid more than $3 million for it. Rolls management jumped to it when the Sultan requested a special car and satisfied just about his every whim. In return, he was very good to Rolls-Royce and family business including orders worth tens of millions from the Sultan's brother, Prince Jefri and his son Prince Hakeem, were major factors in keeping Rolls-Royce going in the early 1990s when it was in deep financial trouble. More than $150 million-worth of orders from Brunei, including $45 million in one year, were a lifeline.

Scores of one-off cars costing a ton of money were built for the Sultan, including the only two six-door sedans ever produced by Rolls-Royce. Many special cars, incorporating unique features, occupied craftsmen for months and ran to several million dollars apiece. As many as sixty specially commissioned cars a year were built for the Brunei royals, providing a cash-flow that kept the Company's head above water and helped finance future mainstream models.

It may come as a shock to many aficionados who believe that only one Bentley Java concept car was created to learn that the Sultan got two. This was the stylish coupé/convertible that caused a sensation at the Geneva Motor Show in 1994 and was used as a tantalizing stalking horse to measure public reaction. The car never went into production because much needed new sedans had first call on development money. But Java triggered a media blitz of news stories 'oohing' and 'aahing' over the exciting small Bentley. The public never got to buy one, but the Sultan just had to have the Java. In great secrecy, in a secure block to which only those with absolute need were admitted, they were fully engineered as normal working cars and, predictably, cost a fortune. Each car was a huge profit generator and bore a plaque on the engine announcing that it had been 'specially constructed for the Royal House of Brunei'.

Journalists, aware of the Sultan specials and looking for a shot of the latest unusual Rolls or Bentley, would post a photographer at the front of the Dorchester in London's Park Lane, the upscale friendly wayside hostelry which the Sultan happened to own, and await the arrival of another unique car bearing his number plate. For several years in the 1990s, the Sultan, according to *Forbes* magazine, was the world's richest man, worth upwards of $40 billion, until Bill Gates got his act together. But the Sultan was not hurting – that was until the price of oil, his principal income stream, fell by 40 per cent, as the Asian economy tanked.

Brunei, for the first time in memory, fell on relatively hard times. By 2002, the Sultan's assets were reported by *Forbes* and the *London Sunday Times* to have dwindled to about $10 billion and he had dropped to No.25 in the 'Rich List'. His finances weren't helped by his younger brother, the car-mad Prince Jefri, who bought exotic cars by the shipload. He took off on a spending spree believed to be unprecedented in modern times.

Jefri bought Garrard, the Crown jewelers in London, and lashed out more than $370 million on Asprey the ultra-expensive bric-a-brac shop on Bond Street, whose windows display more over-priced stuff that you can do without than any place I can think of. Like some modern-day financial Tarzan, Prince Jefri mounted a buying-spree of staggering velocity, drawing on the Brunei International Investment Agency, which he supervised until the cash draught began to be felt at home and he was fired by the Sultan.

With losses estimated at $16 billion the failure hurt the country's economy and caused a spectacular row within the royal family. Jefri agreed to return a huge amount of booty comprising cash, hotels, aircraft and cars. The state froze his assets, accusing him of improperly using its funds. It was unclear whether the assets included the cars, several homes and a luxury yacht he had acquired. Jefri was put on a paltry monthly $300,000 allowance to keep body and soul together for himself and his four wives. He was stranded in inhospitable places like Paris where he happened to have bought the Plaza Athenee and the United States where he had invested in two outstanding refuges, New York's Palace Hotel and the Beverly Hills Hotel in California. Whatever his indulgences, you couldn't fault his taste in pubs.

The family car collection amounts to an astonishing automotive empire. No one is sure what belongs to the Sultan or what was ordered in his name by Jefri and his car-obsessed eldest son Prince Haakem. The vast collection contains a 542hp twin-turbo Rolls-Royce, claimed to be the most powerful Rolls ever built, and several larger and longer-than-normal Phantom VI limousines. For good measure, the Sultan's private museum also boasted Formula One championship-winning cars from the 1980s.

In addition to the hundreds of Rolls-Royce and Bentleys in acres of underground parking, were hundreds more to make automotive enthusiasts swoon, like eight McLaren F1s, scores of Ferraris, Mercedes, Porsches and more than 200 Aston Martins with special interior, engine and suspension features, many with unique bodies like shooting brakes and sedan coachwork by Italy's Pininfarina. The Sultan underscored his authority to the people, and his brother, in 2001 by holding the most extravagant garage sale in history. The merchandise filled several warehouses. And the media turned up to ogle. Auctioneers came from Britain to organize the sale of thousands of items ranging from simulators for a Comanche attack helicopter and an Airbus A340 jetliner, to two unused Mercedes-Benz fire trucks, and an F1 racecar. Also on the block, a 16,000-ton stock of marble which could have gone some way to building a second Taj Mahal; a 12ft-high bronze rocking horse and a collection of grand pianos. It took nearly a week to get through the inventory, which raised a fraction of the cost, about $8 million, leaving a few billion, give or take, on the downside.

Brunei, a small former British colony, became rich through huge offshore oil and gas deposits discovered just as Wall Street was coming apart in 1929. The population, one third of a million, has lived an insulated life for three-quarters of a century, paying no taxes and enjoying free education and healthcare. For the royal family, the energy resources yielded riches almost beyond comprehension. It was a bit like the movie *It's a Mad, Mad, Mad, Mad World* – only gloriously madder. The polo-playing Sultan and his high-living relatives built palaces, and along the way acquired, as the auction demonstrated, gigantic quantities of expensive baubles.

The Brunei household's vast fortune was a major artery to Crewe's beating heart. You can imagine the consternation when the Rolls-loving Sultan, learning that BMW engines would power the next generation sedans, said he would not have German engines in his cars. When this deeply worrying subject came up at a marketing meeting, I queried why we couldn't keep the Sultan happy by putting the old and proven 6.75-liter British-built engine into his cars. The magnificent, but ancient block, they said, wouldn't fit into the new Seraph and Arnage models.

A little while later, however, there was an urgent rethink when Bentley sales went into free-fall, customers complaining that the Arnage's BMW engine did not have the power or speed demanded by Bentley buffs. Needs must when the Devil drives, as they say. 'Old Bessie's horsepower was boosted to 400 – no mean achievement for an engine whose basic design could be traced back more than forty years and she was shoehorned into the Arnage. The Bentley grille once again fronted an engine worthy of its heritage and the newly named Bentley Arnage Red Label was hurried to market for the 2000 model year and hit the spot – just what Bentley aficionados wanted. Thanks to the Sultan of Brunei, the old thunderer was back – a real Bentley engine, built at Crewe where all the engines should be made, and nary a German nut or bolt in sight!

Saddam Hussein, another *Arabian Nights* figure, became a multiple Rolls-Royce owner – but without any spare parts – thanks to his military. During the first Gulf War his troops looted the Rolls-Royce dealership in Kuwait, taking all the cars. Most were in for service, while their owners fled the summer heat for the fleshpots of London and Paris where they conveniently kept other Rolls-Royce. The Iraqis retreated in style after blowing up the parts department, destroying transmissions and other expensive spares useful in a hot, sandy climate. The penny probably dropped when they got home to Baghdad.

When Rolls-Royce learned that seventy-seven prize motor cars, worth more than $12 million had been abducted by the Iraqis, company spokesmen clucked appropriate murmurs of sorrow at such distressing losses sustained by valued Kuwaiti customers, while their marketing colleagues quietly viewed the plunder with the pragmatic anticipation that when the good times rolled again, there were seventy-seven immediate new Rolls purchases to be had off the bat.

Money was the last consideration when ordering a customized Rolls and sometimes the results were funny. The Saudis ordered a Phantom VI – the luxurious flagship of the Rolls-Royce fleet. The car, a year in the building, was carefully transported to Crewe for dispatch to Riyadh. Then, panic stations at the export depot. A Hercules had arrived unexpectedly at Manchester Airport to pick up the limousine, and there was a message that the car must be on its way to Saudi Arabia immediately. Colin Yoxall, an energetic and experienced fixer who never hesitated to do the unconventional to satisfy a customer, pulled the paperwork and set off in the Phantom, driving at speeds the designers of such a huge and heavy tank probably never envisaged. He made the urgent dash to the airport in what must have been record time – about forty minutes.

Then there was a new problem. The Saudis, fearful of scratching or damaging the car, refused to sign for it, until it was in the aircraft and secured. Yoxall sighed and positioned the Phantom some 50 yards from the steep ramp leading up to the Hercules's hold. This was going to take some skillful driving. He would have to 'wind up' the three-ton behemoth; gun it across the tarmac and once atop the ramp, stand on the brakes if aviation history was to be avoided. One miscalculation and Manchester Airport would be able to boast the only plane with its own built-in flight-deck Rolls-Royce. The Saudi staffers, stiff with fear that their mission could end in disaster, watched apprehensively. Either their silent prayers were answered, or Colin Yoxall really was as skilled a driver as he always claimed. He floored the pedal and as the car was about to reach the summit, hit the brakes. The black projectile did a sort of elegant wheelie, soared over top of the ramp and hurtled into the cargo hold like a semi-controlled locomotive. It whistled through and came to rest a foot or two from the flight-deck door. Colin put the transmission in park, handed the keys to a grateful Saudi and said 'sign here', quietly reflecting that he had probably saved his own job and maybe a much more severe fate for them.

8

STRIVE FOR PERFECTION
SAID HENRY

> You see things, and you say 'Why?'
> But I dream things that never were,
> And say 'Why not?'
> *George Bernard Shaw*

Shaw could well have been referring to a youngster named Frederick Henry Royce, who started work at the age of ten, selling newspapers and delivering telegrams, who taught himself electrical engineering, and went on to realize dreams of making mechanical devices work better and last longer. He was a visionary, an engineering pioneer – some have said genius – but he always called himself simply 'Henry Royce, mechanic'.

However one describes him, there is no question that he was driven by an unswerving zeal to create the very best of its kind, which made his name a worldwide benchmark for quality. He established standards and a commitment to excellence that endure today. 'Pa Royce', as he was known in the factory, transmitted this commitment to the loyal people who worked with him and it carried through to those who came after. Indeed, you could gauge the meaning, the depth of the pride in what they did, by asking a man in the street in the towns of Crewe or in Derby, where he worked. 'I work at Royce's' would be the response. That's the way they acknowledged the revered engineer who founded the Company, set the bar high, and insisted that nothing was ever right or good enough.

I remember a craftsman being asked why he was putting so much time into meticulously shaping a swivel-ashtray for a Silver Shadow. 'Mr Royce would have done it this way', was the reply. Mr Royce's principles and influence endured for many years after his passing. Managers would quietly point to the fact that right up to 1980 when the carburetor gave way to fuel injection, a beautifully engineered device called a throttle-knuckle joint that Henry Royce had designed three-quarters of a century before, was still being fitted to every Rolls-Royce motor car. The reason was not sentimental. It was simply that nobody had come up with anything better. They would chuckle that Mr Engineer Royce would have liked that.

Edwardian and Victorian England were harsh times in which to grow up, unless you had money, an economic benefit enjoyed by relatively few. True, the country had come quite a way from the appalling *Oliver Twist*-type days of workhouses etched so eloquently by Charles Dickens, but for most people, life remained a hard grind. Indeed, the anti-slavery campaigner William Wilberforce, died only thirty years before the birth in 1863 of Henry Royce, who would grow up to make the world's finest motor cars that only the very wealthy could ever have a hope of owning.

Royce struggled with poverty as a boy – his widowed mother had a tough time making ends meet and on many days, young Henry's food intake ran to little more than a couple

The factory in Cook Street, Manchester, where the first Royce cars were built.

of slices of bread soaked in milk. It was about as far a cry as you could imagine from the privileged world of the man who later became his business partner.

The Honourable Charles Stewart Rolls was born in the right bed, as they say, the third son of a wealthy landowner, Lord Llangattock, but, like Royce, was a visionary. He rejected the indolent route adopted by aristocratic fops living it up on family money in Edwardian London. He had dreams of doing notable things in the fledgling automotive and aviation worlds and achieved much in a tragically short life, becoming a successful businessman, balloonist, racecar driver and pilot.

He had a 'blue-blood education' – Eton College – then Britain's 'Ivy League' Cambridge University where he took a degree in Mechanical Engineering and Applied Science, while Royce, fourteen-years older, was already making his way in the engineering world.

Henry, the fifth son of James Royce, a farmer who came from a family of millers, was born in 1863, at Alwalton in Lincolnshire, about 100 miles north of London. His father, showing mechanical interests that clearly passed on to the son, saw steam as the ideal energy source for the mills and tried to convert them. It did not work out, so he sold up and moved the family to London when Henry was three. But they were tough times and when he died six years later, Henry had to give up schooling and do some breadwinning.

His telegram-delivery route took in Mount Street in Mayfair, the elegant district of the rich, bounded by Park Lane, Piccadilly, Regent Street and Oxford Street, where you can smell the money on every street and where the luxury cars he was eventually to build would become the carriages of the wealthy for many decades.

Young Henry Royce was probably the Post Office messenger who delivered a telegram to the Rolls family's Mayfair townhouse in 1877, announcing the birth of Charles Stewart Rolls.

Sir Frederick H. Royce, Bart.

A smiling Henry Royce after being knighted
for his services to engineering and to Britain.

Those who dabble in the occult would probably say that this was fate at its most influential. It's an intriguing possibility, and as Rolls-Royce-lore aficionados would say: 'If it is not true, well, it orta be!' Even in those boyhood days he was intrigued by mechanical devices and when he was fourteen, an aunt back in Lincolnshire found the £20 a year – a fair sum then – to pay for an apprenticeship at the Great Northern Railway Works in Peterborough, not far from the village where he was born and later the birthplace of another leading figure, though only a politician: Margaret Thatcher.

He lodged with another apprentice whose father taught the teenaged boys how to use tools and a lathe, and the importance of doing a job thoroughly. This possibly was the foundation of a zealous commitment to 'getting it right' that became the principle by which he lived his life.

As well as hands-on engineering, he studied its science along with electrical engineering and algebra and even languages. But, after three years, his aunt could no longer afford the apprenticeship fees and Henry set out on foot for the north of England. There was little work and he walked all the way to Leeds, about 100 miles, where he got a tool-making job demanding fifty-four hours a week in return for a wage of 11s ($3). Some days he worked from 6a.m. until 10p.m., but he learned his craft and moved on to London to join the Electric Light & Power Co., and took evening classes to broaden his education. At nineteen, in 1882, he was promoted to chief electrician at the Lancashire Maxim & Western Electric Co., in north-west England, and two years later, having amassed a little capital – £20 – he and another engineer, Ernest Claremont, who had about £50, decided to go into business together.

They pooled their savings and in 1884 started F.H. Royce & Co., Electrical and Mechanical Engineers, in a workshop in Cook Street, Manchester where Royce would make his first car

Henry Royce in the Phantom prototype at his home at West Wittering in 1925.

ten years later. No one ever discovered how Henry, putting in much less cash than Claremont, managed to persuade him that the firm should bear only the Royce name.

The two young entrepreneurs lived over the workshop and the early days were tough. Business improved when Henry designed a household electric bell-set and as more customers came along, he was able to expand the firm's industrial interests, perfecting a sparkless dynamo that was a boon to factories, shipping and mining where a spark could cause an explosion. The dynamos were reliable and well-engineered and gained the Company a reputation for first-class products. One minor new business disadvantage lay in the fact that they never seemed to wear out – a quality that marked everything Royce was to make.

Ruminating on his calling, Henry Royce, who seemed to have a gift for one-liners that would have made Johnny Carson proud, once said: 'Perfection lies in small things. But perfection is no small thing.'

Striving for perfection, in fact, committed him absolutely to his work. It was an obsession: inventing, designing and building, and he neglected his health, working long days and into the night, eating only when somebody brought him a sandwich, a sausage or a couple of eggs cooked over a flame on a bench and this punishing way of life – minimal nourishment and no exercise – affected his health. Royce and Claremont were so focused on the business, they did not get out much to meet the young ladies of Manchester, and eventually settled for a sort of package deal – marrying two sisters.

Their company was making electric cranes and doing so well in the early 1900s that Royce was able to afford a house in the posh Knutsford area in Cheshire, a short drive out of Manchester. Brae Cottage had a beautiful garden which he delighted in when he made the time and he made a home there for his mother who had spent many years in London, eking out a living as a housekeeper.

Then came the event that turned out to be the embryo that spawned an industrial dynasty. He bought a used French car, a 1901 Decauville, for his daily commute. It was noisy, vibrated annoyingly, overheated and had an unreliable electrical system – a particularly offensive crime in the eyes of Royce the perfectionist. He took the car to bits to try to correct its faults and was able to make some improvements, but the Decauville still fell short, as any Englishman will tell you about French products! He determined that starting from scratch was the way to go. He would build a car himself and the rest, as the cliché goes, is history.

Royce, now forty, decided to make three experimental cars and in late 1903 designed and built, mostly by himself, a car with a two-cylinder 10hp engine – the first Royce – which was running on a test bed by March 1904. It was ready by the end of the month and took its first test drive on April Fool's Day, which would have been an unfortunate choice had it failed to proceed. Lore has it that the record keeping was massaged by a few hours to avoid the risk of ribald comment, especially from across the Channel. Thus, many people pay lip service to the car that it made its first outing on 31 March.

Whatever the date, the whole thing came together beautifully and even Royce allowed himself a smile and a satisfied nod. The engine fired easily and, cheered on by the workforce, he drove out of Cook Street and was so pleased with its smooth performance, he kept going, driving the fifteen miles all the way home.

The English would be loathe to admit, but might concede if pressed, that French ineptitude and a Gallic willingness to settle for less, was the genesis of the Rolls-Royce motor car. Without the spluttering, vibrating Decauville, who knows, there might never have been a Rolls-Royce? The incentive to make a better car would be the only thing for which the English would grudgingly thank the French, in addition perhaps to champagne and cognac.

Now equipped with a reliable car that ran quietly and smoothly, Royce set about improving automobile technology. He designed his own carburetor which had a throttle arrangement controlled by a governor. With this, a driver could maintain a constant speed whether the car was going up hill or on the flat and might well be described as the world's first cruise control – a feature that did not appear on other cars for many years.

Royce also designed an ignition system and a clutch to provide a smooth take-off, brakes that were much better than anything else on the road and springing that gave the car a good ride.

Sir Henry Royce (right) with the first experimental Phantom I, which was also his personal car, pictured at Le Canadel, his home on the French Riviera.

Charles Stewart Rolls in his French Wright bi-plane was the first Englishman to die in a powered aviation accident. He was thirty-two.

This commitment to excellence was the origin of one of his famous quotations:

> Strive for perfection in everything you do.
> Take the best that exists and make it better.
> When it does not exist, design it.
> Accept nothing nearly right or good enough.

He came up with another classic one-liner after stopping his car on one of his daily journeys to Knutsford to help a clergyman using colourful language about a broken lawnmower that might have startled the Archbishop of Canterbury. He took off his jacket, got out his tools, and fixed it. The Reverend was impressed. 'I have to say, Mr Royce, it is gratifying that an engineer of your eminence would deign to attend to something as mundane as a lawnmower.' Royce is reported to have uttered the immortal response that would have qualified him for the PR business: 'Whatever is rightly done, however humble, is noble.' The impressed vicar had the phrase inscribed in Latin on a panel of wood and gave it to Royce, who placed it on a mantelshelf in Brae Cottage:

Quidvis recte factum quamvis humile praeclarum

Royce now had the car bug and quickly completed the second and third cars. One went to his partner Ernest Claremont and the other to one of their stockholders, Henry Edmunds, later to become known as 'The Godfather of Rolls-Royce', being the man who arranged the historic meeting between Hank and Chuck, as they would say in Wyoming.

His involvement in motoring events sponsorship had brought him into contact with Claude Johnson who had been secretary of the Automobile Club of Great Britain & Ireland, which later became the RAC. Johnson, who was running Charles Rolls' car importing business in London's Mayfair, C.S. Rolls & Co., was to be the cement that held the Rolls-Royce Company together, and later was to be known as 'the hyphen in Rolls-Royce'.

Rolls was enthusiastic about the potential of the new horseless carriages but was concerned about the unreliability of the French and Belgian cars he was selling. His first car, a 3½hp Peugeot – the first car ever seen in the university town of Cambridge was a real clunker and kept breaking down. One 150-mile journey to his family home at Monmouth in Wales, took nearly three days, with brake failure and lots of roadside engineering needed to keep it going. Little wonder, then, that after starting his car business in 1902 he began looking for a quality British car that would be a big improvement on the foreign models he was selling.

Meanwhile he had begun to make a name in car racing as one of England's most skilled drivers and set several world speed records and raced all over Europe, competing in races from Paris to Berlin, Madrid and Vienna. His exploits got him into the record books of the adventurous. Noted as a colorful Edwardian adventurer, he also racked up a couple of motoring convictions, one as early as 1896 when he was nineteen, for failing to display a red flag in front of his Peugeot and for speeding at a dangerous 30mph.

One incident that caused press comment involved a collision he had in 1902 with a horse and trap when he was driving home with a girlfriend from a ballooning competition. A journalist wrote:

> The Hon Charles Rolls, who was thrown from his motor car, and at the same time overturned a dog cart, injuring one man's back and ankles, and giving another concussion of the brain, described the accident as 'alarming, but not serious'. One wonders what the Honourable Charles would call a serious accident.

Between times, Rolls was selling cars to various people of royal blood, a clutch of Princes, including the Crown Prince of Rumania, and virtually a listing of members of the House of Lords, Dukes, Barons and Knights who felt they should get in early on the motoring era. But

Charles Rolls at the wheel with Claude Johnson, known as the hyphen in Rolls-Royce, in a 1905 four-cylinder 20hp TT car.

'Little Sue', SU 13, the 1905 10hp Rolls-Royce was donated to the Company after covering well over 100,000 miles. Rolls-Royce engineers would say, straight-faced: 'She is now out of warranty but can still drive at 20mph plus.' She lives proudly alongside the Silver Ghost at the Crewe factory. Though in retirement (sort of) she and the Ghost will still fire up as soon as their engines are primed.

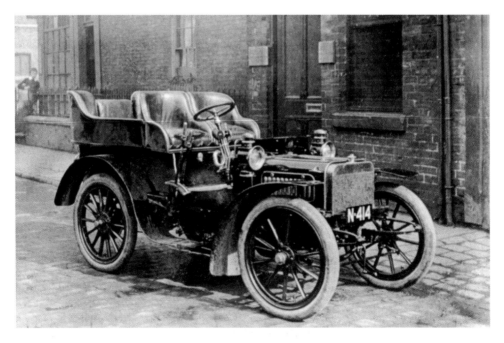

The first car built by Henry Royce pictured outside the factory in Cook Street. Designed and built by Royce to overcome the overheating and other shortcomings of the French Decauville car he had bought, this was one of three 10hp cars he built in 1904.

he continued to look for a superior British product and Johnson and Edmunds told him about the engineer in Manchester who was making cars of remarkable quality.

Royce was also recognizing that he needed somebody to sell his cars while he got on with the far more absorbing job of designing and engineering, but would not take the time to travel to London to talk to Rolls. So Edmunds persuaded Rolls to go to Manchester, meet Royce for lunch at the Midland Hotel and drive the car. Rolls suspected it would be as noisy and inefficient as everything else on the road, but, within moments of taking the wheel, he knew his search was over. He marveled at the smoothness and quietness of the engine.

Back in London, an enthusiastic Rolls hauled Johnson out of bed in the middle of the night to demonstrate the car through the empty streets. 'Henry Royce is the man I have been looking for,' he said.

Royce too, saw it as a good fit. Rolls was the man to do the marketing. They agreed that Rolls would have an exclusive right to sell all the cars Royce could make and just seven months later, in December 1904, five exhibits were shown at the Paris Salon – 10 and 20hp cars along with 10 and 15hp chassis and engines and a 30hp six-cylinder engine. They won a gold medal, impressing public and journalists and two days before Christmas, a contract was signed in which it was stipulated that all the cars would be called Rolls-Royce.

Though the industry was in its infancy, 800 companies were making cars by 1905. Rolls could have chosen any, but he saw the supreme quality and potential of the Royce and made probably the most inspired decision of his life. Royce believed that only the highest standards of engineering were acceptable and Rolls said that silence and smoothness were what customers were looking for – qualities that became the Company's cornerstones.

A Hollywood scriptwriter could not have dreamed up a better partnership – a gifted and dedicated engineer applying the highest quality standards to make better cars than the world had ever seen and an energetic sportsman and businessman with unmatched connections and a flair for demonstrating how good the cars were. They worked together for only six years, Rolls dying tragically young, but the partnership created a storybook legend.

Charles Rolls packed a lot into a short and exciting life. He set speed records, winning a string of demanding races and driving competitions including the great Thousand Miles Trial in which he beat sixty-four competitors, and he drove a 20hp four-cylinder Rolls-Royce to victory in the 1906 Tourist Trophy race in the Isle of Man, finishing twenty-seven minutes ahead of the field. He told a motoring reporter who congratulated him: 'Thank you, but as I had nothing to do but sit there until the car got to the finish, the credit is due to Mr Royce, the designer and builder.'

Later that year, deciding the New World should know about the great cars his partner was making and sensing a lucrative market in the United States, he embarked on the first sales promotional show, shipping a 'light twenty', a 20hp Rolls-Royce to New York.

He won the Five Miles Silver Trophy for 25hp cars at the Yonkers Empire City raceway after a bruising race in which other drivers aggressively tried to force him out. The advanced Royce-designed suspension gave him an edge around the bends and averaging close to 60mph, he finished twenty seconds ahead of a 30hp Packard behind which were other even more powerful cars: a 45hp Peerless and a 60hp Renault.

The race planted the seed of America's love affair with Rolls-Royce and led to the first sale, a Captain Hutton from Texas buying the Yonkers-winning car and Rolls set up a North American import company with agents in New York and Ottawa. An immediate problem was to convince skeptical United States licensing authorities that such quiet cars were gasoline-driven vehicles and not electrically powered. Winthrop and Nelson Rockefeller had no doubts. They ordered the first Rolls-Royce to be exported to the United States, a 40/50hp, similar to the Silver Ghost, which arrived in New York in late June 1907.

This beautiful old car, with original wheels, wicker picnic baskets and acetylene gas headlamps, was shipped back to England on the *Queen Elizabeth II* in 1979 to take part in a memorable seventy-fifth anniversary celebration, 'Rolls-Royce on Wheel and Wing', where 336 classic motor cars gathered at the Battle of Britain airfield at Duxford in Cambridgeshire.

The restless Charlie Rolls never married, nor did he bother with foxhunting or shooting which occupied many of his wealthy contemporaries. He was a doer, a man who believed in climbing the fence, peering over and jumping. He was fascinated by air travel, became a pioneer balloonist and crashed many times as he taught himself to fly a glider. He saw a bright future for aviation and urged fellow directors at Rolls-Royce to build the Wright Brothers' biplane under license. They said no, but he determined to press on after being taken up for his first flight by Wilbur Wright. He asked the Short Brothers, then making balloons, to build a Wright biplane for him, learned to pilot it and, on 2 June 1910, he caused a minor sensation by making the first non-stop double crossing of the English Channel in a powered aircraft. At a celebratory dinner he joked: 'This was the first time I've ever gone into France and out again without paying tax on the petrol.'

By now, Rolls was consumed by aviation and was losing interest in demonstrating cars to potential buyers. He reasoned that Royce and Claude Johnson were running the Company so well, he could step away from selling and also his duties as technical managing director, but he retained his seat on the board.

Sadly, his adventurousness cruelly cut short his life. On 12 July, a little over a month after the historic cross-channel flight, he was killed at an air show in Bournemouth on England's south coast when his French-Wright biplane crashed during a landing competition. Rolls had rejected appeals from friends to wait until strong morning winds abated. He took off and was fighting the gusts as he aimed for a touch down in the center of a 100-yard circle. Some thought the steep dive to make a pinpoint landing, following maneuvers to keep clear of a crowded spectator area, was too much for the fragile aircraft. Others believed an experimental tailplane assembly failed. Whatever the reason, there was a sharp cracking sound, part of the tailplane broke off and the plane turned upside down before hitting the ground. Rolls was thrown clear but suffered a head injury from which he died within moments.

The accident robbed him of savoring the enormous success of the Company he had founded with Henry Royce only four years before and doing so much for Rolls-Royce as it geared up to become a world-leader in aero-engines. The man who said he preferred flying to driving 'because there are no policemen in the air' might have qualified as a playboy – he had the money – but he preferred traveling fast and getting involved in the exciting beginnings of powered aviation. Certainly he took advantage of his privileged start, but he wanted to do something meaningful with his life and he was a dreamer, looking for challenges, putting his energies into getting the best out of the machines of the day and trying to improve them – aspirations he shared with Royce. Charlie Rolls' valedictory act, ironically, was to establish one more record, the melancholy distinction of being the first Englishman to die in a powered aviation accident. He was a few weeks short of his thirty-third birthday.

A friend, Eustace Miles said of him: 'I never heard anyone say anything against him except that he had too much to do.' Another described him as: 'Earnest, persistent, courageous and modest – a man who did rather than talked. Charles Rolls was of the stuff of which the best Englishmen are made.'

He might have been happy with that as an epitaph.

The early Royce cars were two-cylinder, 10hp and sixteen were produced at the Cook Street workshop, of which three survive. One of them, treasured by the Company, is SU13, Little Sue, a four-seater built in 1905 for a Mr Sydney J. Gammell, who drove her all over Scotland for fifteen years, clocking well over 100,000 miles. He could not bring himself to sell what he had come to regard as an old friend and donated the car to the Company in grateful thanks for many years of faithful service. Mr Gammell drove her from Aberdeen to Derby to make the presentation on 21 June 1920.

I was asked by a reporter, a few years back, why, having made so many wonderful cars, Rolls-Royce did not have a fabulous museum. 'There is a museum,' I replied. 'It can be seen every day, out and about on the world's roads.' It was said of Sir Christopher Wren, whose

Rolls takes the Wright brothers for a spin in the Silver Ghost.

architectural triumph was St Paul's Cathedral: 'If you would see his monument, look all around you.' The motor cars of Henry Royce are certainly his monument.

The 'mobile museum' has been one of Little Sue's roles since she came home. She has graced enthusiasts' events in many countries, including the London-to-Brighton Vintage Car Run (and with a decent tailwind, can still clip along at better than 20mph which is not bad for an old lady with 100 birthdays behind her) and in 1979 we took her to the world's leading *Concours d'Elegance* at Pebble Beach, to mark the seventy-fifth anniversary of the first Royce.

At the nearby historic car races at Monterey, with her bright bodywork gleaming in the California sunshine, she led a cavalcade of vintage cars to cheering crowds around the famed Laguna Seca track and to demonstrate her docility and smooth running, David Roscoe, my colleague from Crewe, jumped out of the driving seat and loped alongside, as she phut-phutted along, sounding like a smooth mobile sewing machine. Then he climbed aboard again to steer her around the remainder of the circuit.

The technically minded will be thrilled to know that she has a cast-iron engine, an aluminum crankcase and a crankshaft of nickel steel forging with bronzed bushed bearings and a gallon oil reservoir under the crankcase with an overflow tap to check the level. Little Sue and her 10hp siblings were followed by three-, four-, six- and eight-cylinder cars over the following two years, then the legendary 40/50hp Silver Ghost series, of which more than 8,000 were built between 1907 and 1925.

The Silver Ghost, which figures in another chapter, is believed by many to be the greatest car Henry Royce ever built and his great monument. Certainly it is the Company's most beloved heirloom. With more than 500,000 miles under her wheels, she still comes out on 'high-days and holidays' as the English say, a constant testament to the quality, durability and reliability of the great man's work.

From the outset, Royce was utterly loyal to customers, proclaiming that the sale of a motor car was not the end of it as far as the Company was concerned, rather the beginning of a relationship. Anthony Bird and Ian Hallows, in their book *The Rolls-Royce Motor Car*, long regarded as the bible of fact, said that if the Silver Ghost had not been supported by adequate service it would not have succeeded as it did. The service departments, school for drivers and annual inspections at customers' homes, if necessary, were as important as the car itself.

When the First World War started the Company stopped making chassis for cars except for military and official use – armored, ambulances and staff cars. Some of the armored variety

From car to aircraft power, Henry Royce designed the engines that enabled Alcock and Brown to make the first non-stop flight across the Atlantic.

The famed Merlin that powered RAF fighters and bombers in the Second World War.

– the type used by Lawrence of Arabia in desert warfare – and fitted with Vickers machine guns, were still in service in the Second World War.

As the First World War got under way, the government asked Henry Royce to build the qualities of his car engine into aero-engines. In just six months, the Eagle was running, a forerunner of twin Eagle motors that in 1919 carried the British flyers Alcock and Brown in a converted Vickers Vimy bomber on the first non-stop air crossing of the Atlantic – Newfoundland to Ireland – in just over sixteen hours.

Royce had a genius for developing engines to generate much more power than was originally designed into them. His R-type aero-engine which achieved more than twice its original engine power with only 1.3 per cent increase in weight, established world speed records in the air, on water and on land, won the Schneider air-race trophy three times, reaching a record speed of 340mph and led to the Merlin, which powered the fighters and bombers that inflicted so much damage upon Britain's enemies in the Second World War. It was Henry Royce's most valued gift to the most important cause of all.

The 'R' raised the world's air-speed record to 407mph in a Supermarine S6 seaplane in 1931, a staggering achievement in those days; powered the *Miss England* racing boats in the early 1930s; was driven by Sir Henry Segrave and Kaye Don to water speed records and, with a supercharger fitted, propelled Malcolm Campbell's *Bluebird* to a 272mph land-speed record at Daytona Beech in 1933. It went on to push the record beyond 300mph two years later.

Many legendary engines were to follow, including the development with Frank Whittle of the revolutionary jet engine, but though the Rolls-Royce RR badge has adorned engines powering generations of airliners, including the Boeing 747, the Concorde and the gargantuan Airbus 380, it is the motor car that comes first to most people's minds when the name Rolls-Royce comes up.

For somebody who regarded engineering purity as the Holy Grail, Henry Royce took a surprisingly cavalier attitude toward his own health. For many years, he overworked and neglected his diet, and this took a damaging toll. In the early years, fifteen-hour days were the norm to build the business and ensure its survival. Later, knowing no other way of life, Royce continued to grind away, putting in ridiculously long days and intense effort. He became very ill and Johnson, a sort of good shepherd as well as managing director, took him to London, seeking the best care. Doctors doubted he would live more than a few months, but Royce summoned inner-strength, rallied and agreed to take a holiday, traveling first to Egypt, then to the south of France. Johnson arranged to build a house in France, at Le Canadel, with an office from which the sick, but still zealous Royce belabored company managers back in England with streams of comments, engineering drawings and instructions. They accepted the onslaughts, critiques and guidance from afar, preferring them to bombardments from just along the corridor. He continued working, but never returned to the factory at Derby.

After his death, in 1933, the red lettering on the RR badge on the radiator was changed to black, mythology having it that this was done as a sign of respect to the founder. Not true. Royce himself had instructed, a short time before, that 'black lettering is more suitable than red to conform to myriad color schemes'.

Henry Royce was made a Baronet in 1931, a fitting acknowledgement of his contribution not only to the British motor and aviation industries, but to world engineering standards. That of course was when knighthoods were awarded in recognition of outstanding achievements that benefited the world in the most practical ways. Notable examples were Alexander Fleming, who discovered Penicillin, Frank Whittle, the genius behind the jet engine and Winston Churchill, whose powerful wartime leadership recently earned him the accolade 'Greatest Englishman of the Twentieth Century' in a nationwide vote.

Since then, in the view of many in Britain, knighthoods have been devalued, the title being dished out to pop singers, sportsmen, television news presenters, disc jockeys, a sprinkling of actors, political cronies and heavy contributors to party funds. The achievements of Henry Royce were exceptional. He set new goals in quality standards for an entire industry and in

THE ROLLS-ROYCE CAR.

SILENCE.

All who have tried one of these cars declare it to be the quietest yet produced. It is certainly unique in this respect.
The engine is so accurately balanced, and the carburation so perfect that when the car is standing still there is an entire absence of noise and vibration, which makes it almost impossible to tell whether the engine is revolving or at rest.

Direct Drive.

The top speed is a "direct drive," and when running, not a sound can be heard but the rush of air past the car or the "swish" of the mud on the road.

Gear Wheels.

The teeth of the gear wheels are cut by special and very expensive machinery, which ensures the most accurate work, a very high efficiency, and silence of running.

— FINALLY —

THE ROLLS-ROYCE CAR IS NO EXPERIMENT

Having covered 15,000 miles, and having been submitted to EVERY KIND OF TEST, before being placed on the market.

FULL DETAILED SPECIFICATION
——— OF THE ———
ROLLS-ROYCE CAR

Will be mailed free to any part of the world on application to
C. S. ROLLS & Co., 14 and 15, Conduit St., Regent St, London, W.

NOTE.—Every ROLLS-ROYCE Car is sent out complete with full kit of tools and spare parts, two magnificent brass headlights with double lenses, horn, and regulation tail lamp, WITHOUT EXTRA CHARGE.

6

TERMS OF BUSINESS.

PAYMENTS.
Orders for cars must be accompanied by a remittance of one-third of purchase price, the balance being payable when the car is ready for delivery at our works.
Cheques should be made payable to "C. S. Rolls and Co." and crossed "Barclay and Co., Ltd."

CARRIAGE
On goods forwarded by us is payable by Consignee. Parts sent to us for renewal or repair must be carriage paid and bear the name and address of the Sender.

PACKING.
Goods are packed by us with great care ; we do not, however, hold ourselves responsible for any loss or damage in transit.

CASES
And Packing are charged for at cost, and are not returnable.

DELIVERY.
All quotations are for delivery at our Works in London, unless otherwise specially agreed by us, and goods are forwarded by rail or road at purchasers' risk, responsibility, and expense.

GUARANTEE AS TO ROLLS-ROYCE CARRIAGES.
In the manufacture of our cars we use all reasonable care and skill to ensure the selection and use of the best materials and the best workmanship. Accordingly in lieu of the warranty or guarantee as to the fitness for the purposes for which they are sold or otherwise implied by Common Law, Statute, or otherwise, which warranty or guarantee are in all cases excluded, we give to those purchasing from us the following guarantee with all new ROLLS-ROYCE cars purchased from us :
If any part of a new ROLLS-ROYCE car supplied by us should under normal conditions be found to be defective within three calendar months from the despatch thereof through faulty material or workmanship, we guarantee and agree, provided notice of the defect be communicated to us in writing at our head office forthwith on its discovery, with the number of the car and date of sale by us, and the car or the defective part unaltered and unrepaired by others than ourselves and such other parts as we may require be delivered to us carriage paid at our works with all reasonable despatch, to repair the defect FREE OF CHARGE or we will similarly supply a replica of the part.
Our guarantee does not apply to tyres, lamps, batteries and other articles not of our manufacture.

CUSTOMERS' CARS
Are driven by Members of our Staff at Customers' own risk and responsibility.

MODIFICATIONS IN CATALOGUE.
This Catalogue is subject to modification without notice.

7

those early days a century ago, he transformed the motor car from a clanking, temperamental plaything into a safe, smooth silent comfortable and practical means of transport. He demanded dedication, patience, integrity and commitment to excellence, and refused to accept that what was already done well could not be made even better. There was only one way to approach a task and anything less amounted to unacceptable compromise.

Charles Rolls was taken from the Company all too soon. It is true that his interest in cars was waning as he turned to other exciting pursuits like ballooning and flying, but his contribution to Rolls-Royce was a major one. Without his panache, his monied contacts in society and his marketing flair, the Company might not have flourished and blossomed. Somehow, I feel, its splendid name would not have had quite the same ringing impact if the founders' names had been Schmidt and Kohl or Mitsu and Saki.

The many accomplishments of Henry Royce and the notable contributions he made to engineering could give rise to a multitude of epitaphs. Perhaps he would be content with something written by Ronald W. Harker in his book *The Engines were Rolls-Royce*:

The name Rolls-Royce stands not only for
Excellence but for honest endeavor, fair
trading and good behavior. It is a name
to conjure with and one for future
generations to revere and emulate.

9

YANKEE DOODLE ROYCES – JUST AS GOOD AS THE HOME-GROWN ONES

Lore has it that only bands of little, wizened old craftsmen, tapping, shaping, leather-sewing and veneer-matching can build a Rolls-Royce, and the genuine article could be made in one of only four places in England: Manchester, where the first ones were built; Derby, where Royce took the operation in 1909; Crewe, where the cars were made after the Second World War and the Mulliner Park Ward coach-building works in London. But there is another place – the only one in the world where Rolls-Royce motor cars have been built outside their homeland and it is in the United States, at Springfield, Massachusetts, a community with two other claims to fame – being the birthplace of basketball and home of the famous rifle. For ten years, Rolls-Royce made motor cars in Springfield and accepted opinion has it that the 'American Rolls-Royce' was every bit as good as those made in England.

Just under 3,000 were produced – 1,703 Ghosts and 1,241 Phantoms. That they were built to the highest Rolls-Royce standards, set out in tablets of stone in England, was evident in a letter from an owner. He told of 'driving my Springfield car from Philadelphia to Los Angeles and back, laden with wife, daughters and luggage'. He described traversing roadless prairie, dried-up river beds and mountain passes: 'And the only attention the car required was fuel for the entire 6,627 miles.'

Charles Rolls spotted the potential of the American market in 1906 and appointed representatives in New York and Ottawa to cover the North American continent. As could be expected, New York City – Baghdad on the Hudson – where you can buy or trade anything, became a key center in Rolls-Royce sales development in the United States, but not for a decade. The enthusiastic Charlie Rolls' sales estimates had been more than a trifle optimistic and it was not until after the First World War that serious effort was put into developing the United States market.

Fewer than 100 cars were sold before the war, but the list of heavyweight buyers was impressive, among them Flo Ziegfeld, the show business czar, S.J. Bloomingdale, the department store chief, and the investment banker J. Pierpont Morgan, the man who coined the immortal phrase: 'If you have to ask the price, you can't afford it.' He was talking about a yacht, but his words have often applied to Rolls-Royce.

Sales were gathering pace by 1919, and North Americans were buying more cars than the rest of the world combined. So it was decided to do something momentous – make cars beyond England's shores and Massachusetts was selected for its availability of skilled workers and closeness to two major markets, Boston and New York. It was the only place, it turned out, that Rolls-Royce ever built cars outside England.

There was another reason for selecting the east. It was felt that it would not be a good idea to make waves like setting up shop in Michigan, which had become the heartland of the American automobile industry, particularly in the light of comments by the CEO of a

United States luxury automobile manufacturer. He told a journalist that if the cars were made to the same quality standards as the English Rolls-Royce, they would be a serious threat to top-of-the-line American cars. If they were produced on American lines, they would not be true Rolls-Royce and he would have no concerns.

The Springfield plant, formerly a wire-wheel works, took the strain off the Derby factory, which had a two-year order backlog and also got around high import duties, as most materials were sourced in the United States. A band of engineering missionaries, fifty-three engineers and supervisors, who between them were expert in overseeing every facet of the building of a Rolls-Royce, traveled with their families from England and brought along engineering drawings and samples of every part of a Rolls-Royce at each stage of its construction. These were the templates against which all locally made parts were examined. If ten separate operations were required to make a part in England, the process was replicated at Springfield. The same strict quality standards were applied to steel which was inspected during manufacture, again when it arrived at the factory and yet again as it was used to make components.

The company was sensitive to reservations about the American-built cars. It addressed the situation in terminology that had a whiff of Empire about it:

> The genuine Rolls-Royce is being built in America under strict English supervision. There will be no 'English and American' makes – just the one authentic chassis. Experts will be challenged to detect any difference whether produced in England or America.
>
> The British experts in America will send their handiwork to England and Canada as well as to patrons here. In the past Americans tried to build foreign cars, but now the English are building the English car. Furthermore, the old handicaps of a changing design, a foreign tongue and a confusing metric system are absent.

Despite this declamation/mission statement, it was a struggle to convince potential buyers that the cars were the real McCoy. Competitors had the nerve to suggest that the American Rolls-Royce was a shallow imitation of the genuine article produced in Derby, England, and the quiet bad-mouthing campaign was reinforced by United States owners of the British-built cars, with an eye to their investment.

Rumors about the United States-built cars being inferior to those made in England were way off the mark. To ensure that English factory quality standards were achieved and maintained, the chief engineer at Springfield ran what today would be called seminars for the Massachusetts-recruited workforce and did not find them wanting in any way. In fact it is acknowledged by many aficionados that the Springfield cars were every bit as good as those in England and some years, let it be breathed softly, were regarded as better. The bottom line is: if you are into classic cars and have the money, grab a Springfield Rolls.

Who were the customers for these trail-blazing American Royces? I am indebted to my friend, John de Campi, one of the most knowledgeable Rolls-Royce experts around, who wrote a fascinating book, *Rolls-Royce in America*, and painstakingly tabulated details about the cars made in Springfield. Celebrities who ordered Springfield Ghosts or Phantoms included America's sweetheart, the actress Mary Pickford, who bought a beautiful Salamanca soon after the factory rolled out the first cars. Gary Cooper had one and the movie moguls, the brothers Warner, owned several, one of which they gave to Al Jolson. Charlie Chaplin owned a Ghost and one of the last Phantoms made in America; Jackie Coogan owned two Ghosts and Fred Astaire, Harold Lloyd, Mack Sennett, Greta Garbo, Tom Mix, Douglas Fairbanks, Zeppo Marx, Irving Berlin and Howard Hughes all drove American-built Rolls-Royce. 'The Manassa Mauler', heavyweight boxing champion Jack Dempsey, owned a 1924 Piccadilly-bodied Ghost. Even the bootleggers in the south, who clearly were drivers of good taste, used Springfield Rolls to outrun the Revenoo agents. Henry Royce would have enjoyed that.

A handful of Springfields found their way to England, including a Ghost for the Marquis of Cholmondley, (pronounced Chumley, just to confuse the foreigners). Back in New York

City, deep-pocketed non-showbiz owners included the steamship magnate W.R. Grace, who bought two Phantoms, S.R. Guggenheim and Marshall Field. Tight-fisted bankers are noted for being willing to lend you an umbrella on a sunny day, but they do splash out now and again. The president of the Fifth National Bank gave a 1924 Ghost fitted with a Mayfair-body to a Mr C. Kaye – no information is recorded as to why. The president of the Metropolitan Life Insurance Company, a Mr H. Fisk got his 1923 Ghost the same way – from an appreciative vice president. What was that all about?

Also, in Manhattan, where nothing should surprise you any more, a Mrs B.T. Schulze acquired her Springfield Ghost as part of a divorce settlement. Friends gave President Woodrow Wilson a 1924 Ghost and a model of the same vintage, owned by a Mr C.H. Geist of Philadelphia, was previously rented for $7 a day, including driver. That must have been the best bargain in Rolls-Royce history.

On car care, owners were advised that 'cylinders may require regrinding after years of use.' The company also told them:

> The car does not require any more attention or skill than that demanded by any other car to maintain it in perfect condition. It will run longer and better than any other car even in a neglected condition but naturally, it will not run like a Rolls-Royce if it is neglected. To run perfectly, it is only necessary to lubricate where indicated and keep the working parts clean.
>
> Owing to the extreme silence and smoothness of the car, a neglected part will announce itself by some kind of small noise or slight harshness in running. Such small defects, of course, in other cars could not be detected as no other car is so smooth running.

A key element in laying the foundation for what was to become the largest single Rolls-Royce marketplace in the world was appointing custom coachbuilders who would meet the highest-quality standards. and several were found, the best known being the Brewster Company of New York which played a significant role in creating unique bodies. British engineers were impressed by the quality of the work being turned out in the United States. Ernest Hives, head of the experimental department at Derby, who later became a legendary Rolls-Royce chairman, reported that the workmanship of custom-body builders in America was excellent and the best were better made and finished than those in England.

The start up was gradual, no cars were ready to go until 1921 when 135 were produced, the first being a Ghost whose sticker, had it possessed one, would have sought just under $12,000 from the buyer – slightly less than the price in England. That could have been put down to the influence of American marketing techniques: not exactly a loss leader (who would dare say such a thing about a Rolls-Royce?), but make the price attractive to stimulate a market. Production grew by two cars a week the following year and again in 1924. The numbers gradually increased, many going on to be fitted with Brewster Piccadilly roadster bodies. They were some of the most outstanding cars produced by the Company and were noted for their quality and many different styles of coachwork.

Rolls-Royce of America, as the United States company was called, bought the Brewster Company in 1926 after the coachbuilder had run into difficulties and for the remaining five years of production nearly all Springfield cars were Brewster-bodied. An unspoken requirement was that the Springfield cars should replicate their British siblings, but one major concession was made to the peculiar American habit of driving on the wrong side of the road.

The steering wheel on the right, as in the imported cars had a degree of snob value, but really was a bit of a nuisance, adding an additional complication for the driver. So, early in 1925, about four years into production, left-hand drive became standard, but for a year or so was described as a modification while stocks of right-hand drives were cleared.

During a five-year production run, the Ghosts, though required to comply with technical manuals from England, were engineered to suit American road conditions. Changes were made to the gearbox, suspension, and wheels. When Springfield began to build the Phantom

I in 1926, American refinements included advanced components like thermostatic radiator shutters, a carburetor air cleaner and a central chassis-lubrication system. The lubrication design was brilliant. No longer did you (or probably your unfortunate chauffeur) have to roll about under the car to find awkward places that required oil. You merely lifted the hood, inserted an oil-filled syringe into a couple of tubes and the job was done. A good example of Yankee ingenuity of the sort that made Bill Boeing and Henry Ford industrial titans.

The Phantoms weren't race cars, but they could move. Arthur Soutter, the general maintenance manager at Springfield, writes in his book *The American Rolls-Royce*, of tuning a Brewster Speedster Phantom 1 and reaching 86mph – a respectable performance for the 1920s.

A string of American coachbuilders were subjected to gimlet-eyed scrutiny by Rolls-Royce managers who would have refused to release a chassis if they had had reservations about the quality of the body to go on to it. Any concern was misplaced. The American companies produced a range of magnificent bodies for the Ghosts and Phantoms engineered in Springfield. There was the occasional outlandish body that escaped. One was named 'The Windblown Coupé', by its American owner, William Brewster, because it was only partly completed when he took it on a trip around France. There, he said, it looked like 'a windblown privy'. It became the 1930 New York show car – after the body had been attended to.

John de Campi says it was designed to be a striking show-stopper but the body was not a practical one. The seats were so low that the driver sat nearly on the floor, and still the head room was minimal. The steeply raked door was difficult to close. Despite that, the first buyer to step up was the playboy Tommy Manville, he of multiple-marriage fame.

One owner had a pickup truck body fitted to a Phantom chassis, which a purist would aver was tantamount to wearing a Savile Row suit under your overalls. The only feature to distinguish it from other trucks was the Flying Lady hood ornament. Of course, there was another less obvious, but splendid benefit – it drove more smoothly and quietly than any other truck on the road. The American Rolls-Royce company, selling 300 cars a year by 1928, and looking for more, decided to romance the advertising and move away from traditional nuts-and-bolts copy with a more appealing, almost seductive approach. A Springfield advertisement, placed in *Vogue* in 1929, showed three stylish Phantoms and their luxurious interiors. It was headed:

'Little nothings', the French call them – but they're everything to a motor car.
     Our gloves, your bag, your scarf – '*ces petits riens*'. But what big 'little nothings' they are. They can make or mar a costume. They simply must be right!
     Years ago, Rolls-Royce learned this lesson from women and applied it to motor cars. Every detail of a Rolls-Royce – every 'little nothing' must be right.
What do we mean by 'right'? First of all, everything that goes into a Rolls-Royce must be superlative in quality. You will find no imitations in this car. Upholstery fabrics and rugs must be the finest the world produces. Hardware and fittings are never copies – they must be original in design.
     And these 'little nothings' must be impeccable in taste. No note of the bizarre ever creeps into a Rolls-Royce. Paint, trim, upholstery, hardware and fittings – even the vanity and the tassels on the curtains, must be in perfect harmony.
     But most important of all is the infinite care with which every 'little nothing' is fitted into the car. The upholstery is tailored with the same painstaking exactness that goes into an O'Rossen *tailleur*. Many a finished Rolls-Royce has been torn down and built again because the top did not have the proper slope or the seat backs did not have the proper curve.
     Because of this insistence upon perfection in details, you can be certain that the Rolls-Royce you purchase will be exactly as you would wish it to be in every way. You can be sure that, when it stands proudly before your door, you will behold a masterpiece of blended beauty.

When the copy addressed the experience of riding in the American-built Rolls-Royce, it confided:

> Somewhere between you and the graceful little figure-head that rides the radiator, you know a powerful motor is purring. You know it by the ease with which you glide up hills and by the swallow flight of the scenery. But you have to strain your ears to hear the motor. Even the din of city streets seems far away. Inside your Rolls-Royce, all is quiet. All is peace. So restful – like a countryside at twilight.
>
> Such is Rolls-Royce – the world's most magnificent motor-car creation. Swift and silent and strong. And as exquisitely tailored as the figure that looks back at you from your mirror.

Lyrical copy and much further over the top than Rolls-Royce advertisement messages in later years. But a moneyed lover of prose and romanticism might have considered it worth buying the car just to read about it! Alas, even beautiful advertisement copy and the magnificent motor cars themselves could not save the Springfield factory from closing only a decade after the start-up. Sales in 1930 dropped by one third to 212 and mustered only seventy-three the following year. Then production stopped with the books showing losses totaling $1.7 million.

The superb quality of the Springfield cars was not enough for survival. The Great Depression had much to do with the closure, but several other factors played a part, like heavy debt inherited from the purchase of the Brewster coach-building company and lack of new model investment funds. Even though the plant had been profitable on about 300 cars a year, the operation was too small to sustain the expense of tooling for new models.

Nonetheless, the Springfield plant made a significant contribution to Rolls-Royce ownership in North America and created a momentum that the British company picked up. In later years, the United States became the largest single market for Rolls-Royce and was the major cash-cow until the 1990s when another combination of economic pressures took the wheels off, as described in a later chapter.

Just as the 1920s advertising was soulfully crafted, so were other communications, even to bill-dodgers. Springfield faithfully followed standards of propriety laid down in England. After an inordinate amount of time had elapsed and it was deemed imperative to chase the bilkers, the Massachusetts management, genetically incapable of unpleasant terminology, insisted on maintaining a gentlemanly English tone in pursuit of monies due. Arthur Soutter, who was at Springfield from start to finish, recalls the phrasing of dunning letters to customers with overdue accounts:

> Dear Sir or Madam:
>
> We have the honor to present for your attention a statement showing the balance due on your account.
>
> No doubt, due to the multiplicity of demands upon your time, this has escaped your notice. We would be pleased if, at your convenience, we might receive your check in settlement.
>
> Thank you very much.

Had such letters been penned 200 miles south of Springfield, in the Soprano territory of New Jersey or New York, the terminology would likely have been less polite and the message more to the point. It would have advised the debtor that if he did not pay up, pronto, two associates would call round with baseball bats to do him grievous bodily harm.

10

HOW TO OUTFOX HIJACKERS AND THE SCHOOL FOR GENTLEMAN CHAUFFEURS

'Don't even go there' was the unspoken stricture for many years at Rolls-Royce whenever certain taboos looked like creeping into a conversation in the power corridor. It was deemed to be quite vulgar to talk about money or how expensive the car was, but even more disturbing were emotive words like hijack or car-bomb. As the world became a more dangerous place, however, executives delicately discussed the specter of the ungodly out there attempting harm on the great and the good and the rich.

The unmentionable was reluctantly raised in *The Chauffeur's Handbook*, a unique document that is classic Rolls-Royce. It recognized a new climate of potential violence and that wealthy and high-profile people seen about in luxury cars should check out their security – or at least, their drivers should. So the gold-embossed, red-bound handbook, normally devoted to etiquette, telling chauffeurs how to properly deport themselves, maintain the aura of elegance and give passengers a smooth ride, suddenly introduced jarring references to mortality. This is how it was phrased:

Explosive Devices:

Become fully familiar with the underside profile and wheel-arches of your car, as this is the most likely location for explosive devices to be planted.

Approaching the car:

1. Observe the car from all sides, looking for bags, packages or wires.
2. Slowly walk around the car and scrutinize closely, paying particular attention to the wheel wells and tires.
3. Carefully inspect the underside of the car, including brakes and electrical components.
4. Inspect the interior before opening the doors. This will be easier if it is kept clear of clothing, rugs, boxes and newspapers.
5. Keep a pocket flashlight for night inspections.
6. Listen for unnatural sounds, such as the ticking of a clock.

Remember – a cautious person continues to live.

Utilizing central door locking should become a natural extension of preparing to drive off. The safety of your passengers in a kidnap or hi-jack situation may depend on the inability of assailants to gain access through the doors or to throw a device through the windows.

It is recommended that as soon as the passengers are comfortably seated, the driver closes all the motor car's windows when traveling at low speed in high-risk areas. At high speed in low-risk areas the doors should be unlocked to enable easy access to the car in the event of an accident.

Several years later, the Company came up with a practical means of addressing an increasingly worrying reality with a security course that trained drivers to recognize potential threat or attack. They were taught evasive and aggressive driving, including high-speed reverse, braking and swing around, of the sort you see in movie car chases. I personally had a taste of such alarming driving with Peter Perris, chief of the Rolls-Royce School of Instruction, which drivers must attend if they are to call themselves Rolls-Royce chauffeurs. We were at the Lime Rock motor racing circuit in Connecticut, running a two-day version of the school for a small group of American journalists. Peter startled the journalists by hot-rodding a 385hp Bentley Turbo R around the track at alarmingly high speeds. Was a big sedan tipping the scale at 2½ tons, one mused, really designed for this type of white-knuckle driving – squealing-tire trips of the sort usually indulged in by helmeted men cocooned in low-slung racecars?

But, right in tune with its deceptively high-performance capabilities and adaptive suspension, Perris took the bulky Bentley close to its limits, smilingly noting that we would know that we were close if the tarmac scraped the chrome off the door handles! At speeds that made the passengers reflect apprehensively on their chances of surviving this jaw-clenching experience, he skillfully mapped the line into each bend, drifting the Turbo through in a Schumacher-esque style that doubtless would have elicited an approving nod from the Bentley Boys whose legendary victories at Le Mans in the late 1920s blew the competition away and forged a special place for Bentley in the annals of motor racing.

Back on the straight, Perris gave us a remarkable demonstration of high-speed reversing that would most likely have ruined the day of any hijacker. I could not believe what was happening. Glancing over his shoulder, he hit the gas and the car shot backward in a straight line at something approaching 40mph. Then, a sudden palpitating maneuver – a flick of the wheel and touch of the brake achieved a violent and screeching 180-degree swivel and in a flash we were continuing in the same direction, only now facing forward. It was an impressive display of deft handling that few could hope, or perhaps would wish, to try to emulate. The journalists later wrote up the experience, averring that the professional drivers at Rolls-Royce were the guys they 'would most wish to be with in a bad situation'.

It reminded me of an anti-hijacking course run on a private estate in the south of England by a former officer of the SAS, the elite British Army Special Forces unit, whose professionalism and reputation for tackling difficult and dangerous projects is unmatched. A key section was reported thus:

> The driver shouts a codeword the moment he suspects an emergency and the passenger spreadeagles himself across the rear seat and braces for some elaborate maneuvers which might include a 'front-end throw' in which the car is spun through a 180-degree turn, or a sudden switch into reverse for a 35mph sprint backwards.

Only the British can put sentences together like that.

In a very English understated way, this is how Rolls-Royce described a major objective of its Security Training Course:

> The student will be able to demonstrate a high standard of vehicle maneuverability at low and high speed and high stress in both forward and reverse directions, and will be able to accelerate, brake and steer in a manner sufficient to extricate himself and his vehicle occupants from any situation.

Before being accepted for the course, a chauffeur had to be a graduate of the Rolls-Royce School of Instruction and to have driven for three years or 30,000 miles to the written satisfaction of his employer. He was also required to keep his car in such pristine condition that it would pass meticulous inspection by a company expert. After this rigorous examination of knowledge, competence and driving skills, he would join an exclusive group. Since 1919 when the school started, fewer than 100 people a year have been granted the prized Certificate of Merit and numbered silver cap badge. These awards set them apart from other professional drivers, signifying that they have been trained at the finest school of its kind. The cap badge, in fact, reveals more about the wearer than any commendation. In the Company's own modest words: 'It signifies that he has successfully undergone the finest tuition in order to take proper charge of the finest motor car in the world.' The really adventurous would aim for the ultimate Rolls-Royce accolade, the Advanced Driving Certificate. This involved passing the demanding test required of police drivers, a sixty-mile road trip and a mandatory running commentary lasting half an hour. Anybody who has tried to control a car on a skidpan knows how difficult it can be. But a skilled driver like David Harrison, the school's senior instructor, who was born almost within sight of the Rolls-Royce factory in Crewe, makes it look simple.

David, in charge of the advanced driving course, also knows a lot about outfoxing hijackers and finessed skidpan driving. The journalists at Lime Rock were amazed as he took a Silver Spur in a controlled, continuous circle around the greasy pan, where the rest of us had been sliding helplessly onto the grass. The same fingertip judgment applied to parking and reversing where we had to drive the car with only an inch or two of clearance between poles representing garage door limits.

Despite an acknowledgment that uneasy lay the heads of some nervous high-profile owners in the light of terrorist concerns, Rolls-Royce was skittish of publicly talking about supplying armored cars. Some were built at enormous cost, both in cash and weight and, with different driving characteristics from the norm, were better handled by a chauffeur who had been through security training. A Silver Spur in a state of semi-completion would be taken under wraps to a company south of London that specialized in materials like Chobham armor and other sterling stuff that protects military vehicles from anti-social devices like mortars. Over several months the work-in-progress would be transformed into the nearest thing to a Vickers Challenger tank, sporting a Rolls-Royce grille. The result was euphemistically referred to as 'a protected car'. The steel floor pan was fitted with so much explosive-proofing, one insider told me that if a 'reasonably powerful bomb' went off beneath it, the car would likely rise only two or three feet into the air while retaining structural integrity – another euphemism meaning it would not disintegrate. The undignified jarring when it crashed back to earth, however, was troublesome, in that such a violent bounce was not the Rolls-Royce way of doing things. Thankfully, no human beings found themselves in the position of putting any of this to the test.

The bulletproof windows were so thick, they made those pebble-glasses worn by one of the three stooges look like near-invisible contact lenses and so heavy they could not be raised or lowered. So, in the United States, where one of these four-ton battle-cruisers was used by the British Ambassador, the chauffeur had to open the door to pay tolls. This perhaps was the only possible security weakness in an otherwise impenetrable mobile bank vault.

The Mulliner Park Ward coach-building division's 'peace of mind, armor-plating and protective measures service' stated in a discreet brochure: 'In every Rolls-Royce and Bentley motor car there is one component we value more than any other. You.' Buyers were assured that the work would be strictly confidential. Planners identified the United States and Europe as fertile ground for the armored cars and forecast that these could amount to one quarter of the cars going to some markets. True to their word, they kept the numbers and the destinations off limits.

If you have acquired a 'Proper Motor Car', as a Rolls-Royce is referred to by aficionados, lore has it that you ensure that it is always driven and maintained correctly. For about $2,000 the School of Instruction would teach drivers how to get the best from their cars as well as how to comport themselves in a manner worthy of the magnificent carriages they were piloting.

Dignity at all times was a principal point in the unspoken mission statement. This stemmed in part from driver behavior in the early days when the case for formal tuition in driving and caring for a Rolls-Royce 'in the required manner' became evident as chauffeurs made the difficult transition from horse-drawn carriages to mechanically propelled vehicles.

Even a Rolls-Royce, the horrified company learned, was not immune to some indignities such as the habit of one ex-coachman-turned-chauffeur who drove the motor car through a pond at the foot of a long hill, to cool the brakes – just as he had in the days when he drove a coach and four. One of the first rules is that you must never garage a dirty car. No matter how late, it must be washed with running water and real sponges and chamois leather, the upholstery cleaned, and the edges of the windows wiped free of fingerprints and smudges.

In the school's early days, soon after the end of the First World War, chauffeurs were advised always to carry overalls in the trunk as they would be expected to work on the car, making minor adjustments, lubricating joints and, of course, tire changing. Many years later, even as the end of the century approached, students were told:

> This advice is as valid today as it was then. Any notion that chauffeuring merely entails collecting hampers from Fortnum & Mason (also known as the Queen's Grocers, in London's Piccadilly) or film stars from the Dorchester is of course, nonsense. Duties like these are just a small part of the job. Chauffeurs spend much of their time getting their hands dirty – sometimes very dirty – and a suit of overalls is still essential equipment.

When a student signs up, he is given overalls since the classes involve working under the hood and beneath the car. The first part of the course, five or ten days depending upon driving experience, is spent on learning maintenance and how to care for a motor car that has a lot more features to do with passenger comfort than almost any other on the road. Driving skills are not taken up until later because, to quote school principal Peter Perris: 'There's no point in learning how to glide smoothly away from the curb without first knowing a lot about the car.'

Students have not just included novices eager to obtain a qualification that would get them a top-drawer driving post anywhere, but experienced chauffeurs coming back for refresher courses or to learn about the new car their employer had ordered. The royal family's drivers were required to be graduates of the school. Many owners who like to drive themselves have also enrolled over the years and have left proudly clutching the grey cap and badge. For those without the time for a week's tuition, there was a one-day Owner Appreciation Course. For a modest few hundred dollars, it covered vehicle and driver capabilities and how to get the best out of a Rolls or Bentley. Owners were given a clear understanding of the car's controls and a polite, but valuable assessment of their driving abilities. One owner I knew who lived in London, a partner in a head-hunting management consultancy, would often wear a chauffeur cap when driving his Silver Shadow. He swore he was shown more courtesy and consideration by cabbies and other professional drivers on the crowded streets.

The red book includes rules about clothing and appearance that most of us do not have to worry about, like wearing a dark grey suit, white shirt, black tie, black shoes and a peaked grey cap. Leather gloves must be worn when driving and the cap worn at all times. The Rolls-Royce book of driver etiquette instructs that:

> The Rolls-Royce chauffeur is cautioned to ensure that fingernails are clean and well clipped and that nose hair is not visible. Also he should use medicated shampoo to avoid any possibility of dandruff on the shoulders of his immaculate attire. He must not slouch or drive with an arm on the windowsill.

The tome admonishes: 'Remember, if your bodily attitude is sloppy, people believe your mind is in a similar state.'

While awaiting a passenger, recommended reading is the chauffeur's manual or the highway code rather than a tabloid newspaper. The discovery of a copy of Rupert Murdoch's racy British daily, *The Sun*, noted for pictures of buxom and scantily clad ladies on page three, would, one suspects, be reason for a trip to the guillotine for the hapless fellow. There is a special note about talking to passengers, chauffeurs being instructed: 'Under no circumstances should you enter into conversation unless first addressed by the passenger, and your reply should be brief but courteous. Conversation should not be continued unless encouraged by the passenger.' While designed to ensure that a journey in a luxury car is smooth and enjoyable, the chauffeur's book offers a long list of driving safety 'dos and do nots' that apply to all cars and their drivers, such as:

Use your driving mirror as your third eye, checking it before every maneuver.
Check tire pressures regularly.
Signal clearly and in plenty of time.
Never cut in and out and always allow room to pass.
Do not sound your horn needlessly or aggressively.
Brake early and firmly but not savagely.
Maintain a good posture that will help concentration and alertness.

Here is one you might not have thought about: 'When alighting, it is important that the driver maintain complete control of his door at all times against wind force or possible surprise attack,' warns the manual:

Tightly grasp the interior door handle with your right hand and at the same time operate the release handle with your left so that your arms momentarily cross. Continuing to grasp the interior handle, once outside, pivot around and take hold of the exterior door handle with your left hand before removing your right hand from the interior handle.

When helping passengers alight, he may offer an arm but not a hand, and must always avert his eyes from lady passengers wearing short skirts or other revealing clothing.

Never smoke in the car. If someone has been smoking, open the windows and clear the air before picking up your next passenger. And empty the ashtrays. Special note: In the case of half-smoked cigars, do not assume that the owner has finished with it until a reasonable period of time has elapsed.

It is smooth, well thought out anticipatory principles like these that probably make the Rolls-Royce experience unique.

Driving members of the royal family also has its own code. The chauffeur must remove his cap immediately the royal personage appears and the cap stays off until he drives off. Upon arrival, it comes off again and is not replaced until the royal personage has disappeared from view. It is not required that you leave your seat to attend to the royal personage unless there is no other person present to do so.

The best-known employer of chauffeurs is probably Queen Elizabeth II and in some respects her drivers are the envy of the profession. As their cars have a police escort they need focus simply on gliding smoothly along and never suffer the hassles of their non-royal brethren who not only have to find safe parking and sometimes fight with officious uniformed hawks eager to slap a ticket on the windshield, but have also to watch over the car to prevent predators from damaging it. People holding a resentful view of the wealthy will vent their feelings by giving an expensive car a stark new continuous coachline by running the sharp end of a key along the bodywork. However, there are numerous compensations for the downside. Rolls-Royce chauffeurs enjoy a special position – being universally regarded as being at the pinnacle of their calling.

Whether driving the Queen, a captain of industry, a movie star or a wealthy aristocrat, a graduate of The Rolls-Royce School of Instruction can take pride in being one of the world's best-trained chauffeurs, and this is publicly acknowledged every day as he is entrusted with the safety of leaders in their fields and with the world's finest formal motor car.

11

THE BLACK ART, SHAPELY LADIES AND OTHER WONDROUS THINGS

A cheerful man with a cherubic face, Tony Kent lifts his copper soldering iron off a gas burner, squints down the edges of two flawlessly shaped pieces of stainless steel and joins them with skill that makes the seams undetectable. His measuring instruments are hand and eye, supported by intense concentration and thirty years' experience of the black art that has more to do with ancient metal crafting practices than a car factory.

It takes nearly a day to prepare and soft-solder the eleven pieces of hand-formed metal, about one-tenth of an inch thick, which make up the main structure of the classic hallmark of a Rolls-Royce: the radiator shell. Though simply put together with a traditional pointed iron, heated over an open flame, the connections are very strong and virtually invisible.

A falling flagpole at Buckingham Palace once dented the grille of one of the Queen's Phantom limousines but every joint held. The grille was repaired quite easily but the flagpole, it was sadly reported, was never the same again. The most famous radiators in the world are completed with painstaking care, supreme skill and accuracy, and as Tony puts it, 'with a little optical-illusion help from the ancient Greeks'. Though they appear to be perfectly straight and flat, all the lines and surfaces are in fact slightly curved. A ruler indicates a millimeter of light beneath each edge.

The Greeks called this geometric distortion, a combination of bowed lines and shiny surfaces 'entasis' and the principle, well over 2,000 years old, was used by Kallikrates when he designed the subtle curves into the Doric columns of the Parthenon, probably Greece's most famous symbol, unless that be the Olympic rings. Story has it that Charles Rolls, on vacation, made the long climb to the summit of the Acropolis and the soaring columns of the legendary Greek temple inspired the design of the grille that fairly soon afterward became a hallmark of the motor cars.

The grille is the DNA or personal 'fingerprint' of every motor car that was made at Derby and Crewe. They appear to be identical, but as with human fingerprints, no two are exactly alike. And it has always been proudly claimed that if one comes back damaged, it will be repaired by the man who knows it best – the craftsman who made it. And, if he has retired, the work will be entrusted to somebody he taught, as his methods will be identical.

Over the years, as model-styling changed, so too did radiator-shell dimensions, but the basic profile has been a constant since the early part of the twentieth century. This meant that the craftsmen enjoyed variations in their work, producing one of a dozen different types going back to the 1950s. For decades, only ten men in the world, with special skills knew how to craft the radiator grille of a Rolls-Royce. Most of them served the Company for more than a quarter century and would tutor apprentices who would be their successors, revealing the techniques and the wrinkles as the craft was learned and skills honed.

Though seemingly silver, the radiator's almost mirror-finish came from five hours of polishing the steel until it gleamed brighter than chrome and, in addition to the famed RR

Left: The Rolls-Royce radiator grille.

Below: Tony Kent, one of the few men in the world with the skill to handcraft a grille with stainless steel. Each required a full day's work.

badge at the front, each grille bore a secret second set of initials applied by the craftsman, a neatly inscribed 'trademark', two, sometimes three, letters on the back. These monograms were the signature by which he took personal responsibility for his work. 'I'm proud of what I do,' Tony Kent allows. 'It's more than a job, it is pride of workmanship, and when I see a Royce on the street I often wonder if the grille is one of mine.' He could easily find out. His trademark initials, *TT* are chiseled on the back. Colleague Dennis Jones would proudly tell visitors: 'The finest joints we can hope to get are about the thickness of a human hair. That's what we aim for.'

We flew Tony to the United States to demonstrate his art at the Los Angeles Auto Show and several other events round the country and he fascinated the crowds with his dexterity and skills. He told reporters that though he was an experienced metal worker, it took about twelve months before he was able to complete a radiator grille at the first attempt to the satisfaction of the inspector. Over the following twenty years he crafted about 4,000 radiators, a production speed of about four a week. Although his handiwork adorned the finest motor car in the world, he never had the pleasure of driving one, having never learned to drive and used a bicycle to get to and from the factory.

The company, noted for being serious about its mission, did crack occasionally. In an advertisement extolling the unique features of the product, it intoned: 'It takes one man a week to make a Rolls-Royce radiator. Most craftsmen make one a day.' The stylish radiator shell is just one of many reasons why a Rolls-Royce is different from other cars. Such detailed and time-consuming processes go some way toward explaining the high-cost, handcrafting skills that prove to an owner that he has a motor car embodying qualities and workmanship that set it apart from all others.

For example, no motor car in the world has ever borne such a distinctive and elegant hallmark, a radiator of such appearance and substance, it is possibly the most striking of industrial sculptures.

IS THAT A WOMAN IN HER NIGHTIE ON THE FRONT OF YOUR CAR?

After the famous badge was soldered to the front and the polishing done, one task remained – the fitting of the *Spirit of Ecstasy*, the Flying Lady – about which there are many stories. The most intriguing suggested that the model for the racy statuette was Miss Eleanor Thornton, an attractive young lady in her early twenties. An indelicate afterthought was that she was the mistress as well as personal assistant to the Honourable John Scott-Montagu, founder of *Car Illustrated*, Britain's first motoring magazine, later the second Lord Montagu of Beaulieu, whose ancestral estate in Hampshire today houses a classic car collection. An interesting twist to the story was that they were introduced by Claude Johnson, secretary of the Automobile Club, who later became Rolls-Royce managing director. Company publicists hesitated to venture into Eleanor's relationship with his lordship, merely describing her as 'a close friend', though she was once daringly described as his paramour and their affair was pretty well-known among the chatterers in London society.

The scantily clad statuette that was to become the instantly recognizable Rolls-Royce symbol slightly shocked Edwardian England and hardly surprisingly, no young lady stepped forward at the time to admit 'It is I'. After a year or two, someone worked out that Eleanor Thornton, an unusually liberated woman for her time, was the model. Sadly, just three months shy of her thirty-sixth birthday, she died along with 334 fellow passengers and crew, when the P&O liner, *Persia* was torpedoed by a U-boat off the coast of Crete. Eleanor was due to leave the ship at Port Said, while Montagu continued to India where he was the Inspector of Mechanical Transport. Badly holed, the ship listed to port, preventing the launch of lifeboats – ironically similar to the fate of the *Titanic* three years earlier – and Montagu and Eleanor, hand-in-hand were swept overboard as they tried to climb the sloping deck. Montagu

Rolls-Royce photographer Richard Smiles took this innovative photgraph beneath the twin towers of the World Trade Center.

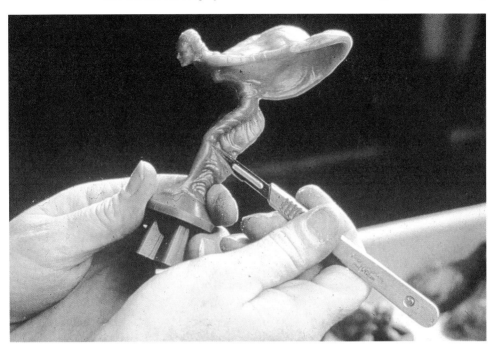

Crafting the *Spirit of Ecstasy*.

survived, thanks to a new variety of safety device given to him by a cousin, who happened to be an admiral. It looked like a suit vest but was inflatable and, more buoyant than a lifebelt, it shot him back to the surface. Eleanor's body was never found. A plaque in the parish church at Beaulieu expresses Montagu's gratitude for his deliverance and poignantly records: In memory of Eleanor Velasco Thornton who served him devotedly for fifteen years. Drowned 30 December 1915.

'Nellie in her nightie' as the irreverent among Rolls owners referred to the Flying Lady came about when Rolls-Royce became concerned about frivolous ornaments with which drivers were decorating radiator caps – figures like toy policemen and black cats. The board went so far as to make a statement in *The Car* and *The Automotor* pointing out that the appearance of a Rolls-Royce should be elegant and have purity of outline. Any figurehead appended to a Rolls-Royce should be uniform and a credit to the philosophy. The directors lyrically determined:

> … it should be one of beauty and convey the spirit of the Rolls-Royce name, namely speed with silence, absence of vibration, the mysterious harnessing of great energy, a beautiful living organism of superb grace, like a sailing yacht.

So they commissioned a leading artist and sculptor, Charles Sykes of the Royal Academy, to design something suitable and he 'experienced a spirit of ecstasy' during a drive in Montagu's 40/50 Ghost, envisioning:

> A sylph so light in her movements that she seemed about to fly away – a figure of grace, force and *joie de vivre* who has selected road travel as her supreme delight, and alighted on the prow of a Rolls-Royce motor car to revel in the freshness of the air and the musical sound of her fluttering veils. She is expressing her keen enjoyment, with arms outstretched and her sight fixed upon the distance.

...and the finished product.

The inspired Sykes determined the mascot would symbolize the silence, smoothness and subtlety of the great gliding English chassis. A wonderfully quaint description of Sykes' epiphany, as he searched for an emblem encompassing grace, movement, beauty and strength says he was:

> Awestruck upon the visage of Lord Montagu's secretary, a Miss Thornton while having tea with his Lordship and Claude Johnson. Dazzled by her beauty, he leapt up from the Queen Anne chair and twirled her about until he had positioned her delicately on her toes, her arms sweeping in a backward attitude. He then ripped the soft, silk draperies so abundant in the office, and thrust them upon a startled, bemused Miss Thornton. Flinging open the windows to welcome in the lusty winter winds, the ensuring gusts set Miss Thornton, hair and costume in ephemeral motion. The pose, the delicate material provocatively yet aesthetically outlined her slender body.

You do not often come across copy like that these days.

Eleanor first appeared atop the radiator in February 1911 and has symbolized Rolls-Royce ever since, though over eight decades was reduced from her initial height of seven inches to four. It is a sad irony that the energetic, fun-loving Charles Rolls, whose vision, enthusiasm and marketing flair did so much to help Rolls-Royce make its mark, never experienced the pleasure of gazing down the long bonnet at the beautiful creature that exhilarated Sykes and triggered his creative juices. Rolls's fatal air crash happened seven months previously.

More than one aristocrat insisted on imposing his artistic talents on mascot design. The Duke of Gloucester fitted a gun turret on the radiator of his 1939 Silver Wraith and later, on his Phantom V, a bird of prey. Montagu had Sykes sculpt him *The Whisperer*, a way-out bulky version of the Flying Lady with forefinger touching her lips. Princess Margaret who, like her sister had a Phantom IV, ordered a winged-horse ornament, Pegasus, for the radiator cap.

The kneeling *Spirit of Ecstasy* which has
attracted controversy at times.

Various metals have been used to create the *Spirit of Ecstasy* – white metal, then bronze, a mixture of copper and zinc and some of nickel which did not need plating. Others were chromium plated, or finished in silver plate, but never solid silver, as one of many myths has it. It is an unfortunate misconception which may explain why she has been an attractive target for acquisitive non-owners. Her gleaming finish has always come from hours of polishing, just like the radiator. For more than half a century she has been cast in stainless steel, using the lost wax process known as *Cire Perdu*, that was invented by the Chinese to produce works of art around 4,000 years ago.

Accurate to five-thousandths of an inch, it is still regarded as probably the most accurate means of reproducing a design and so detailed that the precision-components foundry at Crewe also produced thousands of nozzle-guide vanes for Rolls-Royce jet engines. The lost wax technique was also used to make artificial hip joints. Many a recipient smilingly swung a leg back and forth, saying delightedly: 'I've got the Rolls-Royce of hips.' Other, more mundane items like golf-club heads were also made but could not guarantee that the owner would produce the Rolls-Royce of golf performances.

The process is intriguing. A wax model of the Flying Lady is covered with plaster. Heated to more than 1,000 degrees centigrade, the wax melts out, leaving a cavity into which molten metal is poured. When cooled, the plaster is chipped away and you have a replica of the original wax figure, precise in every detail.

While all the mascots look alike, many, like the radiator shells, vary slightly, according to how the model was prepared.

The key is making a good wax original that can be worked on with a knife before casting, correcting tiny flaws or bubbles and ensuring that each one is a perfect copy of those that have gone before. There can be subtle differences, which support claims by some Rolls-Royce owners 'that the Lady on my car has characteristics that are unique'. Small differences in the hands, feet, flowing robes or facial expression would drive Sykes crazy. He regarded the facial expression as crucial and, for seventeen years until 1928, personally checked every model before it left his foundry. Those with imperfections were destroyed.

The Flying Lady gave each driver a bonus, company executives claimed with a twinkle in the eye. She was, they said with a straight face, almost the perfect shape for deflecting flying snow from the windshield. Oh yes, and if that holds, it is suspected the believers might be customers for the purchase of a bridge over the East River.

HEY – IS THIS DASHBOARD PLASTIC?

More than one buyer, marveling at the highly polished instrument panel and gleaming cocktail cabinet, has made a salesman flinch by echoing: 'Can this be plastic?' The question was asked sometimes by journalists uninitiated in the quality principle laid down by Mr Rolls and Mr Royce. The striking natural beauty of veneered burr-walnut covering the fascia and, on occasion, entire door panels was highlighted by master craftsmen who skillfully stained and brought out the patterns before lacquering and polishing the wood to a glass-like finish. I would joke with reporters that Detroit spent a fortune trying to make plastic look like wood while Rolls-Royce seemed to do just the opposite. The great strengths of Rolls-Royce have always been beauty, craftsmanship, quality, durability and exclusivity, backed by unmatched woodwork, leather upholstery and Wilton carpeting. For many decades, this panoply set the motor cars apart from all others.

Just as the Chinese of old gave the Flying Lady her perfect shape and the ancient Greeks came up with *Entasis* that inspired the lines of the radiator grille, so the Egyptians, nearly 3,000 years ago, made their contribution to the Rolls-Royce of the twentieth century with the art of veneer. Veneers begin life in unlikely places, often, like vintage wine, maturing for years in dank storage cellars. Every year, two emissaries from Crewe would visit Milan seeking grey, dull-looking wood and California, between autumn and spring, when the walnut trees have stopped growing and buyers from specialist companies scour hundreds of acres, looking for trees with concealed beauty. They even examine soil to judge how much clay or water might have influenced the quality of the burr and will back their opinions with a valuation that can go beyond $70,000 for one tree.

The burr comes not from the trunk but from a spherical growth at the base, reaching below and above ground, varying in diameter from about four times the size of a soccer ball and perhaps seven or eight feet high. These large bowls hide patterns of burrs and knots ranging from black and through browns, reds and amber and a few hues in between. Cut from the tree, the root ball spends a week in warm water to nurture the colors within, then is reduced by a giant lathe-like cutting machine to a large number of paper-thin veneer sheets. These are steamed for several days and change color from grey-green to hues and patterns hinting at a richness waiting to be offered up. Some of those dowdy looking, but preciously thin wooden pieces can be upwards of 100 years old.

The factory experts pore over whorls and patterns, searching for tree warts, unique blemishes from which skilled craftsmen, using traditional tools, coax beautiful natural patterns. The quality of the veneer for the following year's motor cars depends wholly upon the expertise of the buyer and the woodshop foreman. This is the caviar of the timber world. Scores of bundles of the thirty or so veneer leaves from one log are meticulously examined – only complete logs are considered to ensure the continuity of attractive figuring meet the highest quality standards. This means one, perhaps two sheets in 100 is Rolls-Royce quality.

For many years, the mission was to select about 70,000sq.ft of burr walnut – enough to cover nearly two football fields. Thousands of square feet of leaves would be examined, hardly perceptible patterns being sponged to see if the batch was good enough for a Rolls-Royce. Only now and again would they nod approval and buy. It struck me that the eyes and sense of aesthetics of the Rolls-Royce veneer experts were to be compared to the valuable noses

The *Spirit of Ecstasy* in her early days was huge and perfectly proportioned for the big Phantoms. But over the years became more compact to the point where some view the shrinkage on the current mascot on the Phantom produced by BMW as being overdone.

of the old wine sniffers of Bordeaux. They were evaluating the future and in this case judging colors and patterns that would only be revealed later, after Dave Martin flicked through piles of veneers and unerringly selected exact matches that made for the symmetry of the instrument panels.

The woodwork of a Rolls-Royce is probably the finest since Chippendale was around and Rob Chapman, a young woodworker whom we brought to the United States with Tony Kent, showed how a master of the craft with a sharp knife and straight edge could create intricate patterns that no two cars would ever share. He matched up to eight small sheets of veneer, connecting each seamlessly to the next and joined in the center to create a mirror-image effect running the length of the instrument panel.

Picnic and writing tables and the center console also are made from the same log, but before being applied to base wood, veneer is kept flat under pressure until a meter confirms moisture content is less than 10 per cent. After sanding, staining and priming there is a sixty-hour drying period, then three coats of lacquer, several days of air-drying and more sanding and buffing. The veneer is then polished to a glass-like finish that allows all the beauty of natural wood to shine through. At the end, the gleaming fascia, better than anything you will find anywhere in the world, is ready to be part of a Rolls-Royce. The flawless surface, almost as hard as glass, can withstand the stubbing out of a cigar should some Philistine choose to put it to the test! Just as the skilled people who distil malt scotch pay serious attention to storage, so timber and veneers are kept at precise temperatures to maintain prime condition. This means a cool, dark humid atmosphere to keep them supple and moist.

For three-quarters of a century, the patterns were recorded in each car's history book and left over pieces numbered to identify with each car so that should replacement be needed years down the road, veneer from the original log could be found in the storage sheds. The careful

Where the skills of the veneer and leather craftsmen come together.

storage of remaining pieces for years afterward reminded me of a wonderful phrase murmured by a Scottish distiller whom I interviewed for a BBC television program. After seeing the fermenting and the stills, he took me across the yard to a long, dark building where the raw, later to be golden, spirit matured slowly for ten years, often more, in oak sherry casks. Then we climbed a nearby hill to inspect the spring supplying water to the distillery and he pointed to the roof of the storage building below, which had once been green but was now quite dark. 'That's the effect of years of whisky vapor gently escaping the casks,' he said in his soft Scottish

Rob Chapman – a wood artisan creating a magnificent veneered interior.

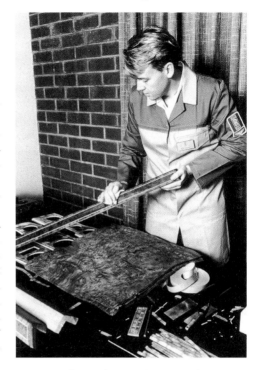

burr. 'We call that the angels' share.' These are magical moments which I believe we should treasure in a much-changed world where machines can do almost anything – and sometimes more – than a human can achieve. But it is good that age-old skills handed down over the centuries are still at work.

Rare black walnut, used on Phantom limousines and the Corniche convertible, was grown especially for Rolls-Royce in Missouri. Though Milan has long been regarded as being to veneer what Antwerp and London's Hatton Garden are to diamonds, the quest for only the very best would go far beyond Italy and the American Midwest. Californian black walnut, West African mahogany and Australian striped walnut came together for glove box and other lids and the waist rails where the door interior met the windows.

Just as the woodshop sought the finest veneers, so the craftspeople use other natural materials that have long been Rolls-Royce hallmarks; leather and wool, which give the car so much of its luxurious ambience. They use only the best and that means Connolly and Wilton.

The hides, brought to England from Scandinavia by John and Sam Connolly of London, would not have made it were there the slightest blemish like insect bites or scratches and that is why they looked to cattle bred in remote areas of northern Europe where the cold is inhospitable to insects and you do not often come across barbed wire. The Connollys were curing and dying fine leather for bespoke shoes, saddles and cavalry harness and fitting out horse-drawn carriages a quarter of a century before Henry Royce built his first car. The tanning company that supplied the hides, Williamson & Sons of Canterbury – another family firm – was plying its trade nearly a century before that and tanned the leather for army boots and saddles in the Boer War.

Generations of Williamsons prepared the raw hides in a tannery that looked like a Dickensian movie set and the brothers Connolly then finessed them 'curing and dressing' the leather in a nineteenth-century converted corn mill in Wimbledon, an area of south-west London, to become famous years later for an energetic sporting activity. It was a civilized business relationship, both families being committed to producing leather of the finest quality and in the relaxed British way of doing things it took a lengthy courtship of about fifty years before consummation. In 1963 they merged to create Connolly Brothers, which, to create a trademark infringement, might also have been called 'the Rolls-Royce of leather producers'.

Williamsons numbered and graded every hide and earmarked the best for Connolly's at Wimbledon where, still looking like a bunch of wash leathers, they were subjected to further indignities – oiling, dying, squeezing and stretching, and going through a curing and dying process that would take about three months. Rolls-Royce demanded luxurious appearance and softness, selecting only a handful of a batch of several hundred. Makers of expensive handbags and other carmakers snapped up the remainder, but polite society does not talk about that. Connolly Brothers, however, still found enough fine quality leather to meet the upholstery needs of the Prime Minister's residence, 10 Downing Street, the House of Lords and the Norwegian Parliament chamber.

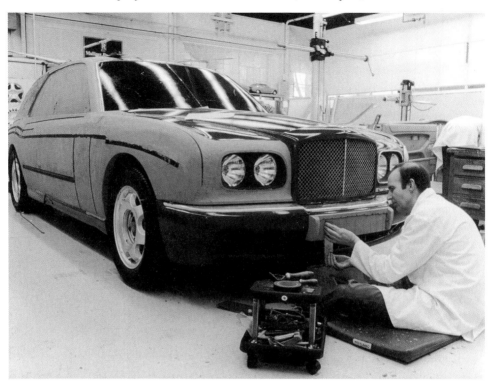

Creating a clay model of the Bentley Arnage.

A dozen cows gave their all for each Rolls-Royce, their hides, carefully matched for color and texture, covering close to 500sq.ft. A further 200sq.ft might be needed if a customer insisted on leather headlining for the passenger compartment, door-pad surrounds, seat-belt reel covers and a leather-covered horn button. About 250 pieces of leather were hand-cut and sewn for each seat, which is where the ladies of Rolls-Royce came into their own. Sewing machines played a part, but nimble fingers were the only answer to some of the complicated tailoring and fitting.

Brian Foster, who joined Rolls-Royce because he liked working with his hands, was in charge of the trim shop, where fifty highly skilled men and women created the magic of motor car interiors. His philosophy was simple: 'We can't afford to have a stitch out of place. Our customers pay a fortune for the finest materials and craftsmanship. Our aim is to ensure that they never find anything to fuss about.'

Just as the wood and leather benefited from skills passed down through the ages, so it is with the luxurious carpeting in a Rolls-Royce, coming from a mill that began weaving the highest-quality English Wilton before Victoria began to Queen it over the British Empire, using looms similar to those that have been used for centuries. The pernickety quality experts at Crowthers of Kidderminster, where soft, yet hard-wearing Wilton has been woven for nearly 300 years, would consider wool only from hardy sheep that had lived rough on three continents.

The weavers slowly made their rolls of Wilton which then went to finishers who would correct by hand any minor imperfections, even on the back. Such a commitment to that degree of hand-finishing has been the norm in the manufacture of a Crewe or Mulliner Park Ward coach-built car for generations.

And that's why about seven out of ten of the motor cars bearing the names of Henry Royce, Charles Rolls and Walter Bentley, are still around today.

12

OF GHOSTS, PHANTOMS
AND CLOUDS

She is called the Silver Ghost. A hundred years old, she is the most famous Rolls-Royce and probably the most valuable motor car in the world and we sort of hijacked the Golden Gate Bridge with her. We 'innocently' held up traffic to the point where for a minute or two, a half-dozen Rolls-Royce cars, spearheaded by the gracious, aged matriarch were the only moving vehicles on the span. We were probably lucky not to be arrested and the cars impounded. This is how it happened:

After a media event at San Francisco's Palace of Fine Arts where journalists were given rides around the Marina area in the Silver Ghost and the latest Rolls-Royce models, we thought it would be a nice gesture to drive her at the head of a Rolls-Royce cavalcade up the hill and over the famous bridge. I asked our photographer, who was shooting from a car in front, to picture the Ghost with the bridge's great towers as a backdrop.

To give him the space and time needed, and also capture the phalanx of new Rolls-Royce in his shots we had to drive quite slowly. We needed a start, so John Bingham, our Northern California zone manager summoned the nerve to stop the traffic by actually pulling a Silver Spur halfway across the road, and then cruised steadily back and forth across the lanes to ensure that cars and trucks that were not of the Rolls-Royce persuasion were held back. That was chutzpah and the maneuvers risked the whole lot of us being pulled over by a cop and told to take a sobriety test.

The outrageous blocking ensured we had the famous Golden Gate almost to ourselves with no traffic behind for quite a distance as our procession crossed the bridge. We should have asked permission, but probably would have been turned down, and if the authorities had agreed, the hassle, the paperwork and arrangements would have taken us into a bureaucratic jungle. In any event, it was a spur of the moment urge. For the toll collectors, it was probably a first. A drying-up of vehicles heading out of San Francisco does not happen in the middle of the day. Crossing the bridge, with the Ghost leading her imperious way, with only $2 million-worth of new Rolls-Royce motor cars in sight, was eerie. By the time the authorities might have stumbled upon what was happening, it was all over, but we were fortunate to get away with blatantly interfering with the traffic flow over the Golden Gate.

We pulled in at the Marin County side to position the Ghost for more shots – then the California Highway Patrol showed up. Fortunately, the officer seemed to have missed our traffic infractions on the bridge that I am sure would have generated a ticket or two, but was concerned about the 'Rolls-Royce cars and media invasion' of Vista Point park area immediately north of the bridge without a permit. I told him about the historic Silver Ghost – how it was beyond price and how it had traveled all over the world over the past ninety years or so, underscoring the reliability of Rolls-Royce motor cars.

He shut down his motorcycle engine, took off the shades, and walked around the car. He could not believe that any car that old could look so good, let alone motor, especially up the

Escorted by outriders of the San Francisco Police Department at the Palace of Fine Arts in San Francisco, the Silver Ghost with John Craig (former Rolls-Royce apprentice and later chief executive of the Canadian and Pacific Rim regions) at the wheel and Reg Abbiss in the passenger seat. The officers had finished their duty at the end of the publicity event, so did not see the Silver Ghost drive silently away to 'hijack' the Golden Gate Bridge.

long hill leading out of the city to the bridge. 'Would you like a ride in her?' I asked enthusiastically. He was astonished, and appreciated the offer, but really did not have the time. But he did sit behind the steering wheel for a few moments so that he could tell his family and the guys back at the station house about the car. He spent a little longer than he intended, however, as John Craig, a forty-year Rolls-Royce veteran who was driving her that day, complete with Edwardian clothing, gave him a detailed rundown on the Ghost's technical attributes. I suggested to the officer that he was fortunate to have a patrol area that encompassed what was probably the world's most famous bridge. He said it was and the work was more interesting and certainly less harrowing than his previous job, as a guard on death row at San Quentin, a few miles to the north. After learning more about the amazing history of the Silver Ghost, he returned to his gleaming bike. 'Have to go, but do not be too long before moving this circus out will you?' he called, as he roared off. They have some laid back cops in California.

The Golden Gate gig was a blast and I have also had the privilege of crossing the Sydney Harbor bridge with the Silver Ghost and walking alongside her in New York in Macy's Thanksgiving Parade with Miss Piggy and Kermit as the honored passengers while Rolls-Royce engineer Cal West, wearing the mandatory cap, goggles and early twentieth-century rainwear, nursed her down Central Park West and Broadway. I say nursed, because driving some distance at walking speed raised the possibility of overheating a nearly 100-year-old engine and suffering the public indignity of 'failing to proceed'.

As a precaution, we had hired four off-duty New York cops and dressed them in Edwardian English bobbies' uniforms to accompany her on the parade route, ready to push her into a side street should such a misfortune occur. But the old trouper gamely made the distance and safely delivered the Muppets to Herald Square.

There are many reasons why the 1907 Silver Ghost is revered. She has given more loyal service to Rolls-Royce than any company could ask – a flagship that has done more to establish the Company's reputation for quality, reliability and engineering excellence than any other. She was Henry Royce's masterpiece and one of the few cars driven by both he and Charles Rolls.

She shrugs off her age, and like all Rolls-Royce motor cars is meant to be driven spiritedly, not cosseted. Going back as far as the era of the Wright brothers who were given a trip out in her by Charles Rolls, she is entitled to be treated respectfully, but we never hesitated to drive her in city traffic.

She has cruised easily through Manhattan, the freeways of Los Angeles, the lake front in Chicago, downtown Boston and even tackled the New Jersey and Pennsylvania turnpikes. To reduce the danger of being clipped by another car, we would follow her fairly closely with one of her modern siblings. This also made a great picture for newspapers and television – two examples of Rolls-Royce engineering, separated by just a few feet and about ninety years. When we flew her to the United States in a new-fangled 747 for a tour to celebrate her seventy-fifth birthday, we worked out that the odometer, had she had one, would have indicated that she had been driven more than 500,000 miles over her very long life. 'Just nicely run in,' mused the engineers.

Henry Royce's beautifully engineered six-cylinder 40/50hp engine ran as sweetly as on the day he drove her out of the workshop, but the years had taken a toll of her wooden wheels which were tending to shrink, allowing the tires to slip unless we stood them in water overnight. That most certainly would never do, it was decided, and new wheels were ordered from a specialist coachbuilder in England with the instruction that they be made exactly to the specification laid down in 1907.

She has no ignition key or starter. Old-fashioned elbow-grease is needed to bring the engine to life, a powerful swing of the starting handle with the thumb carefully tucked away to avoid kickback and possible dislocation. Before this action, fairly complicated preparations have to be carried out in precise sequence. The mechanical ritual begins with priming the fuel

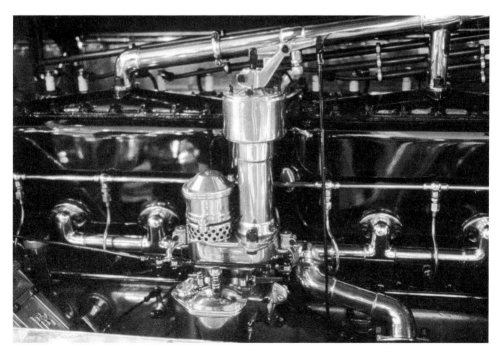

The Rolls-Royce Ghost engine.

The Silver Ghost stops for a breather after hauling up the hill leading to the Golden Gate and crossing the famous bridge.

She climbed further steep hills to a vantage point overlooking the Golden Gate.

system. The bonnet is raised to reach the priming button and check that the carburetor float chamber is full, then you have to suck the mixture through to Mr Royce's powerful cylinders by slowly turning the starting handle. The ignition switch is turned to the 'on' position, the throttle governor set slightly above zero and the ignition retarded almost to the fully 'late' position. The engine, now ready, usually rumbles gloriously and smoothly into life with the first swing of the starting handle.

But you are not done yet. The ignition must be advanced to the normal running position and the engine allowed to warm up for a minute or two before moving off, and the driver must not forget to remove a piece of wood holding the clutch pedal in the down position. This is to keep the leather faces of the cone clutch apart when the car is at rest.

To ensure travel continuity, the driver must regularly pressurize the fuel tank with a hand pump to keep the gasoline coming and adjust the spark-and-fuel mix as he goes uphill. The brake and gearshift levers are floor-mounted outside the right-hand front door and to the right of the steering wheel, which is also on the right. However, the driver has to enter from the left because the spare tire is mounted on the driver's door. How is that for confusing your enemies? And just to make life interesting, the bulb-horn is also mounted outside, slightly behind and to the left of the front passenger.

This remarkable motor car will begin to roll in any of its four gears, a governor preventing engine stall, but gear changing is tricky: 'You have to pay attention,' says Dennis Miller-Williams, the Company's London PR manager, who for many years drove the car probably more often than anybody else. To avoid nerve-jangling gearbox-crashing, you have to make sure the speeds of the mating gears are synchronized before moving the selector lever through its gate. But you do not need to do this too often. The Silver Ghost's big-hearted engine is so flexible, it will accommodate top gear over a wide range of speeds and, once in top, the old girl will bowl along at a splendid clip. Those who take care of her at Crewe have always described the 'air-conditioning provided by nature' as 'copious' and the lack of in-car entertainment 'unimportant'.

The rush of air passing the windshield would dominate the stereo system if there were one and drowns out the occasional creak from the wooden wheels when passing over bumps in the road. Though a very far cry from today's motor cars with ignition keys, starters and creature comforts, Royce designed an amazing range of advanced components – the engine governor is one example – that others had not even dreamed of in the early 1900s and all have served her well down the years.

Built on chassis number 551 and bearing the number plate AX 201, she is the original Silver Ghost and is named as such on a plaque in front of the windshield. Purists argue that there is only one Silver Ghost and that is AX 201. Having said that, many of the 7,874 Ghosts that followed over an eighteen-year production run, of which about a quarter were made in Springfield, Massachusetts, were referred to people in the Company as Silver Ghosts and given the prefix Silver by their owners for the cachet.

She was the greatest promotional tool the Company ever devised, a publicity brainchild of managing director Claude Johnson. He realized that if the Company was to flourish, the world had to be told about Royce's remarkable cars so he mapped out a program of challenging journeys to highlight the fact that Royce was making the best-engineered cars the world had seen. He determined that AX 201 also had to look spectacular, and silver-plated its carriage lamps and other fittings and finished the coachwork in aluminum paint or 'aluminium' as the English say. Johnson had an Edwardian penchant for giving names to his cars and this one, being so quiet and free of vibration, he called the Silver Ghost.

She was fast, luxurious and quiet and so far ahead of everything on the road, her qualities mesmerized the Press. *Autocar* magazine, in April 1907, eulogized that it was the smoothest

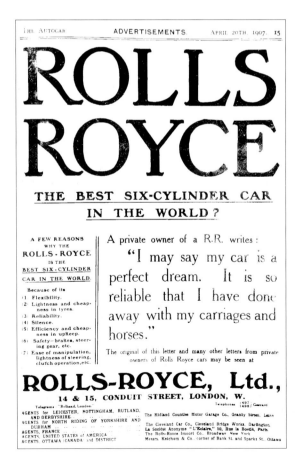

A 1907 advertisement
quoted a delighted owner.

Carefully secured, the Silver Ghost is ready for another transatlantic trip.

car it had ever experienced: 'There is no realization of driving propulsion. The feeling as the passenger sits either at front or back of the vehicle is one of being wafted through the landscape.' This journalist's reference to the sound of the clock inspired the legendary 'ticking of the clock' Silver Cloud advertising half a century later.

Charles Rolls and Claude Johnson took the car on steep and rough hill climbs and long runs to prove her mettle and her performances astounded the fledgling motoring world. Record-setting runs included a 750-mile Scottish reliability trial in which Johnson proved the car's stamina by negotiating the infamous one-in-seven 'Rest and Be Thankful' hill with its sharp hairpin bend, three times forward and twice going up backwards. It handled the remainder of the punishing course without difficulty and with but one hiccup – a fuel tap shut itself off after Johnson had negotiated the notorious Devil's Elbow on bumpy mountainous roads between Perth and Aberdeen. It was fixed in a few moments and the Silver Ghost was on her way again.

The Silver Ghost was doing remarkable things to spook other carmakers. It traveled in top gear all the way to Scotland from the south coast of England and was timed at 52.94mph over a flying quarter mile. Her most notable trip, however, was an unprecedented 15,000-mile run, back and forth between London and Scotland to double the existing long-distance record and more than 14,300 miles of the marathon were completed without an involuntary stop. Sunday stops had to be made at the insistence of the Lord's Day Observance Society which carried considerable clout in those days.

With passengers and luggage, the big open car weighed in at nearly two tons, yet got 20.86 miles to a gallon – pretty good for a 7-liter engine and a lot better than many of its successors with 6.75-liter engines achieved more than a half century later. During the record-setting London-Glasgow shuttle, when the Ghost shattered the 7,089 miles reliability record, the Company produced a poster proclaiming: 'The World Record for a Non-Stop Motor Run Broken.'

Above and below: New York media event: Dennis Miller-Williams takes young ladies in Edwardian costume for a spin through New York's Central Park.

This poster featured the car and Henry Royce, as designer and engineer in chief, and the four drivers, telling us in typically precise Rolls-Royce fashion that Claude Johnson had driven 2,635⅜ miles to date, the Honourable C.S. Rolls, technical managing director, 1,249½ miles, chief tester Eric Platford who prepared the car for the trial 2,629¼ miles and mechanician Reginald Macready 1,329¼ miles. The 15,000-mile record-setting outing was supervised by the Royal Automobile Club, whose engineers afterward dismantled most of the car for a thorough technical examination.

They reported that no wear measurable by micrometer was found in the engine, gearbox, rear axle or brakes. 'Had the car been in the hands of a private owner, no replacements would have been considered necessary,' said the RAC report. It was great testament to the quality of Mr Engineer Royce's work. Shortly after, Rolls-Royce became known as 'The Best Car in the World.'

About a year later, the call of commerce beckoned and the Silver Ghost was sold for £750 – less than $4,000 – but still expensive for a car in a period when Henry Ford had just amazed the world by raising the pay of his assembly-line workers to $5 a day. The buyer was Daniel Hanbury, who owned the car for forty years and left her to his son-in-law who did a part exchange with Rolls-Royce. He accepted a 1939 Bentley, and the Silver Ghost came home to the Company in 1949.

The Rolls-Royce London service depot overhauled the engine and bodywork to restore her to her former glory, then the Company began to proudly show her off and she reverted to the publicity role first initiated by Claude Johnson.

There is a magic about the Silver Ghost that no other motor car enjoys. In the 1960s she was featured in the movie *Those Magnificent Men in Their Flying Machines* and sailed to the United States on the maiden voyage of Cunard's *Queen Elizabeth II*. Dennis Miller-Williams drove her down the ramp and along the potholed streets on the west side where even New York cab drivers slowed to get a good view and paid their respects by honking and giving her space. Dennis took her on a 1,200-mile tour of the eastern seaboard before returning to repeat her legendary 400-mile Glasgow-to-London run for the BBC.

To celebrate the seventy-fifth anniversary of the building of the first Royce car, scores of enthusiasts drove to Manchester, some with 'young cars a mere sixty-or-so-years old', to meet at the place where it all began at the Cook Street workshops. Then, led by the Silver Ghost, a cavalcade of classic cars retraced the original fifteen-mile journey of the very first car, driven by Henry Royce to his old home at Knutsford in Cheshire. It is impossible to put a monetary value on the Silver Ghost. She is priceless, but we insured her for a nominal $30 million when she came to the United States. She occupies a special place in Rolls-Royce history. With mechanical enhancements, she kept the marque in front of the automotive field and there was a major leap in 1924 when the old acetylene lamps were replaced by 'complete electric lighting by dynamo'. Space shuttle technology was on the way!

Meanwhile, custom coachbuilders were fitting many different body styles: tourer; landaulette; limousine; cabriolet; coupé limousine; and even one called a Torpedo tourer. Whether entitled Ghost, Phantom, Wraith, Cloud, Shadow or Spirit, Rolls-Royce has always given its motor cars celestial names that set them apart from all others as they glided along to their own quiet drumbeat.

The Silver Ghost's touring Roi des Belges body styling – by the Barker coach-building company – is just one of many examples of elegant coachwork that have characterized Rolls-Royce motor cars since the early 1900s and it is doubtful we shall see many more examples of such craftsmanship. If you suggested to a manufacturer today that every car had to look different and designed as a one-off, the response would probably be 'impossible'. But such an amazing record is held by Rolls-Royce over four decades, with the help of England's finest coach-building firms. That is why there are thousands of stylishly different classic Royce to be seen around the world, some of them not far now from their centenary. These are

A New York cop stops to admire the Silver Ghost and chat with two English bobbies (who also happened to be New York cops doing a little moonlighting).

wonderful carriages exemplifying the art of the coachbuilder. For the first forty years it was in business, Rolls-Royce did not build a complete car. It made the chassis, engine and technical components, the running gear if you will. Then the platform – the base skeleton – was taken to a master coach-building firm where the body and interior fitments would be designed to the owner's specification, just as he would go to Lobb in St James's Street for his boots, Jermyn Street for shirts, Savile Row for suits and perhaps the Reform Club for his port.

Years later, when the Rolls-Royce Mulliner Park Ward Division was producing Phantoms, it accommodated owner-whims with special features like a parquet floor, a cat basket with a velvet cushion and silver chain, a stone ashtray for a pipe smoker, a horseshoe from a Derby winner and even a speedometer on the divider separating the passenger compartment from the front seats. One demanding owner required a roof to look like the sky at night, complete with stars. This was managed by fitting a perforated blue headlining about half an inch beneath the roof panel with fairy lights in between. Another owner ordered the faces of Rolls and Royce to be outlined in marquetry on the ceiling of the rear-passenger compartment. A time-consuming task, the Company first had to find someone with the skill to do it. Such a gifted artisan was found and another 'unique Rolls-Royce' was completed.

Each car reflected the individual taste of the owner – foibles would be more accurate in some cases – but almost without exception they were stylish and striking examples of good design and craftsmanship. A stroll along the lines of Rolls-Royce cars at the annual rally of the Enthusiasts' Club on an English summer's day is to walk through the Company's history of fine coach-building and engineering. Like so many crafts in England, coach-building is a fairly ancient art, going back more than 400 years when skilled cabinet makers, trimmers and workers in metal and wood built carriages for the gentry and the coaches that carried passengers and mail between London and major cities like York, Edinburgh, Bristol and Canterbury.

It originated in York in the mid-1500s when Walter Rippon built England's first coach for a Duke and later one for Queen Elizabeth. Four centuries later, the Rippon family were Rolls-Royce dealers. The H.J. Mulliner firm was plying its skilled trade in the early 1700s in Northamptonshire, about seventy miles north of London, and was in good company. They were leisurely days of olde England when contemporaries like the potter Josiah Wedgwood, the architect Robert Adams and furniture-maker Thomas Chippendale were bringing English craftsmanship to the fore. Disciples of form and function, they persuaded those with money, usually lords and squires of the manor, that first-quality craftsmanship was worth paying for. Mulliner got in early when the horseless carriage came along and was followed by the Park and Ward companies producing handsome, customized bodies for the motor cars made by Rolls-Royce.

Peter Wharton, a senior stylist at Rolls-Royce, who had been with Park Ward in the 1930s and helped design two Phantoms for Queen Elizabeth II, treasured a modest booklet called: *An Album of Park Ward Coachwork by Designers whose Productions are Acknowledged to Lead*. The first page carried the humble slogan: 'Submitted with confidence to those who require the best.' The House of Barker, as it was known, established almost 300 years ago by a military officer in Queen Anne's Guards, built coaches for George III and more than twenty coaches and carriages for Queen Victoria, we are told by Lawrence Dalton in his masterful chronicle *Coachwork on Rolls-Royce 1906-39*.

Charles Rolls was so impressed by Barker's work that soon after Rolls-Royce was founded, he instructed that 'all Rolls-Royce cars will be fitted with bodies by Barker'. The skill that had won them a reputation for producing elegant horse-drawn vehicles transferred to the new horseless carriage without missing a beat and they consolidated their position with the coachwork for AX 201 – the Silver Ghost. Coachwork for other customers was sometimes lavish and flamboyant, reflecting the tastes of Maharajahs who vied with one another to commission the most eye-catching and extravagant carriages. Ownership of upwards of forty Rolls-Royce was not uncommon – an acquisitive trait viewed by some as somewhat insensitive in a country where millions had no home and owned little more than the clothes on their back.

An unorthodox state car was built by Barker in 1913 for an Indian who rejoiced in the title His Exalted Highness, the Nizam of Hyderabad and was said at that time to be the world's richest man. Furnished with gold brocade upholstery, lace curtains, a raised ornamental throne in place of rear seats it had a domed roof to allow him to wear his headgear. They said you could see it coming. It was painted canary yellow with gold mountings.

Barker produced the coachwork for a car which, after being used by the Viceroy of India, was acquired by the Raja of Monghyr who had a Calcutta silversmith doll it up into a startling – some might say tasteless – parody of a Rolls-Royce. Over the years, Barker had plenty of competition from coach-building companies with English names that you would have to invent if they had not existed. Pearls such as Hooper, James Young, Gurney Nutting, Thrupp & Maberly, Freestone & Webb, Crosbie & Dunn, Connaught and (odd name out), the Dutch-sounding Vanden Plas vied for Rolls-Royce patronage. They even had a trade association going by the majestic title The Institute of British Carriage Makers.

Of the few of these marvelous old companies that survive, the best known probably is Mulliner, a distillation of Mulliner Park Ward, the coach-building division of Rolls-Royce, whose name has distinguished Phantom limousine and Corniche models for many years. Folklore has craftsmen still talking of the fanatical commitment to perfection by one of the founders – Mulliner, Park or perhaps it was Ward – who examined two wing panels, declared they were not a pair, and angrily used a hammer on one to ensure it would be rebuilt. The outraged panel beater, who had made them, lost his cool, picked up the hammer and dented the other in exactly the same place, shouting: 'They're a pair now.'

In England, in the first half of the twentieth century, the coachbuilders produced bodies with fascinating names: Coupé de Ville limousine, Landaulette, Fixed-top cabriolet, Special

Phantom V Mulline – Park Ward seven-passenger limousine.

Touring cabriolet, Sedanca, three-seater sports coupé, Allweather, Limousine de Ville, Continental Tourer, Touring limousine, Drophead coupé, Pillarless saloon, Concealed-hood coupé. They graced countless Ghosts and Phantoms and Wraiths and Bentleys.

Henry Royce's solidly built Ghost chassis and mechanicals proved to be so versatile, it was unnecessary for the Company to produce any other model until 1920. But, recognizing the need for successors to the Ghost if the Company were to prosper, Royce developed three models in the 1920s: a 20hp known as the Baby Rolls, the Phantom 1, and the 20/25. Anybody seeking an example of meticulous, almost messianic zeal had only to view the bodies and chassis of the Phantom when they came together. The assemblers used compressed air valves that were known in the factory as 'lookalike milking machines'. The piston devices were attached to the body while the mounting bolts were tightened to subject the body to identical stresses at each point. This would minimize vibration when the car was moving. Little wonder that Phantoms were still providing their owners with a smooth ride more than fifty years on.

The Phantom series had the longest run of any Rolls-Royce model name – from the mid-1920s right up to the 1990s – and it was the second model produced at the Rolls-Royce factory at Springfield, Massachusetts, which built the American Rolls-Royce, as it was known, in the 1920s.

Many cars were built to be hearses – others fought in wars. In addition to Lawrence of Arabia's legendary fleet of armored Rolls which were judged to be rather more effective than a camel train, the Duke of Westminster, during the First World War drove to the front in a Rolls with a machine gun mounted at the back. Another coachbuilder recreated the splendor of Louis XIV in a 1921 Phantom 1, complete with cherub-painted ceiling and Aubusson upholstered sofa.

Classic Rolls-Royce Phantom.

The Ghost series gave way to the Phantom I in 1925 and a Phantom II four years later. The Phantom III emerged in the fall of 1935 and continued until the start of the Second World War. So over a thirty-four-year period, Rolls-Royce produced only four distinct mechanical models on which, of course, coachbuilders mounted many wonderfully different bodies. The Phantom III with a mighty twelve-cylinder engine had a top speed of about 100mph, quite a clip for a non-race car in the mid-thirties. It had exceptionally light steering and very powerful brakes, useful technical attributes when you are barreling along at high speed in a car weighing as much as some trucks.

The Phantom IV, which began production five years after the Second World War, was super-exclusive even by Rolls-Royce standards and some were gloriously styled landaulettes sporting coats of arms. Only eighteen were produced for a small customer base restricted to royalty and heads of state. Three were bought by the Emir of Kuwait and three by Generalissimo Franco, the Spanish dictator, whose two seven-seat limousines and convertible sedan were armor-plated. All six had coachwork by the house of H.J. Mulliner. The Shah of Iran bought two, a Mulliner convertible coupé and a Hooper limousine and his Iraqi neighbors, King Faisal II and the Prince Regent, each had a Hooper limousine. Prince Talal of Saudi Arabia and the Aga Khan rounded off the Middle East customer list, while back in Britain, Queen Elizabeth II took delivery of another Hooper landaulette and her sister, Princess Margaret, a Mulliner limousine. The exclusive club was completed by the Duke of Gloucester and the Duchess of Kent.

The second Phantom IV to be built was kept by Rolls-Royce and used as a mobile test bed. Called 'the mule' it had Park Ward 'truck coachwork', certainly the least attractive Phantom ever produced. Not appealing to the eye, but a smooth and silent Rolls-Royce under the skin. After more than 200,000 miles of test-running, it was dismantled.

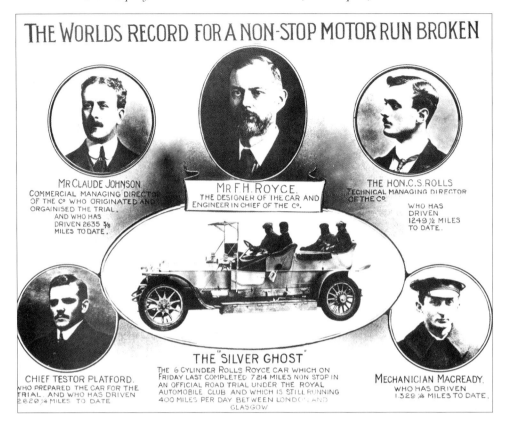

THE WORLDS RECORD FOR A NON-STOP MOTOR RUN BROKEN

MR CLAUDE JOHNSON.
COMMERCIAL MANAGING DIRECTOR
OF THE C° WHO ORIGINATED AND
ORGANISED THE TRIAL.
AND WHO HAS
DRIVEN 2635 ⅜
MILES TO DATE.

MR F.H. ROYCE.
THE DESIGNER OF THE CAR AND
ENGINEER IN CHIEF OF THE C°.

THE HON.C.S.ROLLS
TECHNICAL MANAGING DIRECTOR
OF THE C°.
WHO HAS
DRIVEN
1249 ½ MILES
TO DATE.

THE "SILVER GHOST"
THE 6 CYLINDER ROLLS ROYCE CAR WHICH ON
FRIDAY LAST COMPLETED 7214 MILES NON STOP IN
AN OFFICIAL ROAD TRIAL UNDER THE ROYAL
AUTOMOBILE CLUB AND WHICH IS STILL RUNNING
400 MILES PER DAY BETWEEN LONDON AND
GLASGOW

CHIEF TESTOR PLATFORD.
WHO PREPARED THE CAR FOR THE
TRIAL AND WHO HAS DRIVEN
2820¼ MILES TO DATE

MECHANICIAN MACREADY.
WHO HAS DRIVEN
1329¼ MILES TO DATE.

It was 1959 before lesser mortals than heads of state were able to commission a new Phantom when the Phantom V appeared, one of its many claims to fame being that that it was used to determine the minimum distance between parking meters in Britain. Over nine years, 832 lucky folk were able to buy one before the last of the great Rolls-Royce carriages, the seven-seat Phantom VI limousine, became available in 1968. A fraction under 20ft long, stylish and elegant - the 'P. Six' was majestic and a classic, everyone's idea of a true Rolls-Royce limousine.

The upholstery called for the hides of eighteen cows and the woodwork was of figured burled Lombardian walnut. The Phantom represented everything that was luxurious, solid and durable about Rolls-Royce. It was not a performance car in terms of speed and handling, but when one glides into sight, it is admired as an unmatched example of the art of coach-building. When production wound down in the 1990s, the Mulliner Park Ward coach-building division preserved the last chassis – a steel frame of great strength on which you could probably mount a London bus – should Prince Charles wish to follow family tradition and order what would be the very last Phantom VI. The chassis is in store.

A stroll along the lines of Rolls-Royce cars at the annual rally of the Enthusiasts' Club on an English summer's day is to walk through the Company's history of fine coach-building and engineering. Many magnificent designs have graced the name over the years, but if you were to ask people at random to draw a Rolls-Royce, it is quite likely that they would try to come up with the Silver Cloud. I believe the Cloud was the most beautifully styled Rolls-Royce sedan of them all. Its pure, flowing lines begged the question: How could metalworkers shape such breathtaking beauty? The design seemed to combine all that a painter or an architect would aspire to create. As one aficionado put it to me: 'The Silver Cloud. Now that's a Rolls-Royce!' He was right.

Introduced in 1955, the Cloud had a production life of just over ten years and, as technical and interior fitment innovations were developed, was represented by three versions – Silver Cloud I, II and III. Bentley models, known as SI, SII and SIII, were identical, apart from the radiator grille and badging and interestingly, of the 14,659 built, slightly more than half were Bentleys. This, Bentley enthusiasts would murmur, indicated a certain diffidence on the part of buyers who sought the luxury but a low profile.

This reminded me of a question I asked of a Rolls-Royce sales manager. A member of a family with a world-recognizable name ordered a Bentley. When told that delivery might take a month or two, he asked the Company to fit a Bentley radiator to a Rolls-Royce which in all other respects was identical. Why would he do that? The manager smiled: 'When your name's DuPont, you do not need a Rolls to say anything about you.'

With the possible exception of the Corniche convertible, few Rolls-Royce models in recent years, I feel, have achieved the admiration and special place in people's affections commanded by the Silver Cloud. Today, just as in the 1950s, people will gaze appreciatively when one comes regally into view and often are heard to observe: 'What a beautiful motor car. They do not make them like that any more, do they?' The cars that followed were more spacious and, of course, more technically advanced, adding much to convenience and comfort, but the Silver Cloud, bearing a glorious, ethereal name, has a presence that leaves one in no doubt whatsoever that a Rolls-Royce has just glided by.

The greatest act of Philistinism I can recall was a mechanical change that the Rolls-Royce dealer in Monterey, California, showed me a few years ago. He lifted the bonnet of a Silver Cloud (Clouds do not have hoods), to reveal a Cadillac engine. 'Would you believe that?' he sniffed. It was the work of a former owner, a bandleader, who thought a modern engine would enhance the performance. It struck a jarring note.

I can think of a few diehard enthusiasts, Lieutenant-Colonels and Brigadiers in the Shires of England, who would splutter: 'The chap, sir, should be put to the sword!'

13

PHANTOM CARRIAGES
FOR THE QUEEN

Only in Britain, anglophiles will marvel, will you find a quintet of Rolls-Royce Phantom limousines cheek-by-jowl with ornate horse-drawn state coaches, decorated with gold leaf, recalling days of yore when royalty and the gentry held perfumed lace handkerchiefs to their noses to quell the stench of London's streets. Tucked away in the Royal Mews at Buckingham Palace are more than 100 coaches and carriages: a unique collection spanning 300 years; a working museum of classic eighteenth- and nineteenth-century examples of the coachbuilder's art and still used for royal weddings and other ceremonial occasions.

The oldest, the Gold State Coach that has been on the road for 250 years, was used by George III when he opened Parliament in 1762 and has appeared at every coronation since the early 1800s. The body of the big coach is gilded and needs eight horsepower − literally − to pull its four tons. Only four of the thirty carriage-horses in the royal stables are needed to haul the Irish State Coach − a mere 150 years old − in which the Queen drives to the State Opening of Parliament, accompanied by Queen Alexandra's State Coach carrying the Imperial State Crown. There are several grand siblings - the Scottish State Coach, built in 1830, the 1902 Australian State Landau; the Glass Coach, 1881, and always a part of royal wedding processions and two other landaus, also used in state processions.

Also in the multi-carriage line-up is Queen Victoria's ivory-mounted Phaeton which the Queen uses for her birthday parade. All the carriages and coaches are maintained by craftsmen at the Mews and as if to emphasize that, like vintage Rolls-Royce motor cars, all are able to go at the drop of a top hat, there are two single horse-drawn broughams, closed carriages that can be seen every day carrying royal messengers on their official rounds in London, another quaint custom that is probably unique to the sceptered isle. The Royal Mews, by the way, is open to the public for much of each year and is worth a visit.

Part of the royal collection gets an airing on high ceremonial days like the State Opening of Parliament, when the Queen heads a spectacular procession from Buckingham Palace, down the Mall, through Admiralty Arch, into Trafalgar Square and along Whitehall to Westminster, passing the spot near the entrance to Downing Street where one of her ancestors, Charles I, was publicly beheaded. She is escorted by the splendidly decked-out Household Cavalry, a spectacular and delightful throwback to days of Empire. Looking as though they could add luster to a Gilbert and Sullivan chorus, the soldiers − in their plumed helmets, gleaming breastplates and polished thigh boots, jogging up and down on noble, impeccably groomed horses − provide a nostalgic whiff of olde England, an essential attraction for foreign visitors in the eyes of the drum-bangers of the British tourist authority.

A colorful royal cavalcade through London is like none other anywhere in the world. The Queen wears a selection from the crown jewels, though seldom the huge main crown which is so heavy it could tilt, or compress her head into her shoulders. She is usually accompanied

A Phantom IV state landaulette.

by Prince Philip, the Duke of Edinburgh, who wears a wonderfully anachronistic uniform and sword, bristling with enough medals, lanyards and braid to enable him to double for the bedecked Baron Bomburst in *Chitty Chitty Bang Bang*.

The ancient coaches with primitive suspensions transmit every jarring imperfection in the road and the royals are probably grateful that they do not have to go very far in them, in contrast to the Rolls Phantom fleet, still supremely comfortable despite having been around the clock and beyond the 100,000-mile mark.

Nowadays, to the relief of drivers trying to negotiate the capital's congested traffic, ceremonial processions, coaches, clip-clopping cavalry and the closing off of blocks of streets in central London do not happen too often. When the Queen does move about in public, she usually opts for a less elaborate means of transportation, one of her Phantom limousines, impressive automotive behemoths of great presence and recognizable from afar as the Rolls-Royce of Rolls-Royces. And, because they belong to the monarch, they do not have registration plates.

With huge picture windows, and standing regally and very tall, even for Rolls-Royce, they are imposing examples of coach-building skills. On the roof, at the front, is the royal coat of arms, illuminated at night by a concealed spotlight; also a blue police light, more or less to indicate – coming through! The oldest, a Phantom IV, ordered when the Queen was Princess Elizabeth and built by the famous coachbuilder H.J. Mulliner as a private formal limousine, is of such maturity it was carrying the future Queen about fifteen years before the Beatles shot to fame. One of only eighteen Phantom IVs made and painted originally in the Princess's special dark green color, it was formally described as 'a dignified blend of luxury and restraint'. It can belie its bulk, however, by being able to clock 100mph if required.

The Company extolled the car's virtues:

Phantom VI Special landaulette, limited production and available only to heads of state.

> In addition to the roominess of the rear compartment, one could not but be impressed by such features as an electric sliding roof, electric windows with emergency handles in case of breakdown, electric rear-window blind and a center-rear armrest incorporating a long- and medium-wave radio.

The Phantom was uprated to a state car and repainted in royal black and maroon. It was the first of what was to become a unique group, and was joined over a forty-year period by a stunning landaulette, two Phantom Vs built in the early 1960s and two Phantom VI state limousines representing everything opulent, symbolic, solid and durable about Rolls-Royce. The first P.6, as these models are called, was a gift from the British motor industry to mark the Queen's twenty-fifth anniversary as the sovereign and presented at Silver Jubilee celebrations in 1978. To ensure crowds a good view of the occupants it was fitted with a transparent dome and sunroof and, as the Queen is petite, power to raise the rear seats. These were upholstered in pale blue West of England cloth with mountain blue carpeting and lambswool rugs.

Though the Queen and the Duke are non-smokers, ashtrays and cigar lighters were concealed in the window sills and there was a tug of the forelock to changing times – the traditional magazine rack was replaced by a radio/cassette player and a dictation machine in a wide center armrest. Two forward-facing occasional seats folded flush to the floor. Reading lights, two air-conditioning systems and a glass division to separate the compartments, even a special cover to reduce the size of the rear window for privacy when not on official duty, completed an impressive list of appointments.

The *Spirit of Ecstasy* was different from the customary graceful goddess with outstretched arms. She was in a kneeling position, a variant not seen since the 1950s. This triggered a fuss half a century later when the Saudis ordered a dozen Rolls-Royce with the kneeling lady.

The Company was accused of chauvinism for producing 'a subservient woman to make Arab buyers feel macho'. A female journalist on *The Daily Mail* berated the Arabs and Rolls-Royce for allegedly demeaning women. Embarrassed executives at Crewe protested strongly that the kneeling lady had been available since before the Second World War and had not been specially produced to accommodate philosophies of customers in the Middle East, but depending upon which side you were on, their response had a whiff of 'Methinks the lady doth protest too much...'. They made a note to quietly forget about the kneeling lady henceforth.

Perhaps the most spectacular statuette – the Queen's personal bonnet mascot – which appears on the Queen's limousine on state occasions is a magnificent solid silver miniature sculpture of St George slaying the dragon. The royal Phantoms are probably the greatest mobile public relations tool possessed by Rolls-Royce and for well over half a century they have been at the forefront on most royal occasions. They are serviced by the Rolls-Royce dealer nearest whichever palace, castle or residence the Queen is staying and when retirement time comes, they are not sold ignominiously into the second-hand market – going instead to an historic car collection at Sandringham, one of the Queen's vacation homes.

One of the most striking cars in the royal fleet had a convertible rear roof section, a 1954 Hooper landaulette, the first Phantom IV with automatic transmission. Rolls-Royce often lent it to the Palace, but one embarrassing night, wished it had not. The car refused to start in London's Leicester Square where the Queen had been attending a film premiere. Nobody had told the chauffeur that the engine would not start unless the gear selector was in neutral. After that, a warning light was fixed to the instrument panel as a reminder. Despite the Leicester Square incident, the Palace later bought the car and it gave yeoman service for a quarter of a century until pensioned off.

The last Phantom VI for the Queen, delivered to the Palace in 1987, is a magnificent seven-seat carriage that took the engineers and craftsmen and women of Mulliner Park Ward two years to create. At 19ft 10in long, 6ft 7in wide and 6ft 1in high, it weighs in at more than three tons. Unusually, it has detachable bumpers – the result of an alarming discovery. The gargantuan Phantom was a fraction too long to be stowed on the royal yacht *Britannia*, so it was fitted with quick-release front and rear bumpers that could be removed and put back in minutes. There are some decided advantages to heading a family with the historical power to dispatch those displeasing them to the dungeons of the Tower of London with the shout 'Off with his head!'

The car, in black over royal claret, a color scheme reserved for the monarch, with the rear interior in Baroda blue, the Queen's personal choice, has rear quarter windows extended by 6in to give crowds a good view of the royals and the springs supporting the rear left seat, where the Duke of Edinburgh sits, are softer than those on the right to compensate for his being taller than the Queen. When the car was handed over, after 1,700 miles of road testing, the Company proudly stated:

> Uprated electrical systems ensure that it is able to cater for the heat of Australia, the cold of Canada and the humidity of Singapore, at any speed. As with all state cars, it will either be going very fast on a motorway or almost at a crawl on a state occasion.

A foreign trip is seldom made without a Phantom being taken abroad ahead of time to ensure that the Queen and her family are transported in true-blue British style. On the odd occasion that it is not practical to bring a car from the royal collection, the diplomatic service scouts around for a loaner. On a visit to Bermuda it was decreed that a Rolls-Royce was essential. The only Rolls on the island was owned by a famous British author. He agreed to lend it for the Queen's use, but asked if the Company would provide a plaque for the instrument panel to chronicle the fact that it had been used as royal transportation. As far I can recall, this was done and it probably enhanced the car's resale value.

Above and below: Royal Rolls-Royce Phantoms.

The price of the Queen's second Phantom VI limousine was never mentioned and it is doubtful that a detailed costing was kept, but a Phantom VI buyer, depending upon the specification – meaning, how far over the top he wished to go – could not expect to escape with much change from $1 million. But the result was worth every penny. The construction of a Phantom, the only Rolls-Royce to retain a separate chassis, an aluminum body and using age-old coach-building techniques, involved fourteen months of skilled work. This was sometimes longer if the customer – and some were quite idiosyncratic – specified many extras. These could range from a concealed humidor, liquor cabinet, fridge to hold champagne bottles, fax machine, a miniature home theater, veneer work even more detailed than the norm, exotic weavings or headlining embroidery.

The steel chassis had a strength and weight to do justice to a London bus. The rigid box girder supported an ash and galvanized-steel framework bolted to the chassis frame through special noise and vibration damping mounts. The craftsmanship in the Phantom could be traced back centuries to the stagecoaches of the type that the highwayman Dick Turpin would rob on the way from London to York. The body was formed over an inner cage of corrosion-protected steel and wood, to which a skin of aluminum panels was fitted. Mallets and old-fashioned wringing-machine-like rollers were used to shape the metal, mostly individually beaten light-alloy panels, to create subtle curves and sweeping coach lines and the artisan's hand and eye made the judgment calls as often as measuring instruments. When it was time for the roof, a dozen burly men hoisted a flat piece of steel over the framework and hammer and shape the top from there.

Elbow grease and muscle-power were the energy engines, allied to delicate tapping, filing, smoothing and flatting to create a sculpture of majestic appearance and unlike any other motor car in the world. A craftsman would take four weeks to complete a rear bumper made up of individual sections. Before this he would cut small aluminum pieces to size and hand-beat them with a sand bag. Skilled veneer, wood, upholstery, leather workers and carpet trimmers produced a luxurious interior of equal quality to that found in Phantoms destined for the Queen. The Company modestly described it as 'Truly, the motor car of kings, and the king of motor cars'.

The four-wheel three-ton drawing room rightly occupied pole position at the very pinnacle of powered ground transportation. Skill was required to handle her and it helped if a chauffeur had brawny arms and wrists. It was rather like steering an ocean liner. You stared well ahead and anticipated braking requirements before other drivers might even think about it. Like its predecessors, the Phantom handled a bit like a handsomely upholstered truck and if the car was motoring beyond the mile-a-minute mark, the brakes had to work hard to bring it to a halt. The engineers would grin and tell you: 'Once you've got up a head of steam, you can drive right through a Mercedes without spilling your drink.'

Aside from its beautifully styled coachwork, the essence of the Phantom VI was to be found in its cavernous interior – the unparalleled luxury of exquisitely matched Lombardian walnut, Wilton carpeting and lambswool rugs and the finest hides the brothers Connolly could offer. The last word perhaps was the landaulette version built only for heads of state, with a powered folding hood over the rear compartment.

When it was decided to end Phantom production, the Mulliner Park Ward coach-building division, in typical Rolls-Royce contingency fashion, put a chassis in store – the last one – against the possibility that one day, Prince Charles might decide to follow the royal tradition of having a Rolls-Royce State limousine in the stable. But he had not taken up the option when BMW assumed the name and began making its version of a Rolls-Royce Phantom in 2003. And that's a pity. Should he now do so, the Phantom he would get would not really be comparable to the magnificent examples that have been a quintessential part of British heritage for nearly a century. Being made mostly of German parts, it would be an efficient piece of Teutonic machinery, but I suspect would fall short of the intrinsic qualities of the incomparably crafted Phantoms of the type in the Queen's collection. These surviving limousines stand testament to British workmanship by true artisans who created grand carriages of such quality and presence I cannot see anything quite like them ever being built again.

FOOTNOTE

To mark the Queen's Golden Jubilee in 2002, Rolls-Royce provided another grand limousine, but departing from tradition, made it a Bentley. This decision was influenced by the fact that Volkswagen would be losing the Rolls-Royce brand the following year to BMW and were determined to blindside their German rivals while carving out a foothold for Bentley in the royal fleet.

The limousine, a much-enlarged Bentley Arnage sedan, took two years to build and at three-and-a-half tons, was more than a ton heavier than the Arnage and nearly 3ft longer. The additional weight, leaks suggested, was due to hefty armor plating, anti-mine cladding and bullet-proof glass, to which the official Bentley response was: 'The nature of any security equipment fitted is not for public consumption' – a pompous phrase that could go alongside another Rolls-Royce classic: 'To speak of money is vulgar.'

The car incorporated two novel features – a flat floor, achieved by running the transmission tunnel under the car rather than inside, and rear-hinged doors designed to make exiting easier and to enable the Queen to stand upright before stepping to the ground. There was another departure from the norm, and certainly a first. The car was presented to the Queen at Windsor Castle by a German, Franz-Josef Paefgen, Bentley Motors' new chairman and chief executive. Although more technically sophisticated than the older, coach-built Phantoms and a very comfortable limousine, it bore a large Bentley radiator which did not look as grand as the traditional Rolls-Royce grille and Flying Lady.

The Volkswagen management probably also had in mind that the acceptance by the Queen of a Bentley would assure them of a Royal Warrant of Appointment as a supplier of motor cars to the sovereign. For half a century, Rolls-Royce had been able to display the royal arms, beneath which was the golden statement:

By appointment to
Her Majesty Queen Elizabeth II
motor car manufacturers
Rolls-Royce Motor Cars Limited
Crewe Cheshire

14

ALL THOSE STORIES ABOUT ROLLS-ROYCE – CAN THEY REALLY BE TRUE?

A Rolls-Royce is guaranteed for life… the hood and engine are sealed and the factory keeps the key… a Rolls-Royce can only be sold with the blessing of the Company which will also buy the car back before it wears out.

Many of the stories about Rolls-Royce are true – others, of indeterminate origin, such as those above, have become part of the folklore and fall into the area of Rolls-Royce romanticism and suggest that they ought to be true. One legendary tale that has endured for more than ninety years is that the *Spirit of Ecstasy*, the Flying Lady mascot, is made of solid silver, an unfortunate misconception that probably explains why some have been purloined. This stolen mascot problem was addressed in the 1990s in a way that was uniquely Rolls-Royce. When touched in any way less than gently, the little lady sank elegantly into the radiator shell, while an alarm warned the populace of a heinous crime being committed. But the main reason for making the mascot disappear was not so much to thwart the light-fingered as to meet a new European law banning protuberances that might injure a pedestrian should he or she have the misfortune to collide with a Rolls-Royce. Reflecting on such a distressing possibility, cynics would muse that if you are hit by a two-and-a-half-ton car, a mechanism to take the mascot out of the equation would probably be academic. Much engineering expertise was devoted to creating a silent, hydraulic elevator-system to take her regally into the shell without any fuss.

This solution undoubtedly would have gained the approval of Henry Royce, the perfectionist. He seldom lost his temper, according to factory lore, but did go ballistic one morning when he found minor imperfections in not just one, but twelve cylinder blocks and took a sledgehammer to each one. He was capable of loosening up now and again. Proud of the engineering of his 1907 masterpiece, the Silver Ghost, AX 201, he was fond of balancing a penny on the radiator when the engine was running – a trick, that can still be accomplished today.

The Rolls-Royce owner's dream is to discover an abandoned Royce that has been gathering dust for half a century in an old barn. He charges the battery, turns the key and *voila* – the beautifully engineered motor purrs into life immediately. Such cars have been found and restored to take their rightful place in the historic cavalcade, though the engine's instant firing may be a slight exaggeration.

Kenneth Ullyett, in his book *The Silver Ghost*, recounts that in 1963, at a sawmill in remote backwoods country in British Columbia, a 1910 Ghost engine was doing a first-class job providing power for the loggers. The engine came from one of two cars that arrived in Vancouver in 1910 and were sold about nine years later. One was shipped to Japan and the other scrapped, which seemed to be an extraordinary thing to do to a Rolls-Royce in its prime. The old car came to light in 1959 at Alert Bay, 180 miles north of Vancouver and the engine wound up powering the sawmill, a great testament to Royce engineering and stamina, but not the most dignified way for a Rolls-Royce Ghost engine to end its life.

Rolls-Royce has had its share of demanding and eccentric owners. Extras ordered for Ghosts and Phantoms included a pianola, a bed, hot- and cold-running water and a gilded throne. An African chieftain required a green Rolls-Royce 'because green is the color of nature and that is my color' and insisted also on reinforced running boards for his bodyguards. One lady, rejoicing in the splendid name Mrs Churchill Wylie, decided to tour Africa in her 40/50hp limousine in the 1930s and, being unwilling to sacrifice home comforts, equipped the car with every modern convenience she could think of, including a wind-up gramophone, special cutlery and notepaper headed by a photograph of the car. In the British midlands in the 1920s, an antique dealer ordered the interior of a Rolls-Royce for his wife to be fitted out as a boudoir with tapestries and clocks and, on the ceiling, paintings of naked cherubs. An American lady had a duplicate set of instruments, apart from a steering wheel, fitted to the passenger compartment so that she could monitor the speed. Should the car be traveling faster than she considered to be prudent, she would shout at the chauffeur through a speaking tube that was also thoughtfully provided.

Many years later, in the 1990s, when the Mulliner Park Ward cathedral of bespoke craftsmanship was created, a Bentley Turbo R was converted for the use of a customer who had lost an arm. Special driving controls were fitted, along with another set in the rear compartment which raised interesting speculation about the next move if the one-armed owner in the back did not care for the way in which the car was being driven. Another man, while ordering a Turbo, was so mesmerized by the array of options when he made his pilgrimage to Crewe he almost doubled the price of the car by ordering the full range of additional features. 'Ah, the Bentley Boys survive,' murmured the craftsmen.

Some requests almost defied imagination. A wealthy European came to the factory to order the loudest stereo system imaginable. It required three small suitcase-sized amplifiers in the trunk, delivering 240 watts per speaker. With its sub-woofers (whatever they are), the car could be heard way beyond Hollywood and Vine and set the happy owner back a trifle over $30,000. Steve Watmore, commercial director of the Mulliner Park Ward Galleries, paraphrasing Mick Jagger, observed: 'Customers want satisfaction. They like to feel pride in what they have, and cost is the last thing to come into the equation.' Mulliner Park Ward's talented artisans have provided nervous owners with customized armored blast-proof cars and mobile offices where fax machine, television or cocktail bar glide silently out of sight at the touch of a button. With 'Q' from the MI5 lab-world of James Bond doubtless supervising from above, a separate air supply can be fitted to counter gas attacks, and an 007-like escape system to jettison the windows has been offered with a straight face, along with an aggressive retaliatory system that envelops the area with a huge cloud of smoke. I kid you not. No one would confirm, or indeed deny, that the inspiration for some of these gadgets could be traced to Mr Bond's Goldfinger DB5 and its memorable ejection seat.

The convertible has been a favorite of the famous for well over a quarter of a century. Wayne Gretzky, whom few would dispute was the world's greatest hockey player, plumped for a $200,000 cream-colored Corniche with a tan interior as a wedding present, but he kept it in the family. It was for his wife, the actress Janet Jones. Julio Iglesias, who kept a small fleet at his Florida home, was also dazzled by the Corniche and would treat himself to a car after a hit record broke the two million mark. But he was a bargain hunter and not enamored of sticker-prices. Before he bought the convertible, he made California and Florida dealers compete for the sale. His other cars included a blue Silver Spirit, a red Ferrari Testarossa and a red Volkswagen Rabbit which, a friend said, he loved to drive while practicing his singing. Why drive the Rabbit so often? 'People do not peer through the windows and do not follow him.' Some owners did not mind being stared at. A Silver Spirit was seen in Ohio with a sticker on the rear bumper that read: 'I got this car for my wife. Now how is that for a trade?' Sometimes, one's line of work can provide a terrific perk.

The most impressive was enjoyed by the police chief of Johore in Malaysia, who drove the world's only Rolls-Royce law-enforcement cruiser. Painted in the bright red of the local force, the Silver Spirit had white doors bearing the department crest and flashing roof lights. 'And how did the chief merit such wheels?' a magazine playfully reported:

> Well, it seems he's on intimate terms with the Sultan's wife. Which is okay since it seems he's also the Sultan, and as such owns several other Rollers, including a Phantom V limousine. The moral: If you get a speeding ticket in Johore, we seriously recommend that you pay up.

I would imagine that the car's only drawback would be that it was not the ideal low-profile vehicle for surveillance work.

Aficionados have long argued about where you can find the greatest concentration of Rolls-Royce cars. Hong Kong claims more to the square acre than anywhere else, but for many years the tiny principality of Monaco has been able to boast more per capita than any country in the world. With a population of 30,000, and 300 or so Rolls and Bentleys registered to people with homes there, the ratio of Rolls-Royce to people was one car to every 100 inhabitants. Also, there were about 200 cars registered to non-residents with businesses in Monaco. But local motoring is rather restricted, as the late Prince Rainier's little country is only about one square mile in area. With so many Rolls crammed into such a small space, the exclusivity tends to be somewhat diluted.

The wealthy can be generous at times. An Iranian lady, after major surgery in London, paid cash for a Silver Shadow and left it outside the hospital with a note of thanks to her doctor. In the mid-1980s, a Florida hairdresser and owner of a salon called the Great American Hair Experience, sacrificed his Silver Shadow sedan for the sake of ocean life. Greg Hauptner refused $30,000 and rolled the car off a barge into the Atlantic, a mile off the Palm Beach shoreline. He was calling attention to a need for new reefs where fish could thrive. It joined a 500-ton freighter that had been sunk to form an artificial reef.

With an eye to scuba-diving souvenir hunters, Hauptner had the radiator grille and hubcaps engraved with identification numbers and welded to the body, and, being a diver himself, promised to pop down occasionally to say hello to his old car. Precision has always been critical to the process of creating a Rolls-Royce and the calibrations of all measuring instruments were themselves checked for accuracy in a special 'Standards Room' which had a floor mounted on cork to ensure that it was absolutely level. The hearing of the engineer who listened to the heartbeat of an engine with a dipstick or, sometimes a stethoscope, was checked regularly, although a cork floor was not deemed necessary for the procedure. The end of each dipstick was neatly filed to prevent abrasions that might lead to small metal shavings falling into the sump.

Materials were continually subjected to quality testing – even Connolly's finest leather. During his period as CEO, David Plastow was fond of describing how a motherly lady, Mrs Irma Dougdale, spent her day squirming and bouncing up and down on seats to test durability. When she retired it was decided to go hi-tech and design a machine; a non-stop pulsating gyrating mechanism built to represent a 200lb human with a tough behind; that would wriggle and writhe around the clock for many weeks to simulate usage over one million miles. The machine was affectionately named 'Squirming Irma'.

Wilton carpeting was given severe wear treatment too. A set of powered shoe heels would grind and scuff the beautifully woven carpeting for a week, running back and forth more than 100,000 times. Even the *Spirit of Ecstasy* was not immune. When United States regulations required that anything protruding from the front of a car must give way if a human came into sudden contact, the engineers devised a spring-loaded base which was rigorously tested to ensure that she would do just that. She was subjected to the indignity of being knocked off her perch thousands of times by a swinging rubber hammer.

'Why,' an owner asked, 'are sixty-four nuts underneath my car painted yellow?' He was told gravely that the nuts securing the body to its base sub-frames were tightened to a precise point and painted so that unauthorized meddling or adjustments could be detected. One concern was to maintain the integrity of hydraulic pipes in the self-leveling suspension that gave the car such a royal ride and was finely tuned to compensate for the weight of passengers, and iron out most bumps in the road. Another task taken to fastidious lengths was the final polishing of every piece of glass in the car. Powdered pumice of a fineness normally used for polishing optical lenses was the only material considered good enough.

The only 'acceptable motor car other than a Bentley would be a Royce' according to a Dr Adrian Rogers. He opined: 'My Bentley S3 combines the sobriety required for my profession and the 100 per cent reliability I have to have for night visits.' It hardly needs to be said that he practiced in England where doctors are known still to turn out at night to attend a patient.

After the Sultan of Brunei, the largest purchaser of Rolls-Royce motor cars was the Scottish Co-operative Society, which had 240 – all of them hearses. Another Co-op in the British midlands had nearly as many, underscoring the fact that for well over half a century the British have believed in taking the final journey in great style.

Aside from the attempts of souvenir hunters to bag a Flying Lady, Rolls-Royce cars have for many years enjoyed a singular unpopularity among thieves. Apart from intricate pin-tumbler locks, whose basic design it was claimed could be traced back to biblical times, a back-up system to foil the ungodly was also built into the transmission. This locked electrically when the key was removed which left raising the car off its drive wheels and towing it as the only means of moving it.

Having said that, the Company lost a Flying Lady, and the whole car, a brand-new Silver Spirit, by the simplest of methods. Peter Bancroft, the Mid-Atlantic States zone manager, picked the car up at the New Jersey headquarters and checked into a nearby hotel for the night. The following morning, he was shocked to find the car gone. The police questioned him and then called the FBI because the case qualified as inter-state grand theft auto as the car's destination was Washington. Peter was grilled and he told me: 'They seemed to suspect it was an inside job and I was the collar.' How could the car have disappeared without his connivance? It couldn't be hot-wired. A thief with a key had to be the answer. Then it dawned. Sets of keys for new cars were always placed in the glove box along with the owner's manual. Once the thief had forced a window…

When Peter returned to the office to pick up another car, he was greeted with an ironic round of applause and the observation that maybe this was a technique he could use for inflating his sales figures. The car he had lost, or the body shell, which was all that was left of it, turned up several weeks later near Tuxedo Junction – the affluent area about forty miles north-west of New York City, where the dinner jacket got its name and where the railroad station, I believe, inspired Glenn Miller's *Tuxedo Junction*. Somebody had done a real chop shop number on it. It is said that the components are worth more individually than a whole car, and the expert locusts had surgically picked it clean. Everything that could be unbolted or sawn off had gone – the engine, transmission, radiator shell, instrument panel, upholstery, headlining, carpeting, the wheels and the trunk lid. Only part of the body shell remained. It was decided that in future, spare keys would be accommodated other than in the glove box and perhaps attention should be given to making it more difficult to break the glass.

Proud owners have provided much folklore. One in Florida, it was reported, proudly took his new Rolls to the golf club and on the way home spotted a strolling neighbor. Eager to show off his new toy, he insisted on giving him a lift and that he ride in the rear compartment to savor the luxury. The non-sporty passenger's foot caught a stray golf tee in the lambswool rug, as he settled into the deep upholstery. He picked it up and asked what it was. 'Oh, that's where you place your balls when you are driving,' replied the golfing owner. 'Good heavens,' marveled his guest, 'Rolls-Royce think of everything, don't they?'

And there was the retired colonel at a literary lunch in London, where the port was still being passed around at 3p.m. As he mellowed, the apparent charms of a mature dowager Duchess sitting opposite began to take hold. Downing another generous slug of the wondrous beverage that has been an English favorite for centuries, the fruity old colonel leaned across and murmured conspiratorially, 'I say my dear, when this nonsense is over, why do we not repair to your place and perhaps have a little fun?' The Duchess eyed him for a moment, smiled thinly and said *sotto voce*: 'Well I suppose we could, but I have to tell you that I'm in the menopause.' 'Oh no problem,' replied the old buffer. 'I'll follow in the Bentley.'

It may well have been his Member of Parliament brother, noted for good living and monotonous addresses, who was said to have delivered the 'Rolls-Royce of Speeches' to the House of Commons. It was said to be smooth, well-oiled, inaudible and seemed to go on forever.

ONLY IN NEW YORK

Thus follow two quintessentially New York stories involving Rolls-Royce cars I'd like to think are within the margin of truth:

One concerns a businessman about to fly to Europe. He drove to a Manhattan bank and requested a $10,000 loan. Asked about security, he asked: 'Will my Rolls-Royce do?' The impressed bank official approved the loan and personally drove the car into the basement garage. A month later, the businessman returned to pay off the loan. He was told he owed $10,000 plus 12 per cent interest. He signed a check and picked up his keys. The intrigued bank officer was not done: 'I ran a credit check, and found that you are a millionaire many times over. Why would you need to borrow $10,000?' The customer smiled. 'Where else in New York City could I safely park my Rolls for a month for a hundred dollars?'

The other tale concerns an elderly gentleman, on his way to an appointment in midtown in his Silver Cloud – these were the days when it was somewhat easier to park on Manhattan streets. He spotted a large gap in a line of *New York Times* delivery trucks on West 43rd street. He was preparing to back in when a young man in an MG zipped into the space – vaulted out of the driving seat and told the old boy with a cheeky grin, 'You've got to be young and quick to do that, Pop.' The Rolls driver raised an eyebrow; continued to select reverse and backed the Cloud into the by now quite small gap, crushing the MG against the front of a *Times* truck, severely reconfiguring the sports car's bodywork. 'And you have to be old and rich to do that,' he murmured to the speechless young driver.

15

CORPORATE HITMAN AND…
'THE ROLLS-ROYCE OF MUSTARDS.'

Who steals my purse steals trash.
But damned be he who steals my good name.
Shakespeare

'The Rolls–Royce of Adult Movies' proclaimed the video package shaped like a Rolls–Royce radiator grille, barefacedly using the legendary RR logo, the name and reputation earned over a century to represent the benchmark for supreme quality. 'The Flying Lady hood ornament not only lost her modesty, she was doing things drivers would find distracting,' said a shocked attorney. Then he went after the miscreants, while also chasing some lively entrepreneurs in California, using advertisements featuring well-built young ladies in tight T-shirts bearing the Rolls–Royce logo to advertise: 'The Rolls–Royce of Escort Services – Satisfaction guaranteed.'

If you want to bring a touch of paranoia to a Rolls–Royce lawyer's day, just ask about the trademark infringers. As his eyelids narrow, you'll see distress sear across the retina and, with jaw tightened, he will recount the offensive and demeaning assaults upon the hallowed marks. He will also describe the Company's counter-punching.

Why should anybody be allowed to call his product 'The Rolls–Royce of dentist chairs… of golf carts… or skateboards?' Even McDonald's got a call for advertising the Big Mac as 'The Rolls–Royce of hamburgers'. Kodak, noted for fiercely protecting its own trademark, transgressed with a Rolls–Royce comparison to a camera and when tackled about it was 'suitably apologetic' according to the Rolls legal people.

There are two dangers to ignoring trademark infringements. The public might assume that a product bearing the marks is made by, or connected with Rolls–Royce and worse, might be of poor quality, even junk. Another reason to stop trademark freeloaders is that if Rolls–Royce did not police them, the Company, by neglect, could lose its exclusive right to the name.

Ask the lawyers at Xerox, Hoover and Coca-Cola, who have long fought battles to prevent their products from becoming generic. How often have you heard people say they're going to Hoover the carpet or Xerox a document? Trademarks that were not secured, and fell into everyday use to become generic include linoleum, gramophone, escalator, nylon and cellophane. Companies really have to protect their names from misuse by unprincipled operators in commerce, or risk losing the exclusive right to their marks.

David Roscoe, the Crewe public relations director, was fond of tweaking the noses of the lawyers by observing, 'We try to get journalists to talk about our motor cars, and the legal people want to run out and arrest them.' But advertisers, not journalists, are the main offenders and the Company constantly chased, and sometimes prosecuted, those trying to cash in on the name. We had an up-and-downer with a gallery owner in Beverly Hills who used his Rolls to

Fake Rolls-Royce is banned

Rolls-Royce Motors Inc. has won a legal action against Custom Cloud Motors Inc., of Florida, who were marketing a $3,000 kit to disguise a Chevrolet Monte-Carlo as a Rolls-Royce motor car.

The customising kit contained a copy of the Rolls-Royce radiator grille, a bonnet ornament, tail-lights, fibreglass mudguards and a bonnet unit designed to fit over the corresponding parts of the latest Chevrolet model. "What they took was everything but the words 'Rolls-Royce' themselves", said Mr. Ronald Lehrman, the New York lawyer who took the Company's case to

The radiator, bonnet and mascot of the Custom Cloud are unmistakably imitation of those on the Rolls-Royce car.

court. A survey conducted by Rolls-Royce Motors and entered as evidence, showed that the so-called "Custom Cloud" was falsely identified as a Rolls-Royce car by 65 out of 100 Americans.

In the Federal Court in New York, Judge Thomas Griesa agreed "without hesitation" that the kit "falsely represents that the Chevrolet's origin is Rolls-Royce" and he ordered an immediate injunction while the case went to trial.

Above, left, opposite page and next two pages: Some of the trademark infringers chased-up by Rolls-Royce.

£500 fine for Rolls-Royce imitator

Steel Transpositions' £245 Rolls-Royce conversion kits were manufactured "in deliberate breach of court orders".

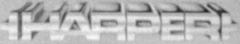

imply supreme quality of his *objets d'art* establishment, and fought to continue publishing the advertisement when told to stop. 'I own the car and can do whatever I wish,' he said. Our lawyers responded that he did not own the trademarks, and these were out front in the advertisement.

In July 2003, within a few days of the oldest profession being legalized in New Zealand, a bordello doing business as 'The White House' shocked the United States embassy by placing newspaper advertisements using an almost identical replica of the presidential seal with bald eagle and the Stars and Stripes. Seeking ladies for the nightclub downstairs, the advertisements were headlined: 'Prostitutes required at Monica's.' Responding to an accusation of poor taste, the owner, according to the BBC, said: 'I run a tasteful, classy business, not a terrible little whorehouse on the corner full of drugs and gangs. It's my crest. It might look like theirs but it is not. Clients from around the world have never complained about the United States theme.' The embassy said it would write to him expressing its 'disappointment and displeasure about his choice of symbolism'.

Rolls-Royce, however, could not afford any ambivalence when people used its name to hawk their products and, in two landmark cases in the 1970s, where trademark infringers blatantly used Rolls-Royce-style radiators and hood-ornament conversion kits, the courts handed Rolls-Royce public and legal recognition of its famed trademarks.

One was the Custom Cloud case, about a $3,000 kit to 'convert' a Chevrolet Monte Carlo into a Rolls-Royce. The customizing package included a fake Rolls-Royce radiator grille, a hood ornament, a CC badge in place of the RR, tail-lights, glass fiber mudguards and a hood unit designed to fit over the corresponding parts of the Chevy. Trademark expert Ron Lehrman handled the case for Rolls-Royce. 'What they took was everything but the words Rolls-Royce,' he said.

A survey entered as evidence showed that sixty-five out of 100 Americans identified the Custom Cloud as a Rolls-Royce. In the Federal Court of New York, a judge agreed 'without hesitation' that the kit falsely represented the Chevy to be a Rolls-Royce and ordered an immediate injunction while the case went to trial. The other trademark case was equally grotesque – a phony Rolls-Royce radiator stuck on the curved front of a Volkswagen beetle. While courts had held that a grille was a functional part of a car, and could not be trademarked, the judge determined in this case that the infringers could not even claim that the fake Rolls grille had a purpose – like sucking air into the engine – as it was stuck on the Beetle's trunk at the front of the car. Finding for Rolls-Royce, he noted: 'The Flying Lady and classic grille do indeed identify Rolls-Royce.' The ruling underscored again the uniqueness and integrity of the Parthenon-shaped grille and radiator.

Some years later, the Rolls trademarks secured recognition in United States federal courts and the Patent Office. There was little doubt that the Custom Cloud and Volkswagen grille cases created precedents in United States law that defined and confirmed the strength and value of Rolls-Royce trademarks and their right to protection under the trademark and unfair competition law. Despite court rulings, and slapping down those trying to get a free ride on Rolls trademarks, there was never a shortage of people coming out of the woodwork to make a buck.

However, Rolls-Royce Motor Cars had a great trademark policeman, Lewis Gaze, an affable, laid-back barrister with a sense of humor, who tragically died all too young. Far from being a stuffy lawyer, Gaze could see the other guy's point of view, and then would seek skillfully to work out the problem without generating rancor. Lewis was variously described by journalists as a 'corporate hit man' or the 'Keeper of the Rolls'. A man with a ready smile, he was the watchdog, gentle, tolerant and always willing to go the extra mile or two to avoid taking the mailed fist to a trademark violator, and hauling him or her into court. Usually a letter sorrowfully outlining the misdeed and asking that they desist would persuade the transgressors not to go there again. If they did, Lewis would go into action.

He never lost a case, but he regarded himself as having failed if he had to issue a writ. In a typical year, he would deal with 500 infringements worldwide, many of them involving trinkets and trash but others perpetrated by not-so-innocent businesses that required a firm approach backed up by the threat of legal action. Jovial though he was, Lewis was unrelenting in his protection of the Company's marks. He told Paul Dean of the *Los Angeles Times*: 'You have to police your trademarks or you lose them. We've spent ninety years building a reputation and you can't expect us to let some entrepreneur climb on our back and start making money in ninety minutes.'

Ruling about a Belgian beer called 'Rolls', with the bottle label bearing the radiator grille, a judge held that the name Rolls was synonymous with the name Rolls-Royce and both names were so equally famous that they should not be allowed on any other products. The judge quoted the words of F.I. Schechter, speaking to an American congressional committee as long ago as 1932: 'Take Rolls-Royce for instance. If you allow Rolls-Royce restaurants and Rolls-Royce cafeterias and Rolls-Royce pants and Rolls-Royce candy, in ten years you won't have the Rolls-Royce mark any more.'

Lewis Gaze smiled like a mischievous schoolboy, when I arranged an interview for him with an *Associated Press* reporter in New York to describe the lengths to which Rolls-Royce would go to protect its trademarks, and the journalist started his piece with, 'If you call Lewis Gaze the Rolls-Royce of attorneys – he'll sue you.' Lewis shook his head and murmured, 'Only in America…'. After that, he made several media tours of the United States where we would fix press interviews and appearances on regional television news shows where, to the producers' delight, he would come prepared with photographs. Carried by the wires, and in hundreds of newspapers, the interviews amounted to a national media megaphone to warn off people who described their products and services as the Rolls-Royce of shoes, pens, cigarette lighters, washing machines and discos.

One celebrated case that went all the way to the London law courts was prompted by a weird pseudo-Rolls produced by a transmission expert in London. He had taken a Merlin engine made by Rolls-Royce to power the Spitfire and other fighters in the Second World War and had built a 'super' car around it.

'He called this behemoth a Rolls-Royce and used it to promote his business,' said Lewis. 'Sure, it had a Rolls-Royce engine, but it was an aircraft engine and the body was definitely not a Rolls body.' The car, allegedly able to reach about 140mph, attracted crowds wherever it went, and marked its departure with a cloud of black smoke. 'Not a very good advert for our motor cars,' Lewis said. The owner refused to stop advertising it as a Rolls, so the Company sued. He responded by producing another 'super' car and a judge cracked down, ordering him not to use it. Still he persisted, putting the car into a classic car show and when it appeared again outside his home, the judge fined him £5,000 (about $7,500) for contempt and granted Rolls-Royce a permanent injunction. The 'super' car broke down outside the law courts near the top of Fleet Street, then the home of Britain's national newspapers and caused traffic chaos throughout one of the busiest areas of London.

A picture of the 'crippled Rolls' enveloped in smoke got major coverage and Rolls executives winced with embarrassment, fearing that people would believe it actually was a Rolls-Royce that had brought ignominy upon the Company. When the judge told the owner not to bring the car to court again, he arrived at the next hearing on a horse. Ah, the eccentric English.

Rolls-Royce also turned its legal eye on another London company that 'converted' vintage Austin limousines into Rolls-Royce-type carriages for funerals, weddings and other occasions where it is important that the occupants travel in style. A conversion kit included a radiator and Flying Lady hood ornament, Rolls-Royce badges, headlights and hubcaps. Lewis recounted: 'There was even an embossed Rolls-Royce plate to go on the engine. Brides thought they were being driven to church in a Rolls-Royce, but it was actually a scruffy old Austin, for which the limousine companies were getting twice the hourly rate.' With the help of a couple of policemen, Lewis raided the Austin Princess entrepreneur and found evidence showing that he had sold several converted cars.

But it was a different story when the 'hit team' went to beard another converter at his yard. The man had a record for violence and lived in a fortress with electric gates and patrolling

Doberman Pinschers. 'There were a few nasty moments when he set the dogs on us, but the police – and they were very large bobbies – stepped forward and firmly told him to lock them up.' When the situation calmed down, the officers found several cars converted with Rolls lookalike parts. Back to court and the judge granted an injunction plus the costs incurred in the pursuit of the infringers. We were intrigued when we heard that a Rolls-Royce Corniche was competing in the toughest of demanding car events, the 1981 Paris-Dakar rally. But the car was not the real McCoy – it was a glass-fiber body on Japanese four-wheel-drive running gear that had never seen the inside of a Rolls workshop. It had been put together in Paris where the owner had persuaded Christian Dior to sponsor him in the Rally to promote the new perfume *Jules*. Dior thought it was a Rolls-Royce.

Explaining how trademarks came to be important, Lewis was fond of pointing out that when wagon trains were opening up the west, the plainsmen hit on the idea of branding their cattle with marks, to prove ownership, thwart rustlers and identify strays. The Roman invaders brought protective branding to Britain with Julius Caesar, a technique they used to differentiate quality Italian pottery and support higher prices and as more business adopted the practice, it extended even to food. As early as 1266, the law required every baker in England to mark his bread, as much to prove hygiene purity as origin. A two-tier system evolved with craft guilds pushing for recognition of quality and national origin; separating the good stuff from run of the mill. It progressed from proof of ownership to a mark of quality and became an essential commercial feature protected by the registration of trademarks in law in the late nineteenth century.

The legal approach is not always spoilsport. Lewis thought it would be a shame if youngsters could not have a Rolls-Royce in their car collection. He licensed a small number of manufacturers to make models provided they were of high quality and an accurate portrayal of the motor car. Lewis Gaze, was the most reasonable and understanding of lawyers, but would throw out immediately any proposal that bordered on misuse or abuse of Rolls-Royce trademarks.

I found myself as his battering ram against Krug champagne. Rolls-Royce Motors International in the United States for several years covered not only North America, but most of Europe and the Middle East which meant I was technically responsible for our public relations and advertising in Riyadh, Bahrain, Paris, Frankfurt and Rome, though my British colleagues were many time zones nearer. Eventually, common sense dawned, and the Swiss office embraced those vast tracts of Europe and beyond.

Before that, however, on an early plane from Rome to Paris, Georges Keller, a Swiss-based colleague who watched over those areas on my behalf, mentioned that he had arranged a meeting with the Krug Champagne Co. which was seeking approval of a special advertisement. Georges had serious doubts about it and had told Remi Krug that there should be input from me as France fell into my bailiwick. We were shown into a magnificent boardroom overlooking the Champs Elysees to be stared at by what seemed to be the full might of the Krug advertising agency. There must have been fifteen people around the table. The advertisement they produced showed a Rolls-Royce Silver Shadow that had been converted into a van. It was parked in front of a chateau with a butler carefully lifting out a case of Krug. Right out in front, dominating the photograph, were the trademarks – the Flying Lady… the RR badge… the radiator grille. The ad agency chief and his colleagues looked expectantly at me. 'Monsieur Krug, ladies and gentlemen,' I said: 'You do not have a snowball's chance in hell of getting this past our trademark lawyer.' Consider, when did Rolls-Royce start making delivery vans? This is a chopped about Silver Shadow and we should probably go after them for decimation of a perfectly good motor car. And if we had built a delivery van, its use like this in an advertisement clearly suggesting that the cargo is the Rolls-Royce of champagne, would be ruled out. The assembled throng was shocked. They had expected that the American/Englishman, seduced by the charms of Paris and majestic surroundings of the Krug/Remy Martin drinks empire, would murmur compliments, give it the nod and beat it back to the Sodom and Gomorrah known as New York. Having delivered the bad news, I tried to be helpful, though I sensed that the ad agency people were not too receptive to any creative input from this philistine who had just booted their work out of the ballpark. 'Why not be more subtle?' I suggested:

> Most people who can afford fine champagne can probably identify the interior of a Rolls-Royce. Why not put a pretty girl in an evening gown and a handsome young man in a tuxedo in the rear seat of a Rolls, raising their glasses of Krug and looking like they're having a great night out?

I added that the sumptuous interior, veneered borders of the corner mirrors and the distinctive Connolly leather would make it immediately evident that they were enjoying their Krug in the most luxurious and prestigious motor car in the world. 'You'd make your point without getting writs from our attorneys.' An alternative could be to photograph a Silver Shadow or a Phantom limousine with the trunk lid raised, and the butler carefully lifting out the case of Krug. No trademarks would be visible, but the inference would be clear that only a Rolls-Royce was good enough to transport this king of champagnes. I had not just shot the whole thing down and exited. I stayed to offer what I believed were constructive alternatives. There were mutters around the table about coming up with further ideas for M. Krug who then graciously took us to lunch at what Georges deliriously proclaimed to be one of France's top three restaurants.

After my outright rejection of their advertisement, it would have been understandable if M. Krug had pleaded another engagement. But he was a charming host and insisted we drank Krug from his private reserve. A somewhat more civilized luncheon of Rolls-Royce caliber that sure vaporized an intense New York or Los Angeles mineral water morality lunch.

The epilogue to this story is that Remi Krug and his advertisement people later got their way for a while. They placed magazine advertisements showing the Rolls delivery van with a chauffeur. The trademarks were still there, adorning the startling Shadow delivery van, and the headline proclaimed: 'The Krugs have always carried their pride to extremes.' The ever-vigilant Lewis Gaze, who had agreed with my assessment of the advertisement, fired off a letter reminding Remi Krug that he had agreed to withdraw it. 'I thought we had reached an understanding concerning the use of our Company trademarks, and perhaps you could explain to me how this delivery van came about and to what extent it is intended to be used,' Lewis wrote. This was his controlled way of putting a trademark infringer on notice. Any time now, brother, we shall be in a room where the proceedings begin with the phrase: 'All rise.' Out of left field came a bombshell. The ageing Shadow, Lewis learned, had been supplied to Krug by of all people, Jack Barclay, the leading official Rolls-Royce distributor in the United Kingdom who had also arranged the conversion. Lewis despaired when he learned that his current Rolls CEO had seen the vehicle and thought it was okay.

Drawing on his wonderful sense of humor, he wrote me: 'I'm off to one of those Tibetan monasteries where you can get in and out only by lowering a basket on a rope. Silent Order naturally. I'll send my forwarding address by pigeon so that you can send food parcels at Christmas. Best regards, Lewis.' Then he sent a whammer to the senior director at Barclays. 'The good dwellers of the Marne,' he wrote, 'may have lost the fight to prevent the Italians, the Spanish and indeed the Californians from calling their dry, sparkling wines "Champagne", but I do not intend to allow this to happen to the name Rolls-Royce. I do not expect our leading distributor in the world to refer to the Rolls-Royce of champagnes.'

To Remi Krug, Lewis said:

> I was most surprised that you had this conversion carried out as we had previously made it clear that we were not happy with the idea of a Rolls-Royce delivery van and you had agreed not to use such an article in your advertising. The fact that one of our authorized distributors has become involved does not alter the situation, as they clearly have no authority to endorse either the conversion of the vehicle or such an advertising campaign.

Then Lewis generously added that as Krug had gone to the expense of having the conversion done, Rolls-Royce would not object to the vehicle being used for promotional purposes, but he insisted that neither the vehicle nor the Rolls-Royce name and trademarks be used in its advertising again.

Now I have a proud confession to make which might torment the Rolls-Royce United States in-house attorneys, were they still around, who would usually slam the door on those who had the temerity to suggest a joint venture. A year or two before they came along, I was instrumental in helping get the famed Grey Poupon advertisement up and running – a campaign that gave Rolls-Royce considerable television and print exposure over many years. I had a call from an ad agency in San Francisco. Could we lend a dozen Silver Clouds for a tasteful advertisement for Grey Poupon mustard? I said I could not help as we had stopped Silver Cloud production many years ago. When they outlined the advertisement, it was clear that Rolls-Royce would emerge with style and frequent exposure at no cost. The opportunity for an open-ended series of advertisements in upscale magazines that implicitly acknowledged Rolls-Royce to be the finest motor car in the world could not be passed up. I put the agency in touch with the Rolls-Royce Owners' Club in California who were happy to polish their cars and turn out for the filming.

They could rustle up only six white Silver Clouds, however, so the commercial had to be cleverly shot to convey twice the number – similar to war movies where they need a number of Huey choppers for Vietnam sequences but can get hold of only a handful, so they shoot them from several angles, coming and going, and when the montage comes together, it looks as though you have a couple of dozen. The advertisements, featuring a cavalcade of elegant Silver Clouds became part of American advertising lore. One Cloud, you may recall, stops alongside another, and the affluent owner, enjoying his picnic lunch but distressed to discover that he has run out of mustard, lowers the window and nonchalantly asks the owner of the other Rolls if he has any Grey Poupon to spare. 'Of course,' is the reply, and a jar is passed through the window. The advertisements were stylish and underscored the impression that Rolls-Royce cars are owned by people who enjoy the good things of life and know how to obtain them.

Certainly, Grey Poupon benefited from the association with the world's best motor car. But Rolls also reaped consistent, positive publicity – important when you have a miniscule budget for which television advertising and frequent color spreads in top magazines are out of the question. A new lawyer arrived at Rolls-Royce after the advertisements had been running for some years and would refer to them with annoyance, but was wise enough not to incur heavy legal costs and ridicule for taking action so late in the game and indeed begging the question: Why on earth would Rolls-Royce want to get the advertisement banned? A fleet of Mercedes could have been used, but the advertisements would not have had the same impact. As a German acquaintance observed: 'Mercedes cars are not exclusive enough. They make too big a range. S-Class owners do not like to think that their top-of-the-line model has a similar Benz radiator and three-pointed star as the clunking diesel taxi standing outside the *Hauptbahnhof*.

Overall, it might sound as though chasing trademark infringers is often a storm in a teacup, and sometimes it is, but overriding is the absolute need to preserve a company's reputation and identity. Nothing is more precious. Without its exclusivity, perception and sterling reputation, what would a Rolls-Royce be worth in the marketplace? Probably not much more than other upscale cars. For a hundred years its unique image has set it apart, and persuaded people to pay a small fortune for the joy of owning one. While protecting the image, we also enhanced it through communications to ensure that new generations of achievers would wish to reward themselves with the car that probably would say more about them than anything else that they possessed.

Having said all that, what do you do about an an enterprising Italian gigolo who advertised himself as 'Signor Rolly-Royce'? That made Lewis Gaze roll his eyes and guffaw, before cheerfully remonstrating with him.

Rest peacefully, Lewis my friend.

1 & 2 No motor car manufacturer in the world could expect to match the glorious State Landaulette versions of the Phantom V and VI which were built only for heads of state. Only sixteen were produced. Visibility of the occupants was a prime requirement but when the huge hood over the rear compartment was lowered the Phantom took on a very different appearance.

3 As the century drew to a close, the spectacular Phantom VI limousine that, unlike some special versions was available to ordinary mortals, gave way to the Silver Spur touring limousine, a more practical carriage for day-to-day use.

4 The Phantom interior, akin to a luxurious gentlemen's club on wheels.

5, 6, 7, 8 *Above, below and overleaf:*
The skills of the coach-builder are
exemplified by the Corniche, an elegant
convertible which combined graceful
styling with supreme luxury.

9 The Bentley Azure, at one third of a million dollars with taxes, was the most expensive Bentley performance convertible offered in the United States. The first year's production was sold out in three weeks.

10 A complex automatic-hood mechanism quickly converted the car into what the company called a 'wind in your hair' driving experience, revealing beautiful leather and veneered interior.

11 & 12 The Bentley TII sedan which had a long production run from the late 1960s to the late 1970s and a successor, the Mulsanne.

13 & 14 The Silver Spirit was designed for the owner-driver. Its longer wheelbase sister, the Silver Spur, was ideal for formal or business use, with or without a chauffeur.

15 The handcrafted Silver
Spur rear compartment.

16 & 17 *Left and below:*
The Turbo R 'Crewe's
missile' was the spectacular
performance car that told the
motoring world that Bentley
indeed was back.

18 & 19 Castle Ashby, ancestral home of the Earl of Northampton, often entertained the annual rally of the Rolls-Royce Enthusiasts' Club. As many as 1,000 owners would drive long distances for a day out polishing their motor cars, picnicking and hoping for an award for the beauty and condition of their prized Rolls or Bentley.

20, 21, 22 The elegant Continental R coupe, the first Bentley in forty years not to share its styling with a Rolls-Royce – a classic coach-built performance car.

23 The Silver Cloud, the stylish and elegant saloon that is unmistakably Rolls-Royce, and revered by aficionados.

24 Highlighting Rolls-Royce engineering halfway through the twentieth century. The Silver Cloud and a deHavilland Comet, the world's first jet-powered airliner.

25 & 26 Classic handcrafted motor cars. *Above:* A Bentley coupe of the '70s from the coachbuilders of Mulliner Park Ward. *Below:* A glorious luxury convertible, the Bentley Azure, among the last of the 1995–2002 series.

27 & 28 The art of coach-building. A touring limousine by James Young and a seven-passenger limousine by H.J. Mulliner Park Ward.

29 A great Bentley name, the Continental, was given to a spectacular coach-built convertible for drivers who desired the craftsmanship of the Rolls-Royce Corniche but opted for a lower profile.

30 The mantle passed in 2007 to a new Bentley powerhouse that would have thrilled the Bentley Boys – the Continental GTC, a high-performance, twelve-cylinder, all-wheel-drive luxury convertible with a top speed north of 190mph.

31 The magic of Brooklands, the cradle of British motor racing. Bentley Motors took its new model, named in honor of the famous circuit, to what remains of the steep banking that challenged the Bentley Boys, way back when. The Brooklands sedan with a classic Bentley racer that has seen more sweat, strain and racetrack mayhem than the sedan's drivers could imagine.

ROLLS-ROYCE
The Best Car in the World

32 Rolls-Royce never missed an opportunity to remind the world of the ultimate accolade.

16

A ROLLS OR A SWIMMING POOL FOR THE HORSES?

Some years ago, there was a comedy series on British television called *Nevermind the Quality, Feel the Width*, or: 'Look how much stuff you are getting for the money'. It was about two partners in a London tailoring business, good friends who argued vehemently but pushed ahead to send the customers away happy. Rolls-Royce, since the early days, and well before the BBC dreamed it up, followed a variation of this philosophy. 'Appreciate the product for what it represents, ignore any technical shortcoming should one become apparent and enjoy the overall experience of owning the world's best luxury transportation package.' And many thousands of owners have been pleased to do that and parade their cars before friends and public. The psychic reward was an agreeable anesthetic to any mechanical irritations or financial toothache. The ethos within Rolls-Royce was that the Company did not sell its motor cars. Rather, owners bought them after giving themselves permission to make the purchase. Seductive promotional work was focused on intensifying desire and transforming inclination into action.

The premise was that a Rolls-Royce was acquired not just as transportation but as a statement signaling, 'I have arrived and this is my reward for years of damned hard work.' After showing it off at the country club, the owner became a sort of 'prisoner'. He had reached the summit and the Rolls marked it. The occasional owner escaped, deigning even to sue Rolls-Royce for a car that blunt English complainers would describe as 'not of merchantable quality'.

It would not be truthful to claim that 'Rollers' as some people describe them, have never been known to throw technical hiccups, or even 'fail to proceed', stranding their exasperated drivers. But in most cases, an owner, in spite of frustration or inconvenience, would go to extraordinary lengths to excuse any mechanical problem. And he would be unwise to mutter any dissatisfaction when socializing at the 19th hole. The response might be: 'You paid how much for it? They must have seen you coming,' or 'Sold the Rolls? Is business bad?'

That's as demoralizing as somebody examining the lapels of your tuxedo and saying, 'Who the hell tailored this? Did he use a knife and fork?'

So with this powerful image and cadres of dedicated owners, why did Rolls-Royce feel a need to put so much effort into public relations, and to a lesser extent, advertising? It is simply because there were other competitors for disposable income, and it was essential to keep the name before the public and constantly demonstrate what a Rolls-Royce signified and what it meant to drive one.

No matter how powerful a product's position in the marketplace, its image dilutes if its voice is not heard. Absence of voice means a loss of share in the public mind. When that happens, people tend to think – if they think about it at all – that you are not around anymore. It is like an actor who is not seen for a while. You assume he has bowed out.

The Rolls-Royce Silver Cloud—$13,995

"At 60 miles an hour the loudest noise in this new Rolls-Royce comes from the electric clock"

What makes Rolls-Royce the best car in the world? "There is really no magic about it—it is merely patient attention to detail," says an eminent Rolls-Royce engineer.

1. "At 60 miles an hour the loudest noise comes from the electric clock," reports the Technical Editor of THE MOTOR. Three mufflers tune out sound frequencies—acoustically.

2. Every Rolls-Royce engine is run for seven hours at full throttle before installation, and each car is test-driven for hundreds of miles over varying road surfaces.

3. The Rolls-Royce is designed as an *owner-driven* car. It is eighteen inches shorter than the largest domestic cars.

4. The car has power steering, power brakes and automatic gear-shift. It is very easy to drive and to park. No chauffeur required.

5. The finished car spends a week in the final test-shop, being fine-tuned. Here it is subjected to 98 separate ordeals. For example, the engineers use a *stethoscope* to listen for axle-whine.

6. The Rolls-Royce is guaranteed for *three*

years. With a new network of dealers and parts-depots from Coast to Coast, service is no problem.

7. The Rolls-Royce radiator has never changed, except that when Sir Henry Royce died in 1933 the monogram RR was changed from red to black.

8. The coachwork is given five coats of primer paint, and hand rubbed between each coat, before *nine* coats of finishing paint go on.

9. By moving a switch on the steering column, you can adjust the shock-absorbers to suit road conditions.

10. A picnic table, veneered in French walnut, slides out from under the dash. Two more swing out behind the front seats.

11. You can get such optional extras as an Espresso coffee-making machine, a dictating machine, a bed, hot and cold water for washing, an electric razor or a telephone.

12. There are three separate systems of power brakes, two hydraulic and one mechanical. Damage to one system will not affect the others. The Rolls-Royce is a very *safe* car—and also a very *lively* car. It cruises serenely at eighty-five. Top speed is in excess of 100 m.p.h.

13. The Bentley is made by Rolls-Royce. Except for the radiators, they are identical motor cars, manufactured by the same engineers in the same works. People who feel diffident about driving a Rolls-Royce can buy a Bentley.

PRICE. The Rolls-Royce illustrated in this advertisement—f.o.b. principal ports of entry—costs $13,995.

If you would like the rewarding experience of driving a Rolls-Royce or Bentley, write or telephone to one of the dealers listed on the opposite page.

Rolls-Royce Inc., 10 Rockefeller Plaza, New York 20, N. Y., CIrcle 5-1144.

An advertisement reprinted from FORTUNE, March, 1959.

A famous advertisement by David Ogilvy – the legendary Silver Cloud 'ticking of the clock' pronouncement.

The choice for the wealthy and privileged has been known to come down to spending it on a Rolls-Royce, a private plane, a second or third home, or a swimming pool for the horses. Apart from seeking converts to the marque, advertising brings a secondary and important psychic benefit to owners. By stroking the great army of enthusiastic non-buyers who respect what a Rolls-Royce represents, those able to afford the car feel even better about it. Recognition and acknowledgement by those who do not drive one is important to those who do.

The Corniche at San Francisco Bay: 'Somewhere above the traffic and beyond the imagination, is a motor car with wings', was the lyrical advertising line for this Corniche advertisement set against the background of the Golden Gate Bridge.

Although Rolls-Royce did not appear to work energetically at it, there was constant striving to stay ahead of the pack, hence the focus on public communication. Rolls has always coyly denied it was the first to claim 'the best car in the world', but once a journalist ventured that opinion, it latched on to it and spread this gospel for decades.

The company started down this road within months of Rolls and Royce getting together, its managing director and first great publicity man, Claude Johnson, quickly appreciating the advantages of drum beating. He began advertising when the Silver Ghost was breaking endurance and reliability records, and the fledgling Rolls-Royce Co. was producing what were undoubtedly the finest motor cars on the road.

The company modestly proclaimed that the Rolls-Royce 40/50hp 'is the best six-cylinder car in the world... the most graceful... most attractive... most silent... most reliable... most flexible and smoothest running.' And it invited people to take a trial run to prove these claims, in London, at the Conduit Street showroom in Mayfair, and in New York at the Rolls-Royce Import Co. on Broadway. In those early days, the publicity was about quality, craftsmanship, reliability and silence, which set the Rolls-Royce apart from the rest. When a reputation for engineering excellence was established, the creative direction shifted to ego-stroking and upscale ownership.

Communications philosophy rejected advertising that sought to sell in competition with other cars by listing automotive benefits, preferring to seduce potential buyers with an emphasis on style, elegance and exclusivity. The advertising principles evolving over the years ruled that a Rolls-Royce advertisement should not look or sound like other car advertisements. The tablets handed down proclaimed: 'We are not in competition; self-confidence and pride in the product yes – arrogance never. Impact must be achieved with style and panache. We must be modern but not avant-garde.'

The mantra:

> We must always be looking for what is special about a Rolls-Royce – how it is made – the people who make it – what it is like to drive – what effect it has on the confidence and status of the owner. If we can substitute another car maker's name in place of our own, then the advertisement has failed.

THE TICKING OF THE CLOCK

One of the most famous of all advertisements was the David Ogilvy Silver Cloud spread, headlined: 'At 60 miles an hour, the loudest noise in this new Rolls-Royce comes from the electric clock.' It is questionable that, put to the test, the case would have been proved, but why entertain such nit-picking when you have come up with one of the greatest advertisement lines of all time?

A commanding attention-grabber, the advertisement is enshrined in advertising folklore, but the genesis of this inspired line could be traced to an *Autocar* journalist, back in 1907. After riding in the Silver Ghost, he enthusiastically lauded the smoothness and quietness of the ride, penning the immortal words: '…there is no engine so far as sensation goes, nor are one's auditory nerves troubled, driving or standing, by a fuller sound than emanates from an eight-day clock.'

The Ogilvy note that 'the Silver Cloud's fuel consumption is remarkably low and there is no need to use premium gas; a happy economy', was probably superfluous. Such minor matters are not usually at the forefront of a Rolls-Royce buyer's thinking. Remember the J.P. Morgan quote about his yacht? 'If you have to ask how much it costs…' Other points made to illustrate the many attributes of the beautifully styled Silver Cloud included the interesting statement that the chassis could be lubricated by simply pushing a pedal from the driver's seat and owners were also advised that they could obtain such optional extras as an espresso coffee-maker; a dictating machine; a bed, hot and cold water for washing, an electric razor and a telephone.

Back in the mid-1950s this was quite a departure for a company noted for its conservatism. It stemmed from the unusual, sometimes weird, extras some early owners insisted on coachbuilders fitting to their horseless carriages. These included a commode, a raised rear-compartment roof to accommodate a top hat and an ivory instrument panel ordered by Egypt's King Farouk. William Randolph Hearst filled each of his Rolls-Royce cars with mirrors, a gold vanity case and a small roll-top desk. Ogilvy also had an angle for the buyer who fancied Rolls-Royce quality, but not the high profile. In the same Silver Cloud advertisement he noted that the Bentley was also made by Rolls-Royce: 'Except for the radiators, they are identical motor cars, manufactured by the same engineers in the same works. The Bentley costs $300 less, because its radiator is simpler to make. People who feel diffident about driving a Rolls-Royce can buy a Bentley.'

For years afterward, some marketing managers at Crewe blamed that line for damaging Bentley sales. It suggested, they said, that if you bought a Bentley, you were a cheap bastard willing to cut the corners for $300. In addition to corporate communications and being spokesman for the Company, I wore another hat for several years at Rolls-Royce: responsibility for advertising. In the United States, the Company's reputation for quality and handcrafting and the mystique surrounding the car meant that something special was expected of its advertising. The ultimate had to be implied without quite saying so and we had to drive the message home that a Rolls was more fun, prestigious and meaningful than a swimming pool or other residential bauble, and desirable not for just a year but for the rest of the owner's life.

Our headlines spoke in a language that was almost unthinkable for any other car, and the writing sought to capture the emotion, pride, satisfaction and romance surrounding Rolls-Royce ownership. Each Rolls-Royce, we emphasized, was a rarity, built by hand and built to last. Each belonged to a long line of motor cars that tended to go on and on, many of them appreciating in value as the years went by.

Warren Pfaff, a gifted copywriter and advertising strategist who headed his own agency on New York's Park Avenue, adopted a lyrical and soothing approach. A subtle commercial message gradually persuaded the reader that life really was incomplete without one of these masterpieces. He also possessed tactical insights that you do not encounter too often in creative people. The theme embodied the quality of a work of art in seven words: 'The heart and soul of a masterpiece', that is built to challenge an unpredictable economy, a motor car that, with care and patience, can appreciate in value long after an ordinary machine is no more. The 'heart' was the sportsman and racing driver Charles Rolls, and the 'soul' the great mechanic Henry Royce.

With new models approaching, we had to move the old ones out in an orderly way to maintain a smooth market. Fire sales were not an option for Rolls-Royce or its owners. We positioned the outgoing models in a way that probably only Rolls-Royce could have pulled off. Beneath the headline: 'The last of the Silver Shadows', the copy reminded us:

> The first Silver Shadows came out of the Silver Clouds. Now, the first of a new generation of Rolls-Royce motor cars is coming out of the Shadows. And now that the last of the Silver Shadows are taking to the road, you can be certain that it will not be the last of them… A masterpiece of a motor car, it is destined to remind you, for years and years to come, that there will never be anything else like it on the road.

Pfaff's writing found the right trigger points with Rolls lovers, and the stocks of Shadows melted away without a blip.

The Silver Spirit, the first new four-door car to be produced in fifteen years, provided tremendous advertising opportunities. Our headline in lifestyle magazines and the *Wall Street Journal*, showing the car moving at high speed, evoked the Cloud's ticking clock. It read: 'The loudest noise in a new Rolls-Royce is the beating of your heart.' We had a twinge of concern when we realized that the message might be an uncomfortable reminder of mortality for owners with pacemakers in Florida and other retirement communities. There were no complaints, but we quietly laid it to rest. Our advertisements were crafted to reflect style and quality with intriguing copy to persuade you to read right to the end, supported by great photography to make the car pop. We sought to create advertisements that appealed to the soul while offering a good, practical reason for buying a Rolls-Royce: 'A Rolls-Royce motor car is a timeless pleasure to drive and a priceless asset to own.'

The success of the Spirit and the long-wheelbase Silver Spur, into which the Company had sunk a development fortune, was critical. We presented them as the newest expressions of a manufacturing philosophy that knew no rival. The advertising expressed a sense of quiet, painstaking evolution rather than sudden invention, detailing the benefits of all that was new in technology, styling, comfort and safety, while at the same time reflecting old-world craftsmanship and tradition. We also addressed the ideal of a motor car designed to deliver more pleasures per mile as opposed to more miles per gallon.

Warren was particularly eloquent when describing the Corniche convertible, arguably the most beautiful coach-built motor car produced by the Company. We had a glorious shot of the car climbing a hill just outside San Francisco, with the Golden Gate Bridge in the background. The premise was the motor car of your dreams and though the main targets were men in the thirty-five-to-fifty-five range, we wove in a strong appeal to women who often influenced purchases of this significance. The headline was a classic: 'Somewhere above the traffic and beyond the imagination, there is a motor car with wings.' The narrative reminded us of a time when it seemed that almost everyone shared a romantic, if unspoken dream, a personal motor car that could welcome the sun and smile at the wind as easily as it could withstand the rain. The motor car was called a convertible and sadly, a changing world had come to call it a rarity. But then, one convertible always was.

The story line described the car's being shaped entirely by hand in the workshops of the Mulliner Park Ward master coachbuilders in London:

> The Corniche is not only a blend of the art of coach-building and the genius of technology, it is a testimonial to a great driver, Charles Stewart Rolls, and a great engineer, Frederick Henry Royce.
>
> One of their dreams pictured a car that would one day take to winding roads with a sense of style and freedom beyond anything they had ever conceived. The Corniche convertible is our newest expression of that dream. Each is five months in the building, and each is a timeless pleasure and a priceless asset in the making.

Warren was adept at crafting copy that made them appear to be two quite different motor cars. The Spirit, he emphasized, was for the owner-driver, the long-wheelbase Spur for the owner who perhaps used a chauffeur for business in the city during the week, but enjoyed driving himself on weekends. Aimed at the CEO club, we showed a businessman walking toward his Spur in front of a gleaming, glass-fronted corporate building in Los Angeles, pointing out: 'The Silver Spur is built for someone who answers to no one.' We were aiming directly at the egos of Tom Wolf's 'masters of the universe', appealing to their sense of aesthetics as well as their financial instincts.

An economic turndown, however, had even the wealthy hesitating about indulgence purchases, asking if they really could justify spending six figures on a Rolls when they could get a perfectly satisfactory Mercedes for a lot less. We took a more assertive tone and took the reader beyond the romantic experience and showing a Rolls to be relevant to business and every day situations. We ran a series of full-page advertisements in the *Wall Street Journal*, *Forbes*, *Fortune* and other business publications, picturing a Silver Spirit on a construction site with the owner and engineers in hard hats studying blueprints spread across the hood. It was an expensive campaign, but a necessary sea change to underscore the relevance and practicality of a large, safe car that would take a businessman quickly and smoothly wherever he needed to go.

At times, of course, we had to change tack and drive home the investment value as a meaningful additional benefit to driving pleasure. A couple of years after the launch of the Spirit and Spur, the copy was written by the flamboyant Jerry Della Femina, who delightedly achieved notoriety early in his career, following his involvement in advertisements to extol the virtues of Japanese electrical products with the provocatively titled book *From Those Wonderful Folks Who Gave You Pearl Harbor*. Responding to changes in the economic climate, the emphasis switched to the strength of the dollar. The headline read: 'There's never been a better time to invest in precious metal. The best motor car value on the road today, The Rolls-Royce Silver Spirit. It's a sterling idea!' It was not the most subtle of messages, but in tune with the tempo of Wall Street and the international financial markets. Unlike your revered grandmother, perhaps, old Rolls-Royce was amenable to hitching up her skirts and skipping along to home in on the avaricious instinct that lurks in most of us.

17

SWEET REVENGE FOR MICHAEL CAINE

Rolls-Royce dealers in Britain were long noted for an intimidating attitude toward people entering the showroom. They implied that it was a privilege to be permitted to pass through the hallowed portals and be considered for a purchase. That is if the visitor got past the gatekeepers, white-gloved, uniformed bouncers disguised as commissionaires whose job was to head off anybody who did not look rich. Since way back, dealers believed that the world would line up patiently for the accolade of the glorious delivery of their Rolls or Bentley. Indeed there was a period when they refused to hand over the new car unless the old one was traded in.

Except for brief periods of recessionary pressure, they were for many years little more than order-takers enjoying a profitable game, insulated from the sordid wheeling and dealing required of those selling lesser machines. A delightful story about cocking a snook to showroom people is told by Maurice Joseph Micklewhite, better known as Michael Caine, who has recounted on chat shows and in his autobiography the enormous satisfaction he got from sticking it to a pompous salesman and a commissionaire at a Rolls-Royce dealership in London's Mayfair.

He acknowledges that he and a friend were unshaven and a little unkempt, but he had reached a point in his career where he could afford a Rolls-Royce and was determined to have one. As they entered the showroom, a salesman signaled the doorman to get rid of them. To the unfriendly question, 'What do you two want?' Caine consulted his grocery-shopping list and told him he wanted to buy a Rolls-Royce. The commissionaire asked sarcastically, 'How many do you want? They're cheaper if you buy more than one.' Caine told him with a short, but telling expletive what to do, and went to another dealer where the salesman recognized him and happily agreed to a test drive during which they swung by the first showroom. Caine saw the commissionaire standing at the door, and as they glided by, the actor gave him not the American insulting one finger, but the equally offensive, traditional British two-fingered gesture that is the reverse of Winston Churchill's 'V for Victory'.

Their lofty attitudes returned to haunt them during the recessions of 1983 and 1990 and when the dot-com bubble burst. These distressing economic circumstances compelled British Rolls salesmen to descend reluctantly from Mount Olympus and painfully suck-up to customers whom they had disdained just a short time before. There was a different approach in the United States where the guys with access to huge wads of the readies often spend the day in jeans and sneakers. Michael Schudroff, who as a child in Brooklyn started out restoring old Rolls and Bentleys and became the most successful dealer in North America, welcomed everybody to his Manhattan showroom. The only exception would be if their appearance clearly indicated insurmountable distance from the socio-economic group able to sustain ownership of a Rolls-Royce and looked as though they might be toting a Smith & Wesson rather than a checkbook.

Occasionally he paid a price for his trust and openness. He had a classic car collection which included a magnificent Rolls-Royce that Mike Todd had had specially built for his

"*Naturally you like it, sir, but I'm not quite sure if it likes you.*"

Recognizing changing times – *The Rolls-Royce Motors Journal.*

then wife, Elizabeth Taylor. Schudroff would put it on show occasionally, with a price tag of £1 million – some way over the top and an indication, perhaps, that he really did not want to let it go. But it added pizzazz to the display of new cars on the floor. One morning a man came in, walked quickly to the Taylor car, raised his arms and brought a bag holding a heavy rock crashing down onto the hood. He then ran out. Schudroff was distraught, unable to understand how anyone could deliberately wreak such savage damage. This I believe upset him as much as the expensive remedial work required on the dented hood of the coach-built limousine.

The open-door, welcome policy, however, paid off in sales. A young man and his father – ordinary-looking people not particularly well-dressed – would often come in to examine the cars and ask questions. This went on over months until one afternoon the son arrived alone, inspected a white Silver Spirit and said: 'This is the car I want and I'd like it to be parked outside and ready to go tomorrow.' He signed a check and returned the next day with his father, whose attention he drew to the car by the kerb and asked him what he thought of it. Then he handed him the keys and said 'Happy Father's Day, Dad'.

Another joyous occasion was engineered for a New Jersey grandmother on her 100th birthday. Her family escorted her to the showroom and presented her with a unique birthday present – a Rolls-Royce. The elderly lady's eyes shone and she asked if they would drive her home in style in her beautiful new car. They did.

One of Schudroff's more unusual customers was a young fellow with well-developed Rolls-Royce tastes who had made a fortune in livestock breeding. He bought about 150 cars over a period of eight years. He would arrive before the showroom opened, carrying a plastic bag containing sponges and wash-leathers, would select a car, often a convertible and insist on helping remove protective tape and covers and wash and polish the coachwork. Then he would hand over a check and drive away. He would buy as many as twenty cars a year, many to be traded-in soon after purchase. The record for a return was a Corniche which came back in the late afternoon of the day it was bought, with the gas tank still half full.

A motor car to make for a very happy Father's Day.

A sensible course might have been to take a car on a dealer plate, qualifying as demonstration mileage, and returning it unregistered which would have been economically advantageous to both the dealership and the customer. Not a starter. Pride of ownership was important – a principle that came expensive, but his business was successful and he could afford to indulge himself.

A visitor to New York provided a new dimension to the famous phrase: 'There are a million stories in the naked city.' In robe and slippers, he walked several blocks from a New York hospital to Carriage House and made his startling entrance. Even in Manhattan, where bizarre sights are commonplace, people in hospital garb are not seen too often strolling through traffic and pushing open the door of a car showroom. The man looked at the cars and told Schudroff:

> I'm seventy-seven years old and I've just been given my life back. I came here for treatment for a tumor that looked really bad. I was just told they can fix it. Now I have a second chance and I'm going to drive home to Boston in my first Rolls-Royce.

The ecstatic patient produced his checkbook and asked Schudroff to meet him with the car outside the hospital the following morning – and away he went, up the FDR Drive, past Yankee Stadium and through the Bronx to the Thruway, heading for the Mass Pike and Bean Town. That, you might say (unless you are a Yankees fan), is really living!

Schudroff, a likeable and shrewd businessman who for years wore his hair down to his shoulders and seldom a tie, was a thorn in the side of the Rolls-Royce Co. until eventually being welcomed into the fold. Car restoring and trading developed into a thriving business and in 1971 aged twenty-five, he rented premises on 73rd Street on Manhattan's east side. Carriage House Motor Cars, a name with a grand, royal ring, soon became the top-selling Rolls-Royce dealership in the north-east.

He would buy new, unregistered cars from less-energetic franchised dealers who wanted to hit sales targets by getting them off their books. Soon, he was selling more cars, new and used, than most of the official dealers. In 1981, just after the launch of the Silver Spirit and

Spur, he achieved a coup that sent the Company into paroxysms. Capitalizing on the United States/Canadian dollar exchange rate, he bought several truck loads of brand new sedans in Montreal, and shipped them to New York. The advertisments he placed in the *Wall Street Journal* and the *New York Times* shook Rolls-Royce and its dealers by both their audacity and business implications. For an opportunistic young businessman, it was the American dream coming alive. 'Brand New Rolls-Royce Silver Spurs at Prices Below Invoice Sticker Price $119,900. Rolls-Royce Dealer Cost $96,899 – Carriage House Price to You $94,000.'

This extraordinary announcement triggered a big-to-do in the Company; uproar among the dealers, and frantic inquiries as to how Schudroff was able to make a profit on brand-new cars while undercutting the United States wholesale price. He had actually purchased them from the Rolls-Royce branch office in Montreal which was delighted to move much of its inventory in one swoop, though the transaction crossed a few internal propriety lines. Calls came in from all over the United States and the episode catapulted Carriage House into the consciousness of every Rolls-Royce enthusiast in America.

Recalling the eruption recently, Michael told me with a laugh:

> One man in Connecticut was so incredulous, he phoned to check that the advertisement was not a hoax, and that I was selling Rolls-Royce Spurs for $3,000 less than United States dealer cost. He said 'I'm coming right down for one,' jumped into his helicopter and I met him an hour later a few blocks away at the 61st Street helicopter port and took him up to the showroom to select a car.

I had asked my marketing colleagues at the Rolls-Royce headquarters why they did not give Carriage House a franchise. The business was growing fast and Schudroff had demonstrated that he was he was better at selling Rolls-Royce and Bentleys than most dealers. But, taking heat from dealers over his freebooting-way of doing business, they wanted no part of him. I argued that aside from his provocative Canadian car advertisements, his advertising, unlike that of many official dealers, was stylish and had always eulogized the Rolls-Royce. Also, he had a large affluent customer base. If we made him official, I reasoned, we would have a powerful new outlet and an element of control. Better have him in the fold than running amok over the landscape. I would not claim that my views tipped the scales, but you did not require a 'PhD in the obvious' to see the logic and that an official laying-on of hands was inevitable. It happened in 1982, a few months after the Canadian caper.

In his first year as a franchised dealer and now in a new building on East 61st Street, which carried an annual rent of $1 million, Schudroff's business really took off. He became number one in sales in North America and second worldwide. His advertising boasted: 'Selling, leasing and servicing more Rolls-Royce and Bentleys for less, than any place else in the world.' For several years he vied with Jack Barclay of London for the title 'Top-selling Rolls-Royce dealer in the world'. He sold more cars than Barclay, but had two Manhattan showrooms, so the Company, keen not to upset Britain's biggest dealer, came up with a sort of Solomon judgment, rendering unto each Caesar an appropriate recognition. Barclay was awarded an annual trophy for the most sales at a single site, and Carriage House one for the most sales overall. Schudroff maintained that position until he fell out with Rolls-Royce during the recession in the early 1990s, left Manhattan, and moved to Greenwich. There, he picked up where he had left off, again becoming the largest non-authorized Rolls-Royce and Bentley trader in the country and still getting brand new cars from lazy dealers in the official network.

Another dealer, whose provocative advertising antagonized his competitors, was Charles Schmidt, a successful operator for several decades in St Louis. 'Carwash Charlie' as he was known – a reference to his first automotive enterprise – was a personable, immaculately turned-out guy and a masterful salesman. He could spiff up a Rolls, persuading you that its age made it a classic and had a talent for writing glowing and lyrical descriptions that would have people eager to buy. Unlike many, this was a dealer who knew how to flourish a pen and finesse the magic. Like Michael Schudroff, he would discount heavily to make a sale and was fiercely resented by other dealers.

The savvy Schmidt also spotted the disparity in the United States and Canadian wholesale prices and dollar values and made several quiet forays to Canada, acquiring cars for several thousand dollars less than the Company was charging dealers in the United States. 'I do believe I spirited down even more Canadian cars than Schudroff, but I did not talk about it' he chuckled.

He added to the irritation by advertising all over the country, way out of his Missouri marketing area and right in the backyards of other Rolls dealers. He was one of the first to advertise grandly that he would 'deliver the motor car of your choice in a private, closed van to any address in North America'. The assumption here was that the closed van deal was to protect the car from damage, bad weather and unnecessary mileage, rather than to be secretive. It can not have been to enable the owner to maintain a low profile. Being seen in your Rolls by your neighbors has long been a strong motivation for purchase. Schmidt made such inroads into other dealers' areas that he began to fear for his safety. He told me that one Rolls dealer in the west had Mafia connections; others had friends in the 'enforcement business' and he was so concerned that he would be pitched overboard during a dealer award cruise, he packed his bags and jumped ship at a foreign port.

Dealers traditionally believe they can write better advertisements than the carmakers, who cringe when a dealer says, 'I've written my own advertisements.' He's invoking the name and reputation of the product, but his handiwork is seldom up to professional writing standard. Every Sunday, newspapers carry 'dealer speak'. No reference to 'used' or 'second-hand', rather 'previously enjoyed' or you are invited to view a collection of 'experienced Mercedes'. Another coy description of a used car tells us 'only 27,000 impeccable, original miles' (what are those?). Land Rover came up with a new one, shilling second-hand models as 'Not Used – Cultured'. A dealer in Miami tried to mask his anxiety to unload stock behind comical, if excruciating phrasing:

Bentley Continental R Sports Coupé Opportunities.
We offer this pair of never-damaged one Florida owner Turbocharged 385hp examples for your consideration. Their asking prices have been adjusted to expedite timely purchase decisions.

I believe he was saying he had slashed prices to get rid.

Upscale car makers try to educate dealers in the art of creating an ambience befitting highly priced cars. Customers expect a civilized atmosphere and to feel comfortable when shopping for a luxury car – even fawned over a little. But 'the special buying experience' carefully cultivated for so many years, can be undermined by jarring come-ons like: 'For a limited time, you can select a new Bentley at Prices too Low to Print!'

A brother dealer proclaims: 'Huge Savings on all new Bentleys. Rolls-Royce and Bentley. Spring Mark-Down Sale.'

With 'Come on in – we'll beat any price'-type advertising, some dealers, or retailers as they tend to call themselves these days, allow their enthusiasm to obscure critically important presentational requirements of the affluent league in which they are playing. They destroy the mystique and cheapen the product. They sacrifice the style expected of a business that is asking you to hand over a $250,000 for a car, in favor of circus barker overtones. When did you last see hectoring advertisements by Tiffany or Rolex? Rolls-Royce, like other manufacturers, tried for years to maintain advertising standards by supplying dealers with advertisementss tailored to local needs They were not supposed to publish their own copy without seeking company approval but some dealers fancied their abilities at doing their own.

In California, one produced an advertisement that offended everybody – the Company and readers of *Palm Springs Life*, including Bob Hope, whose hilltop house overlooked Bob Hope Drive – where else? A Rolls-Royce was shown under the scorching sun, with a not impeccably turned out chauffeur leaning nonchalantly against it and reading a newspaper, while the naked lady-owner curled up on a blanket with champagne and a picnic basket. Headline: 'The Perfect Picnic.'

Bentley Continental R 'bargain' – 'Price adjusted to expedite timely purchase decision', said a Miami dealer loftily.

To make the picture worse from a technical standpoint, it was shot in the middle of the day in the open desert. Photographers will tell you that a car should never be photographed in the sun at noon when every stone and blemish in the immediate area reflects harshly in the bodywork. The soft light and shadows of early morning or evening as the sun is setting give a gentler image and highlight the styling. If the picture has to be taken during the day, then plenty of cloud is needed.

Hope complained to the magazine about its bad taste and expressed surprise that Rolls-Royce would publish such an advertisement. The Company was as dismayed as he and, though innocent, also came in for criticism from the conservative wealthy who have estates there. The dealer had the nerve to bill Rolls-Royce for half his cost. I told him, 'Not a chance.'

We had a dealer in Texas who thought he would home in on investment value. Again, the car was photographed in the glare of the mid-day sun and to compound the photographic felony, the empty license-plate holder which should always be covered with a double-R or at least a black panel to avoid its looking like a missing tooth, was left just as the car had come off the boat. The copy line was a lulu: 'This Rolls-Royce is so valuable it should be in a safe deposit box. It's that good of an investment.'

No one expects Milton or Wordsworth in a car advertisement, and copy should be conversational, but this made the English purists flinch. And yet, the message was unambiguous. The Rolls-Royce could be an appreciating asset, and the investment was available right here. Putting aside reservations about the grammatical and presentational style, this was after all, the Texas marketplace. The advertisement probably got its message over.

Private owners are not averse to indulging in an attractive incentive line and a sparkling example appeared in the Rolls-Royce Owners' Club *Flying Lady* magazine in 2003. An advertisement for a 1958 Silver Cloud advised would-be buyers: 'driven by ninety-two-year-old lady for forty years; no rust.' The car, like the elderly owner, was presumably 'just run in'.

18

YE OLDE ENGLISH SPIN DOCTORS

Spin-doctoring, the manipulation technique used by publicists and 'political whisperers' to change perceptions by suggesting that the reality is quite different from first impression became an unsavory political cliché in recent years. Image-meisters, shilling for administrations in Washington and London, have given corporate as well as political spinners a bad name by 're-interpreting' the facts to the point where statements explaining what their masters meant are often greeted with cynicism.

Rolls-Royce has been in the spin-doctor business for many decades – not the devious kind practiced by the political machines – but what I would call gentle massaging of truth and myth. Putting the best possible reflection on a situation highlighting the many fascinating features of the motor car; quality and craftsmanship, and polishing the mystique. The object – to produce interesting stories for the media, and playing the English language like a symphony. Two examples: 'Rolls-Royce never has a price hike. It effects a tariff adjustment that regretfully is usually upward.' And 'That you are calling about a Rolls-Royce that has failed to proceed underscores how unusual an occurrence that is.'

Harmless word-spinning of this nature could take the sting out of difficult questions about price increases or a report that a Rolls had broken down and was straddling the middle lane of the Santa Monica freeway, backing up traffic all the way to downtown Los Angeles. Such a high-profile failure to proceed did happen on the 405, one of the most heavily trafficked freeways in the world, just east of Los Angeles international airport, when a car carrying the Duke and Duchess of York, Prince Andrew and Fergie, conked out as they headed a procession to a British trade event at Newport Beach. The Rolls-Royce Company was blameless but had to take it on the chin, and the management in England was appalled.

A brand-new Silver Spur had been shipped out for royal events running over several days, but for reasons of diplomatic lunacy, it was relegated to second place without notice. It was like something out of a Monty Python farce. The senior British consular official blindsided everybody by deciding that a 1930s vintage Rolls owned by an acquaintance should be promoted to lead car to carry the royals. He ignored the serious possibility that a fifty-year-old car – even a Rolls-Royce – might have problems on a hot day in fast-moving traffic on a Los Angeles freeway.

A mile or two south of the airport the old Rolls, that would certainly have been checked out by engineers had the Company known of its proposed role, began to feel the heat and decided to call it a day. The cavalcade came to a stop as television traffic helicopter reporters chortled: 'The Royal Rolls has broken down, and officials are escorting the Duke and Fergie to a newer Rolls behind.' Although the 'regrettable failure to proceed' line was chronicled humorously, television and newspaper reports were dominated by pictures of the broken-down Rolls. We could not say that we knew nothing of a decision to switch our new car for a

The new Corniche arrives in Beverly Hills (where else can you smell the money all the way from Pasadena to Rodeo Drive?). Reg Abbiss spins the Bentley story for Steve Parker of KTLA TV.

very old one, so we cut our losses by saying that at the last minute somebody thought that the royals would enjoy gliding down the freeway in a classic coach-built Rolls-Royce. It turned out that the engine overheating was caused by a broken fan belt and we exercised the ultimate spin by pointing out that Rolls-Royce did not make the offending belt. And if we had, it most certainly would not have broken!

Dennis Miller-Williams, the delightful and courtly English gentleman who for many years was the Rolls-Royce public relations manager in London, was beloved by journalists and indeed most people with whom he came into contact. Along with the articulate David Plastow, who was chief executive and very effective front man in the 1970s, Dennis was a stylish and trusted communicator.

I was privileged to know him both as a journalist on the outside when I was at the BBC and as a colleague and friend who skillfully demonstrated the use of certain phrases and nuances when speaking for an august company with a special product and tradition. Dennis always had an acceptable comment even when a reporter on deadline, wanted an immediate answer to difficult questions, and many times, his smooth approach steered away from dangerous scenarios that could lead to a black hole. Spinning came to him naturally, yet he never seemed to be doing it – probably because he did not realize what it was and such a description would have puzzled him.

But he authored some classic one-liners that captivated journalists. The 'failure to proceed' and 'tariff adjustment' phrases were his, and I long marveled at his reply when I asked him before I joined the Company what it was like doing public relations for Rolls-Royce. 'It's rather like being called to the priesthood' he replied softly and respectfully.

A Cambridge-educated lawyer and former RAF pilot, Dennis, with his gray hair and distinguished features, could have doubled for a bishop or a banker and was revered by Rolls and Bentley owners around the world. When John Lennon had a psychedelic paint job done on his Phantom V, Dennis was the man the media called. Feigning distress at what some viewed as the desecration of ten flawless coats of lacquer, but always diplomatic, he selected

Would you entrust this Bentley Turbo R to a reporter who says he's not a very good driver and has had 'a few unfortunate happenings'?

his words with care when asked what the Company thought about it. 'The motor car is Mr Lennon's property, so he is entitled to paint it whatever color he wishes. But it is not a color scheme we would contemplate including in the catalogue.' Tongue firmly in cheek, he added that the Beatle had certainly invalidated the paintwork warranty.

Dennis Miller-Williams epitomized the perception of Rolls-Royce as an entity of gentlemanly tranquility, with the talent to handle virtually any problem without breaking a sweat.

The spin machine really had to crank up when Rolls-Royce came under attack as the poster car for unjustifiably high-fuel consumption. Pressures were developing in the United States to crack down on gas-guzzlers and require carmakers to achieve an average of more than 20mpg over their model ranges. Rolls-Royce, getting a miserable eleven-to-thirteen, was vilified by environmentalists as one of the greatest sinners. In an age when technology could produce small but powerful and economical engines, critics asked how Rolls-Royce could justify putting a large 6.75-liter engine in a car that could do with its own fuel tanker bringing up the rear. They had a point to which the answer was that we could not afford the enormous cost of designing and producing a new engine.

Rolls escaped gas-guzzler penalties on the basis that it was a small manufacturer with basically one large, very heavy car and for which achieving better fuel consumption was technically and financially infeasible. Nonetheless, it was targeted as a gas-guzzling pariah driven by wealthy people who did not care a fig about fuel economy so long as gas supplies did not dry up. How could we spin our way out of that?

We responded with a dual thrust. To critics who said we were undermining conservation efforts, I said: 'The difference between the miles per gallon the government wants, and what all the Rolls-Royce cars in America use, would amount to only thirty barrels of a national daily consumption of seven million. Also, many Rolls are not driven every day, their owners usually having other cars for daily transportation.' The justification question was addressed by

More 'pushing' than 'spinning'. Reg gives the Silver Ghost a helpful push at a media event in New York. The eloquent Dennis Miller-Williams is driving.

highlighting that at the heart of the American dream, hard work historically brought great benefits, and successful people had always rewarded themselves with the best of its kind, be it a house, a plane, a horse-breeding ranch or a car. A Rolls-Royce symbolized the dream.

'What a gray world it would be if luxury cars were driven off the road in favor of econo-boxes, and the sights of ambition were lowered,' George Lewis, president of Rolls-Royce Motors Inc., told the *Associated Press*. 'Entrepreneurs and others who buy Rolls-Royce cars are self-made, successful people who generate the wealth and the jobs in the United States. Surely they are entitled to enjoy what they have earned. And surely, the arrival of about twenty cars a week does not make a meaningful difference.'

To charges that a Rolls-Royce represented extravagance in every respect, we ventured into one of the greatest spin stretches, pointing out that the fifteen or twenty cars, sometimes more, that many people owned over their lifetime, required huge amounts of steel and other materials. 'A Rolls-Royce can be said to be more environmentally friendly than almost any other car because just one can last a person's lifetime and therefore accounts for less of the world's energy and other resources.'

Sometimes the spinners get spun. And I was the victim of a good-humored tugging of my string. Steve Hartman, a likeable and disarming CBS reporter in Los Angeles came to Marina Del Rey to which we had invited press and broadcast media to test drive the 1996 range of Rolls and Bentleys, and take them up the coast road and through Topanga canyon. He hurried up just as I finished an interview and asked about driving the cars. His questions about the arrangements were a bit unusual. The conversation went something like this:

'I've never driven cars as expensive as these and I'm not a very good driver. I should tell you, I've had a few unfortunate happenings.'
    'Happenings?' I replied. 'What sort of happenings? Are you accident-prone or something?'
    'Well, - I've had a couple of accidents and one car was wrecked.'
    'Was it your fault?'

'The judge thought so. After my last crash, he restricted my driving.'

'Restricted? You do have a license?'

'Yes, but I'm not sure it would cover me if I damaged the car.'

'Is it suspended?'

'Well, let me put it this way. Do I need a valid license to drive this Rolls?'

'Yes. Do you have one?'

'Not sure. I do not have the judgment summons with me.'

'Look you've got to have a license. These cars cost $250,000 and with the best will in the world, I can't let you whiz off to Topanga without one. I don't think you would be covered by insurance and we'd all wind up in front of the judge – you for doing it – me for letting you. Can I suggest something? Why don't I drive and you can do your taping, make your comments and ask questions on the way?'

'We could do that, but I really need to be behind the wheel so I can do my story as we drive. Are you refusing to let me drive?'

I had never had such a curious conversation. I was puzzled by its direction and it crossed my mind, fleetingly, that perhaps this reporter was in therapy of some kind, which would not be unusual in California. He did not seem to be quite like the other reporters, and the weirdness of the situation reminded me that some of the strangest people I have ever met have been in La La land. I was trying to work out how to resolve the problem without upsetting him, when I noticed his cameraman, some distance away across the lot, shooting with a zoom lens and realized that Hartman was wearing a lapel microphone. He saw my lights come on as it dawned that this was a bizarre, if gentle, ambush interview, and he began to grin.

'You know,' he said, 'I specialize in an offbeat approach to stories and that conversation we've just had is priceless. You were beginning to look at me as though I'd lost my marbles, and were about to call for men in white coats to take me away.' 'That may be,' I replied, 'but be honest – you were a bit deceptive. Come on. Its not the way a reporter normally starts his coverage is it? You crossed the line about secret recording and that makes a lot of people uncomfortable.'

'Well,' he said, 'it is all in fun and I wouldn't use anything to really embarrass you or the Company.' 'Okay,' I said. 'I'll buy that.' And Steve Hartman was as good as his word. He did an excellent piece, driving a Bentley convertible through Marina Del Rey, marveling at its opulence and asking why it cost so much and what sort of people would buy it. He used a few moments of our earlier 'interview' in which I began to show concern that here was some accident-prone driver without a license, trying to persuade me to give him the keys to a very, very expensive car. It was funny, and gave a gentle leg-pulling angle to his report on the news that night.

The ultimate in spin doctoring is when you can use journalistic experience to persuade a reporter to accept constructive suggestions that shape the story you want him or her to run. I used this 'helpful behavior' technique many times, but my motives were pure – to ensure that we both came out winners. I would distill for them all the material they needed, which virtually ensured that Rolls-Royce got what amounted to a free commercial on regional, sometimes network television.

When we ran a media event, broadcast journalists were invited early so they would have time and space for taping and interviewing without their newspaper and magazine brethren getting in the way with their questions. Often a television reporter would arrive knowing little about the story except that these were the world's most luxurious and expensive cars and cost many times his salary, a point he sometimes made. I would give him a brief rundown and a string of one-liners about why the cars were so special, extolling the wizened old craftsmen tapping away and cutting and stitching and shaping with ancient tools and requiring several months to build just one car, and I would weave in carefully crafted ten-second soundbites that he would not be able to resist. Within a couple of minutes, he would say, 'Hold it. Let's get this on tape.'

This was the trigger point. I was now in a position to help influence the content and tone of the piece that would be aired. And when he gave me the open-ended question, 'What's different about a Rolls-Royce?' we were in spin heaven. I would briefly pinpoint magnificent craftsmanship, veneers, leather, soft lambswool rugs and flawless paintwork, in a chronology that was effectively a roadmap of overlay shots with which the cameraman could illustrate the interview, and I would save a few points about 'the best car in the world' to feed to the reporter for his stand-up link and pay-off pieces.

In about half an hour, I could have him on his way to the next assignment, the Rolls-Royce or Bentley story wrapped up, and calling as he left: 'Thanks for all the help. Really interesting story. Should be on at six.' My colleagues and I, who dealt with these situations were fortunate. We had great material to work with. Doing PR for slotted-angle brackets would have presented more difficulty. But with a Rolls-Royce and its many unusual features to talk about, there was a 'feel-good' atmosphere about the story.

With few exceptions, reporters did not turn up with an agenda to abrasively knock the idea that this was the world's finest car and that we should be in jail for deigning to charge so much. They started from the premise of wanting to know what was so special and how it came to be regarded as the best. When a reporter sought an interview lasting several minutes, the questions invariably included: 'I've heard it said that Rolls-Royce will fly a mechanic to any point in the world if the car breaks down or refuses to start?' The answer was that if a Rolls-Royce dealer was too far away, we would seek a reputable dealer in the area who could probably diagnose and fix the problem with help from a Rolls-Royce engineer via phone or fax. If this did not work, an engineer would fly there as a last resort. This led to an old chestnut about a Rolls-Royce coming to an involuntary stop in the south of France with a broken half-shaft, and a mechanic driving out with a replacement part. When the owner got home, he phoned Rolls-Royce for his bill and was told: 'We have no record, sir, of anyone going to France to fit a half-shaft. Half-shafts in Rolls-Royce motor cars, of course, do not break.' Whether that famous old story is accurate or just part of the lore and mythology, the premise is true. The Company would do whatever was necessary to help the stranded owner, and if it meant a mechanic going out there, he would have gone.

A revered philosophy has always been that Rolls-Royce does not sever connections with the car or the owner when the tail lights disappear out of the showroom. To give some heft to an advertising campaign, the Company decided to break a rule that customers were never discussed. Why not blow the trumpets about the distinguished lineage of owners over three-quarters of a century? Major advertisements appeared in the top peoples' papers listing scores of famous names. They included George Bernard Shaw, Ernest Hemingway, Czar Nicholas II, Benito Mussolini, Rudyard Kipling, Andrew Carnegie, Ronald Colman, Errol Flynn, Mae West, the Rockefeller family and other famous owners a little less long in the tooth like Zsa-Zsa Gabor. The headline was: 'For 78 years, Rolls-Royce motor cars have been owned by the men and women who shape history. They still are.'

Unfortunately, virtually all the named owners had long since passed from this life, and when the advertisements were posted in the factory, a wag wrote on one: 'Beware driving a Rolls-Royce. It could be hazardous to your health!'

A final observation about spin doctoring. Rolls-Royce spinning was harmless, often humorous and I cannot recall it as ever being seriously political or carrying sinister undertones designed to be misleading or hurtful. But, regardless of one's skill in fudging or being 'economical with the truth' as one British Member of Parliament once suggested of a politician on the other side of the aisle, the truth, or much of it, often eventually emerges.

My colleague Ian Kerr, a talented strategist who worked with me for many years on Rolls-Royce communications, could not have downright lied if his career depended upon it. One of the most honest and straightforward men I have ever known, and the architect of many of our successes, Ian could quickly analyze a situation and hit the nail.

Believing in the axiom 'truth will out,' he would say: 'No matter how much clotted cream you place atop a pile of horse manure in the street, the public will see it truly for what it is when the sun comes out.'

19

FRENCH CONNECTION AND
NEW LAMPS FOR OLD

It was perhaps appropriate that Rolls-Royce Motor Cars, which for many represented the admired qualities of traditional England, should be rescued by a quintessential English gentleman, the Receiver, Rupert Nicholson, who looked as though he would fit well into a Dickens novel. Both the car and aerospace companies have much to thank him for. Plunged helplessly into a deadly bankruptcy, workers' and managers' morale was low and there were fears that the cars they were completing were possibly the last.

But Nicholson made a courageous decision just days after the collapse that forever endeared him to 'those who worked at Royce's.' He signaled tremendous faith in the viability of the business, by giving the go-ahead to the launch of a coach-built convertible, a two-door beauty, named the Corniche, and he found the money to do it.

France was the only place for a press introduction, on *Le Grand Corniche*, the spectacular Mediterranean coast road that link Nice and Monaco. Nine of the handcrafted cars were driven to the south of France; two-dozen journalists were flown out for an intensive twenty-four-hours teach-in and ride-and-drive and a model critically important to the Company's future got a perfect send-off.

The automobile writers loved the car, one of the most beautiful convertibles Rolls-Royce had ever built and which, with technical developments and many other refinements, including a turbo, making it the fastest open-top Rolls ever built. The Corniche stayed in production for more than twenty years. Over that time Corniche I, II, III and IV become outstanding examples of the Rolls-Royce philosophy of evolution. The Corniche was a classic and if ever you get the chance to drive or ride in one, or own one, take it. With the top down on a warm sunny afternoon, the breeze in your face and cosseted by the most luxurious of interiors, the sensation almost equates to your first orgasm!

The journalists gliding along the scenic cliff roads leading to Monte Carlo had no inkling that if a satchel of Francs and travelers checks had not been lugged from London, they and the Rolls-Royce people might have faced the indignity of being directed to sleeping arrangements on the beach. The French hoteliers, with an eye on Rolls-Royce being in bankruptcy insisted on cash.

It made no difference that Rolls-Royce and France went back together many years, that Henry Royce had had a home at Le Canadel on the Riviera; that all his cars were given punishing testing on French roads before going into production, and that Rolls-Royce, in love with French names, had named its most beautiful car after the Corniche.

The new convertibles got a great press and back at the factory, David Plastow, who had been appointed chief executive five weeks before the roof fell in, and Bill Harris, his solid and experienced commercial director, were able to use the momentum to map the way forward. They were the right guys in the right place when good planning and motivation were needed

The Silver Shadow morphed into a convertible which became the classic Corniche, the Corniche coupe and the Bentley Continental convertible. The Corniche is regarded as one of the most beautiful examples of the coachbuilder's art. Handcrafted by Mulliner Park Ward master coachbuilders, the body took several weeks to shape before being taken to Crewe for mechanical fitments, then being returned to MPW for interior furnishing and the fitting of the top.

The Corniche pictured with a somewhat older open-air model, the Silver Ghost (about seventy-five years older).

to stabilize the Company and convince the workforce as well as the marketplace that Rolls-Royce was running and very much in business.

Some say that the bankruptcy was the best thing that could have happened from the car makers' standpoint as it released them from having to answer to the high-tech aerospace overlords at corporate headquarters in Derby who tended at times to look patronizingly upon them as wood-whittling, old-fashioned engineering Jed Clampets living in a timewarp and making motor cars one at a time.

It certainly gave the car division a freedom it had not enjoyed since the early days, before aero-engines predominated. For the managers, it was a chance to run and re-build their own company and they grabbed it. The post-bankruptcy period saw intense activity. David Plastow, who had started with Rolls-Royce as a sales representative in northern England had worked his way up to marketing director and now CEO, a job with a high stress factor. The workers, still shaken by the specter of closure and economic devastation for thousands of families in the town of Crewe, still feared for the future. Plastow had to get production on track and prove that Rolls-Royce had a future.

There was another pressing matter to get to grips with – how to extend the life of the Silver Shadow and its Bentley sibling until the next generation cars, the Silver Spirit, Spur

Based on the Silver Shadow, the Bentley Corniche coupe was introduced as the Mulliner Park Ward two-door saloon, the body being built at the coachbuilding works in London. It later became the Corniche coupe.

and Bentley Mulsanne would be ready several years down the road. This meant refining and engineering changes into the Shadow while developing its successor – not a big deal in a large car company but projects of cosmic proportions for a boutique manufacturer of limited resources.

The need for a new shape with improved mechanicals and fuel consumption had to be reconciled while remaining true to Rolls-Royce styling and tradition – nothing so radical as to risk the car's being mistaken for anything other than a Royce. At the same time, the factory was working on the Camargue, a huge hand-built coupé – the ultimate 'personal Rolls-Royce' as it became known. This car had to underscore that Rolls-Royce had come through the bankruptcy trauma and was still the leading player in the luxury car business.

Often described as the rarest Rolls-Royce, the Camargue took its name from an area roamed by wild horses, black bulls and flamingos in Southern France. Codenamed Delta, it was crafted at the Mulliner Park Ward coach-building works in London on the basic Silver Shadow/Corniche base. Plastow was regarded as its 'father', having enthusiastically called for a different type of Rolls for the owner who wished to drive himself – a sophisticated car with the finest interior appointments, hi-tech aircraft-style instrumentation and an aggressive road presence.

Five years in development, Camargue was the first Rolls designed from scratch to meet United States safety legislation. The strength of the bulky body was demonstrated by only one car being needed to meet all United States crash tests. The results were impressive, the roof giving only a half-inch under a 5,100lb load. And the car sailed through other destructive

The Camargue – an exclusive coach-built coupe and named after the region in France that is noted for its wild horses was a major styling departure for Rolls-Royce. Viewed by Crewe engineers as the best-riding luxury tank they produced in the 1970s, it was designed to appeal to Rolls-Royce enthusiasts with sporting instincts who enjoyed driving a car with instrumentation redolent of an airplane cockpit. Only 534 were built between 1975 and 1986.

Today, the Camargue is prized by collectors, particularly a dozen special final edition models built for the United States.

assaults, including hitting a 100-ton concrete block head-on at 30mph and being walloped in the rear by a 4,000lb barrier at 20mph. The dents were hammered out and the car went on to complete a tough crash program. The severity of the crash tests required most manufacturers to use a different car for each one. That Rolls-Royce needed only one for the complete series spoke volumes for buying one on safety grounds alone. With this build-quality the 'heavy metal' Camargue came in as weighty as its price tag – $90,000 at launch in 1976 – which made it the most expensive production car ever sold in America and more than twice the price of the Silver Shadow. Unusually, Rolls sought outside styling input, turning to Italy's Sergio Pininfarina for the main bodylines. The Crewe design department headed by chief stylist Fritz Feller, who also brought in the Spirit and Spur six years later, did the rest.

There were some misgivings when Pininfarina jutted the radiator shell several degrees forward - a radical departure! But it seemed to work, giving the familiar Rolls frontage a new perspective, even though it presented a slab-like appearance. This was the main criticism of the car and it bothered Plastow and his colleagues. Graham Hull, one of Rolls-Royce's most talented stylists, produced what many viewed as more aesthetically appealing lines that sadly, were never seen outside the department. Everything about the Camargue was big and powerful, like gigantic disc brakes actuated by three separate hydraulic systems. Its dual-level air-conditioning system – eighteen years in development and the most technically advanced on the road – later went into all Rolls and Bentleys, following the philosophy that a major new component should first be tried out on small production-run models before being committed to the entire range.

The company did not look upon this as using people paying the highest prices as guinea pigs; rather it was easier to engineer new components on small production runs before committing to the mainstream cars. Eight-and-a-half inches wider than the Corniche convertible, the Camargue offered space, it was discreetly pointed out, for 'an extra golf bag or two in the enlarged luggage compartment'. It was certainly a different-looking Rolls – very wide, with cavernous, heavy doors. One well-known journalist opined: 'Not good Rolls-Royce – not good Pininfarina.' But it was a grand, luxurious motor car that had its fans and engineers at the factory claimed it to be the best-riding Rolls ever. Over an eleven-year production life, 534 were built but only 526 sold. Four were prototypes without chassis numbers and four were production-built experimental cars, subsequently scrapped. One turbo-charged Rolls covered more than 250,000 miles. This powerful missile led to the Bentley Mulsanne Turbo, of which more later. I wrote a brochure for the Camargue toward the end of its production run, targeting collectors who might consider adding this special Royce to their stable. To trigger the saliva glands, I pointed out:

> From the hand-sculpted radiator grill to matched walnut veneers, there is no room for compromise… built with the accumulated skill, experience and knowledge gained over eighty years of manufacturing motor cars of the finest quality, Camargue blends the latest technical thinking with that which is tried and true – an incomparable blend of superb craftsmanship and state of the art engineering.

Camargue was: 'Built as Frederick Henry Royce built his cars – one at a time – and always by hand. Excellence was the norm. Integrity the guiding principle.'

When I wrote this type of material in brochures or press releases, my colleagues would roll their eyes and tell me I had missed my calling, and should be writing new *Wizard of Oz* stuff for MGM against a background of cascading strings. That may be, but it was a magnificent car of great quality and presence, and it is not difficult to get lyrical about something as magnetic as that. The Camargue close out in 1986 was a good example of the marketing techniques practiced by the American subsidiary of Rolls-Royce Motor Cars. Camargues, we proclaimed, were used as personal transportation by kings, princes, diplomats and captains of industry around the world. Now, the United States would receive twelve of a final limited edition of twenty-five to commemorate the eightieth anniversary of the first sale of a Rolls-Royce in America.

The special 'Last of the Camargues' were dreamed up with the United States in mind, with just twelve cars with many additional features, and we put on a media event in the courtyard at the Beverly Wilshire, a favored hang-out of people who are attracted to high-ticket items bordering on the unique. This amounted to bringing an almost irresistible proposition to the very heart of wealth and indulgence where the millionaires of Beverly Hills and its environs were not fazed by a high price provided they were getting something different to make friends' eyes pop at the next Malibu pool party.

The specification was exceptional – as was the price, a whopping $175,000. Features included veneers with silver inlays, a phone, monogrammed silver-plated cocktail flasks, crystal glasses, a vanity set, attaché case and a silver pen. Finished in white with red upholstery, the cars became collector models within a few years, fetching almost $100,000 over the original asking price. How much, I wonder, would the one turbo-charged Camargue built as a Bentley and used only by the engineering department, have commanded? Now that would be a collector's item. But it was never sold.

NEW LAMPS FOR OLD

While working on bringing the Camargue to market in 1976, the factory also focused on how to squeeze another three years of life out of the Silver Shadow. Significant mechanical improvements

The Camargue's luxurious interior.

in a MkII version would be the answer. The engineers drew on the Camargue's impressive list of technical attributes, altered the front of the Shadow with an aggressive air dam and added badging to the trunk, proclaiming Silver Shadow II, Silver Wraith II or Bentley T II.

The Silver Shadow II and a long-wheelbase version, the Silver Wraith II, which we launched in New York and Los Angeles at Easter 1977, were in production for thirteen years until 1980, when the Spirit and Spur finally appeared. Two thousand modifications phased in over ten years, along with the many changes for the MkII versions added up to a major improvement over the original Shadows. The revamped series got powered rack and pinion steering, gas springs in a new rear suspension to adjust the ride to the load and improve cornering; also the Camargue's unique air conditioning which, the Company promised, assured occupants of 'warm toes and a cool head' something medical experts recommended. The system would quietly adjust itself to the heat of Death Valley or the cooler climes of Fairbanks, Alaska, without the occupants having to touch any switches. To emphasize longevity, the odometer was designed to record journeys up to a million miles and the famous ticking clock was finally banished, giving way to a silent digital display.

But the competition was hotting up. Mercedes and BMW were coming out with new models that made our 'makeover' Rolls, for all its many improvements, look a bit like an elderly aunt, wearing new dress and shoes, arriving unexpectedly at a hot-rod track. We emphasized evolution rather than revolution; the Rolls-Royce tradition of taking its time and refusing to incorporate new components unless there was a measurable benefit, like improving safety, quietness or longevity. Dramatic as the technical changes were, the message continued, the joy of the motor car was in holding all the artistry, technology and patience that Rolls-Royce could bring to bear 'in your very hands. And the joy is not fleeting'.

We took an exhausting new model show on the road, hitting cities in North America and the Pacific Rim with customer and media events. We had tremendous print and broadcast

Rolls-Royce Silver Shadow in a natural habitat – New York's Park Avenue.

The Shadow's long-wheelbase sibling, the Silver Wraith, also in New York.

turnouts in New York, Boston, Chicago, Dallas, Houston, Los Angeles, San Francisco, Vancouver, Toronto and Montreal. It was the same in Sydney, Melbourne and Tokyo. The magic still worked. Most journalists seemed to accept that the latest electronic gizmo was not necessary in a car that was really about traveling in unsurpassed luxury and solid safety.

'Glitzy dashboards are not a priority of Rolls-Royce owners,' I told journalists. 'When you glide away in a Rolls-Royce, the comfort, quietness and feeling of well-being are more important than a high-decibel stereo.' But I would also point out that we were not selling a well-upholstered buckboard. Our air-conditioning system was the most advanced you could find and we believed our back-up braking system was unique.

The Shadow II and Wraith II were not only profitable, generating some of the cash needed for their successors, they gave Rolls-Royce an additional three years of productive life from a venerable model, providing the time needed to ready the Silver Spirit and Silver Spur. About 8,400 Shadow IIs were produced, along with 2,135 Wraith II's, and 560 were built as Bentleys. They still look good today, a little dated perhaps, but unmistakably Rolls-Royce and Bentley. The Shadow/Wraith series, of which 31,714 were made between 1965 and 1980, became the Company's most commercially successful car.

20

THE LOTUS FIASCO

The Lotus Élan is the automotive equivalent of a pair of tight pants – bulging with promise, but difficult to sit in. Automotive journalist

Miscalculation is among many of the performance measurements that have marked expensive failures in the British car industry. Testament to that is a graveyard littered with names like Austin, Morris, Riley, Lanchester, Wolseley, Standard and Triumph. In later years, without the deep pockets and engineering expertise of American and German companies, Rolls-Royce, Bentley, Aston Martin and Jaguar would most likely have joined them. Some have begged the question: What possesses a business-savvy company suddenly to veer away from the norm, and indulge in corporate lunacy?

Now and again, like a misguided lover, a company will have a flirtation that has no basis in sense and Rolls-Royce Motors, with eyes assumedly open, entered such a liaison with Lotus, the British sports car maker. The introduction to what became a time-consuming and financial disaster was brokered by the parent company in England, whose judgment must have become slightly unhinged. It was plain to some at the United States headquarters that grief was likely to be the outcome of a shotgun affair with what we saw as an automotive dead man walking. Lotus built so few cars that it seemed Rolls-Royce was General Motors by comparison, and those of us who had experienced the indifferent quality of some products of the British car industry, had reason for anxiety. Getting into bed with Lotus was ill-advised and tantamount to agreeing to buy the Brooklyn Bridge at a midnight meeting at a dubious location in Jersey City.

The Rolls model range was selling well, new ones were on track and there was a good feeling as the end of the 1970s approached. I do not know if the Company's guard was down or it felt it had to cozy up to Margaret Thatcher, Britain's gung-ho 'British is best' Prime Minister, who was shopping around for somebody to save Lotus from going under and Rolls-Royce came into the government's sights as the answer to the problem.

The fierce 'There'll always be an England' Iron Lady, described by insiders as being the toughest ball-buster in the cabinet, punishing ministers who dared disagree with her policies with a steely glare that reduced them to mute attendees, was troubled by the prospect of another British company collapsing. Lotus was some fifteen years out from its great motor-racing days when Jim Clark's grand prix victories built a storied reputation for the tiny Norfolk company and it had fallen on difficult times. A boutique specialist manufacturer, with limited development funds, its range of small, low-slung 'vroom-vroom' sports cars made of glass-fiber were not seen as being sturdily engineered and were overpriced, particularly in the American market. Rolls-Royce also was to be faced later with a pricing problem affecting its own products when overly aggressive sticker policies led even very wealthy buyers to conclude they should hide their wallets.

Rolls-Royce has always been close to the establishment – Buckingham Palace and political and social seats of power – and has always felt a 'terribly British' special responsibility to 'step up and do the right thing'. But this time the Company's altruism cost it a bundle. Lotus, with a huge stock of unsold cars, desperately needed a relevant, coherent model range, marketing savvy and an efficient dealer network in North America if it was to stay afloat. To use a phrase quite familiar in British industry, when a company was in trouble and showed no sign of solving the problems, its activities were likened to rearranging the deck chairs on the *Titanic*.

The first indication of what proved to be a damaging and expensive aberration by Rolls-Royce was a request from England that the United States subsidiary consider becoming the Lotus importer and distributor, utilizing the Rolls dealer network. Car dealers are pretty sharp. They have to be to survive in such a business and Rolls dealers were no different from those selling Chevys. Dealers know how to evaluate a franchise and were aware that Lotus was struggling, asking what was in 1979 an astronomical and unrealistic sum – upwards of $39,000 – for the four-cylinder Elite that was supposed to be a four-seater. It was, as I told our chief executive in England, provided the rear seat occupants were infants or unfortunate double amputees.

Few Rolls-Royce executives in the United States knew of Lotus, apart from its being an exotic sports car. As a Brit, I was more familiar with its reputation and offered the view that we should have nothing to do with it. 'The Lotus,' I said 'is a low-slung, overpriced sports car with a small engine not noted for reliability, and I'd hate to have an accident in one.' I suggested that Rolls-Royce politely advise whichever of Mrs Thatcher's Whitehall mandarins was trying to sell us a bill of goods that we had too much on our plate to take on Lotus and that perhaps some other British engineering company like the money-heavy GKN could step up and come to its rescue.

I had two main concerns – the questionable reputation and durability of Lotus cars that I felt could sully Rolls-Royce by association in our most important marketplace and the strain this would surely put on relationships with our dealers, some of whom would resent being strong-armed to take Lotus on. The possibility of broadening our trading base and developing a new income stream appealed to some colleagues, however. No room for dissent here. So my product-presentation comment in a position paper that went to England was amended to read something like: 'Importing the Lotus will require a distinct shift in our public relations and advertising posture'. I'll say!

The rationale was that both Rolls-Royce and Lotus were British manufacturers of handcrafted, exclusive and individually engineered motor cars, and the synergy could be profitable. As some of my colleagues observed later when the import of what we had been lumbered with began to weigh heavily upon the core business: 'What the hell were they smoking or sniffing in Crewe to even entertain it?'

Some weeks later, as Christmas approached, Rolls-Royce proved to Lotus that there was indeed a Santa Claus. It handed over a check for more than $6 million, yes six million, for the Lotus United States stock of parts and 190 cars. Many of the cars, it was discovered, were eighteen-months old, grimy and standing in warehouses in Baltimore on the east coast and Costa Mesa in California. The clean-up work required before we dared show a car to a dealer was dispiriting and arduous. The tires had flat spots like concrete and the batteries were shot. I seem to recall these were small units made near the Lotus factory specially to fit a tight space. No car could be operational until new ones were shipped from England.

Our engineers, mostly British, and Lotus gun-shy, were appalled at the decision to take it on, and some dealers flat-out refused to have anything to do with it. Some were persuaded, and a network was signed up, based more on goodwill toward Rolls-Royce than perceived profit opportunity. As our warehousemen scrubbed and polished to make the cars presentable, new problems became evident. Many were 1978 and 1979 models and the 1980s were due any time. Talk about a fire sale before we had even got into business! There was no change in the styling and nothing to speak of in the mechanicals to differentiate the model years. But to ask for anything near the sticker for the newer ones meant having to heavily discount the old stock.

Strike one at Rolls-Royce finances. We were the geniuses who had paid full pop to Lotus for the stock. The dealers were amazed and displeased by the model-year mess that we had inherited and looked to the importer, good old Rolls-Royce, to do the heavy lifting, carry the financial burden and slash prices to enable them to move some cars out.

It was an uphill struggle from the outset. There was more than enough work with Rolls-Royce commitments and each executive, trying to focus on Rolls-Royce and Bentley, his primary responsibility, found himself putting in long, additional hours trying to do something with Lotus. Also, we needed advertising and public relations funding – this had to come out of the Rolls-Royce pocket – to tell America about Colin Chapman's sports cars which had virtually disappeared from the radar screen. There was a small Lotus enthusiasts' club made up of drivers of stamina and fervent loyalty to what was a cult car, handicapped by way-too-high sticker prices and minimal expansion prospects and we could not look there for meaningful sales.

We spent $25,000 on a survey to try to get a handle on people's perception of Lotus, which seemed to be the best-kept sports car secret in America. The way to go was to capitalize on its exclusivity and racing heritage, grand-prix engineering lineage and a suggestion that it was the nearest thing to a street-legal racecar. We had to raid the Rolls-Royce budget for many more thousands of dollars to get the campaign going. Warren Pfaff, head of our New York advertising agency, whose creative work earlier in his career had successfully persuaded people that the new Boeing 747 with 'all the room in the world' was the most wondrous airliner to be built since flying began, produced a series of arresting advertisements. One of them showing a Lotus speeding along a California Pacific highway proclaimed: 'From Formula One to US One. A Lotus is a rare sight.'

Warren's line was right on. They were a rare sight – there were so few around. It was also rare in its beautiful styling, its most appealing attribute, and one of the most exciting sports car shapes on the road. We focused our publicity thrust and magazine placement on successful young professionals awash with cash – the Beverly Hills orthodontist, plastic surgeon or hairdresser in his $200 designer jeans, $1000 Rodeo Drive sports shirt, gold necklace and bracelet, strutting away from his parked Lotus hoping passers-by would mistake him for a racecar driver. And we targeted successful lawyers and Wall Street traders, noted for extravagance and automotive indulgence.

At a meeting in England, some weeks after we had started the Lotus campaign, David Plastow, Rolls-Royce CEO, asked me cheerfully if I had driven one and what did I think? Plastow was noted for being able to take a direct answer no matter how unpalatable. I gave it to him. 'I have an advertising slogan that describes the Lotus, but I doubt it'll make a constructive contribution to the dialogue: "If you are rich, vertically challenged and deaf, have we got a car for you!"'

The chief executive broke up. 'You are cynical,' he chuckled. 'They can't be as bad as that!' 'They do not start too well,' I told him:

> They're noisy, and that glass-fiber body gives you the feeling that you have all the protection of a cornflake packet. They're so low, your tailbone feels it is 6in above the road, and that may be okay for whizzing around Laguna Seca, but in the real world, truckers can't see you, and driving a Lotus in heavy traffic on Route 4 on the way to the Washington Bridge is an experience in vulnerability.

I added, 'When you extricate yourself from the Esprit, after a hundred miles – or perhaps shoehorn yourself out is more accurate – you are like some sort of Quasimodo who would welcome the help of an orthopedist to straighten you out.'

But the Company pressed on. It had to. The debit ledger showed a big red $6 million. We put together a small fleet of Esprits, Élans and Elites for journalists to test drive, and all were smitten by the car's racy 'go fast' styling and cornering abilities, but less complimentary about its mechanical reliability. I got more than one embarrassing phone call to say one had conked out – either it had stalled and refused to re-start, or the lights wouldn't work. 'Lucas, Prince of Darkness has struck again,' a phrase automotive journalists with experience of driving British cars were fond of using, referring to electrics manufactured by the Lucas company. Another journalistic joke that went the rounds for many years: 'Why do the English drink warm beer? Because they have Lucas refrigerators.'

The record for a Lotus breakdown was 50ft from our parking exit. The low front, which had only about 5in clearance, a providence-tempter on the potholed roads of New Jersey and New York – clipped a manhole cover standing proud prior to resurfacing. The bump knocked out the electrics in the nose of the car. The journalist reappeared in the lobby a few minutes after setting out and we found him another car, imploring careful negotiation of the high gratings on the street. Not the most auspicious start for a test-driving weekend that you hoped the reporter would write nice things about.

Years later, in 1996, a leading automotive writer, Gavin Green, told readers of *The Independent* newspaper in Britain in a piece headed 'Great body. Pity it always lets me down':

> I write this from the side of the busy Marylebone Road in London on a wet and miserable Thursday night, sitting in a Lotus Elise waiting for the RAC (roadside help) to come. The car has broken down, an occurrence familiar to many Lotus owners (the Company's name is said to be an acronym for 'Lots Of Trouble Usually Serious'). Over the past twenty years, it has probably been Britain's least reliable make of car and that's saying something.'

Sales of the large Lotus inventory that Rolls-Royce, as the new United States distributors had inherited, were slow and the factory was asked not to send more ('motorized plastic skateboards' was a private description at Rolls-Royce) until stocks began to move more quickly. The marketing director, desperate to get some off the books, signed a weird deal with a New York barter company – a frantic Las Vegas-like throw – but even these expert product movers had trouble disposing of them.

Under a complicated arrangement, the barter people promised advertising space in the *Wall Street Journal* and other prestigious publications as part-payment for the cars, which they got at a knockdown price. Our advertising agency had serious reservations, saying it was unworkable. It was. *The Journal* and most other publications repudiated the arrangement that had been described by the barter company. The barter company then offered alternatives as partial recompense for the cars that certainly would have sent Rolls-Royce management in Britain over the edge. Would we be interested in 5,000 hotel bedside clocks or 30,000 tons of bat manure fertilizer that happened to be stacked up in Africa? The overture was declined, due to an inability to identify a use for such products in the business of marketing luxury motor cars. The barter people meanwhile were offering Lotus cars to companies as sales incentives or as raffle prizes. You can imagine how that went down with dealers who were trying to unload Lotus stocks they wished would just go away. It was an embarrassment and a fiasco.

The cost to Rolls-Royce was enormous in cash, time, and wear and tear. Everybody had double duty trying to do justice to two very different products, which had but one tenuous connection – there was a wheel at each corner.

The Lotus range just did not have much marketplace appeal, and it was agreed that turbo-charging the Esprit might boost sales, but astonishingly, Lotus demanded that Rolls-Royce pay the considerable homologation costs involved in testing and proving that the vehicle met the United States government safety and environmental requirements. Rolls-Royce pointed out that it was their marketing agent, not the manufacturer, and technical matters clearly fell into the Lotus bailiwick. This impasse signaled the end and no tears were shed when the importing arrangement that had dragged on for about three years was mercifully euthanized.

The final unfair irony, apart from Rolls-Royce having to write off about $3 million on top of continuous losses since the start, was a lawsuit by a dealer in the west. He sued Rolls-Royce for not supplying turbo-Esprits, though it was argued that Rolls was only the importer and that he should talk to the Lotus company in England. The court found in his favor.

Lotus continued to struggle, bouncing from corporate owner to owner in the 1980s and 1990s – General Motors, Bugatti and then Proton, the Malaysian carmaker. Chief executives came and went as if through revolving doors and the London *Daily Telegraph* commented in 2002:

> It is hard to escape the notion that Lotus is the motor industry equivalent of the Middle East – ungovernable. Lotus's insistence that the departure of the latest CEO, in office for less than a year, is part of a grand plan, looks disingenuous. Companies that know where they are going do not swap chief executives with the frequency of oil changes.

The *Daily Telegraph* referred to upheavals, project delays, job cuts and financial losses and noted: 'Lotus has no known plans to replace the one model that desperately needs pensioning off; the Esprit coupé, whose origins date back to 1975. A $70,000 car with a plastic body simply doesn't hack it in the market these days.'

Sadly for both Lotus and Rolls-Royce, it did not hack it earlier, either.

21

PRIVILEGED JOURNOS AND
THE GLOSSY POSSE

Were it left to me to decide whether we should have a government without newspapers, or newspapers without a government, I should not hesitate a moment to prefer the latter.

Thomas Jefferson

Most journalists are hardworking and underpaid. They chronicle town councils and local events ranging from courts to baseball, and most broadcast reporters, allowing for jazzing the piece up a bit, come through with a fair – if breathless – flavor of the story. But a few privileged corps in the world of journalism enjoy the good life at the expense of car companies, hotels and resorts. And their stuff is not always a mirror-image of the facts.

Automotive and travel writers have come to expect deluxe pampering that might explain gushing pieces about cars and vacation places that sometimes do not quite measure up when you experience them yourself. Now, I'm not tarring all the people who write on these topics with the great brush of freeloading. There are some straight arrows, good journalists who do not accept more than a minimum of largesse and are far from being in the pocket of organizations they are writing about. In the rarified heights of publishing, however, are editors of fashion magazines, which journalist Toby Young once described as the 'glossy posse', and the most powerful cabal in America.

'Glossies and the Good Life', a Young piece in the *Wall Street Journal* in October 2003, highlighted 'the cozy relationship' between fashion-fed glossies and advertisers: 'Magazines' fashion departments are deluged with freebies every day, some of them worth a deal of money.' At *Vanity Fair*, where Young worked for more than two years, he once stumbled across a screwed-up ball of paper outside the office of the fashion director. On the paper was the message: 'a while back, the Diamond Information Center presented you with a diamond solitaire necklace…'

'The fashion director of another glossy,' he wrote, 'was caught trying to sell on eBay a couture coat she had been sent by Chanel. The floor bid was $150,000.'

The CEO of Conde Nast, Young continued, received so much booty he had to hire three town cars to carry it to his house. 'We're talking hand-made suits, cases of wine, sets of golf clubs – not your usual *tchotchkes*. The Lincolns sailed off down Madison Avenue like Spanish galleons packed with treasure. A spokesperson for Conde Nast says that this story, which I had from a closely placed source, 'is absolutely untrue.'

'So what if glossy magazine editors give favorable coverage to those who cross their palms with silver?' asks Mr Young, who authored the book *How to Lose Friends and Alienate People*, a memoir about working for a series of upscale magazines. 'The people who work for glossy magazines routinely lie about what cosmetic products the *fabulosi* in their pages are wearing. Hair stylists and makeup artists will frequently claim to have used a product simply because the manufacturer put them on the payroll, when in fact they've used something quite different.'

The examples quoted by Mr Young are not typical of everyday journalism – real journalism where most writers do an honest job without a trace of graft, unless of course you call it a sin to accept lunch from a smooth PR practitioner. Do not let the foregoing sour your view of journalists in general. Most do not move in the fleshpots of New York, Washington and Los Angeles, where odious lobbyists and publicity agents almost give lawyers a good name. Most newspapers have an ethics code. The *New York Times*, *Wall Street Journal* and other major papers protect their independence with strict standards. They insist that contributors stipulate that they did not accept hospitality or travel-freebies in the preparation of an article. The *New York Times* response to an invitation to join half a dozen North American automotive journalists on a visit to the Rolls-Royce factory in England would be: 'If the story were strong enough, a reporter would be assigned from the London bureau and he would pay his own way there to join in the briefings and tour the plant. That is how it should be, but in the real world other standards and influences apply.'

A carmaker, airline or resort will focus on lifestyle or specialist writers. Freelancers, the principal targets, often recycle their material for several publications, so everybody wins – the hotel or car manufacturer gets the publicity and the freelance is paid by magazines for the piece. A trip financed by the organization the journalist is writing about raises the question of editorial straightforwardness. But it is not as simple as that. While the immensely rich *New York Times*, setting standards of purity can afford its independence, it is not realistic to expect freelancers to shell out hundreds of dollars for a trip to a European resort or auto plant, interview the CEO and drive a few cars. They can't because most do not make enough. Moreover, they certainly would not go out on such an expensive limb unless they had a commission or two and knew exactly where they were going to place the stories. So the companies create a news peg and finance the trip.

With the big papers spurning facility trips as they are labeled, it is difficult for European or Japanese companies to attract a business or motoring staff writer from a major North American newspaper, but they might make a catch if the writer is in the country on another story or on vacation. The buff books – enthusiasts' magazines – have no qualms about manufacturers picking up the tab. They could comfortably afford to pay their own way, which would ensure absolute independence of comment, but I do not know any that do.

Journalists are usually taken first or business class; put up in luxury hotels and looked after in a manner to which many have delightedly become accustomed. Invitations to Europe and Asia can include luxurious side trips and some writers flaunt this privileged VIP treatment to their readers, weaving in references to ancient castle/hotels with four-poster beds that serve old port in front of log fires and flunkeys reloading the hunting rifles so all they have to do is aim. When they have recovered from copious quantities of foie gras, saumon fume and Dom Perignon, they will write esoteric pieces sprinkled with technical jargon that the average car buyer can not relate to.

And though there is supposed to be a distinct separation between editorial and advertising, in these sharply competitive days when every dollar of advertising revenue is fought over, an article highlighting a new car's list of shortcomings would not be warmly welcomed. Automotive writers could spend almost the entire year jetting to exotic locations all over the world, driving the latest European, Japanese or American cars, and when they are not schmoozing in the Alps, Northern Sweden, the Cote D'azur, or the Napa Valley, they enjoy delivery to their door of the latest models. Test cars appear with such frequency, that an automotive writer can just about count on a free car for every week of the year. Some boast that they do not need to own a car. A PR manager with a leading Japanese manufacturer described them to me as 'the cars-for-life brigade'.

Auto writers will thrash cars to within an inch of their mechanical lives. I have seen Bentleys, Jaguars and others treated to a degree of savagery tantamount to trying to destroy them. Of course a car should be pushed hard to judge its performance and attributes in emergency situations, but it seems pointless to try to murder it. People who pay a fortune for a Porsche, Ferrari or Bentley drive very fast when they can – the cars are built for that – and will take them to a track for the exhilaration of high-performance driving. But they do not abuse them as some journos do before writing about back-end wag, G-forces, oversteer, drag co-efficient and other technical stuff the average motorist does not know much about, or indeed have much interest in.

Ideally, a fleet of new models should be available three months in advance of a launch to accommodate car magazines that require ten to twelve weeks lead time if their reviews are to coincide with the introduction. This caused a logistical problem for the important press lead for the Turbo R, the highest-performance sedan in Bentley history. The factory had trouble producing half a dozen suitable cars in time. Two had to be prototypes – rolling test beds – which were still being tweaked and modified. But better have them than just four pre-production models. I took a dozen top automotive journalists to England to sample the car's stunning acceleration and cornering abilities at a former airfield where a half-century previously, Frank Whittle had done much of the testing on his fledgling jet engine.

The day's driving was in two parts: handling tests on the taxiways and high-speed driving on the two-mile-long main runways, followed by a 150-mile drive to the factory. Each car carried two journalists with an engineer in the rear seat. The slalom driving was so violent, one engineer could stand only two or three sorties before he excused himself. 'I think we brought his breakfast back,' laughed one reporter. This was followed by lead-footed driving, in some cases demonstrating more ferocity than skill, and if the Bentley had been a less-forgiving car, some of the journalists might have found themselves in difficulty. One car returned with smoke wafting out of the wheel wells. To cool the brakes and tires, a Rolls-Royce test driver took it for a brisk few laps without touching the brakes. I marveled as he rapidly yet smoothly coaxed the car around the circuit without the lurching and frantic braking we were seeing that morning.

Some maneuvers by the journalists were so violent that a test component fitted to the suspension of a prototype to allow for adjustments moved fractionally. The rear tire touched the wheel arch as the car heeled over sharply during high-speed cornering. I asked one journalist: 'What are you trying to do – break it?' 'Exactly that,' he grinned. The Turbo R was not a race car. It was a very fast, safe, two-and-a-half ton luxurious projectile that would out-accelerate most cars on the road. But this one, as we explained, was a prototype carrying components still being checked out. Some auto journalists tend to lose sight of what I believe most people seek. Readers look for an informed view on how a car performs in real-world road conditions. They want to know how safe and well-built it is; how smooth and powerful, and responsive to emergency handling, and how much it costs to run, insure, and repair. Some reporters write for other journalists rather than the reader – cute, esoteric phrasing to show what erudite scribes they are. They formulate tortuous sentences which I am not sure enlighten those who are not much into tech-speak.

An engineering degree might have been helpful in understanding this critique of the sporty Acura TL Type S in a leading magazine:

This 3.2-liter, 24-valve, aluminum-block 60 degree V-6 makes use of more aggressive camshafts and redesigned intake-valves for increased performance from the VTEC variable valve timing system. It also has a higher compression ratio of 10.5:1, and spin-cast cylinder walls that are lighter and make for better heat dissipation over the standard counterparts. Airflow is increased by a new dual-chamber intake plenum that contains an electric-motor-actuated valve opening at 3,800rpm. Changing the intake path length enhances the natural supercharger effect, according to Acura.

Technical writing like that reminded me of a memorable Orson Welles wine commercial. He held up a glass, squinted, and told us in those wonderful, deep sonorous tones:

Some experts will talk about where the grapes were grown and tell you that a wine has legs, broad shoulders, or a long nose, staying power or a strong finish. Full-bodied and unctuous in feel with a texture tilting to heaviness, but doesn't cross the line because of the depth and energy of its central fruitiness. What they mean is – it tastes good.

Brief, simple, and to the point.

Chummy relationships between journalists and car PR people, can lead to questions about objectivity. One long-standing practice raises a red flag. Some journalists moonlight for car companies – writing press releases or brochures – and may even have 'an extended car loan for product familiarity'. How, you might ask, can somebody take a paid assignment to write promotional pieces lauding a car's attributes when he might later be asked to produce an honest critique, wearing his journalistic hat?

William Jeanes, editor-in-chief of *Car and Driver* and a leading automotive journalist, brought conflicting issues out into the open a few years back. He raised important principles. Apart from telling the truth, journalists should maintain a respectable distance from the industry they covered. He noted that the *Wall Street Journal*, referring to 'a cozy ride', had reported that car magazines had people on their staffs that accepted money for services performed for car companies. 'This must stop,' said Jeanes, who had already decreed that nobody writing for *Car and Driver* could derive personal gain directly or indirectly, from an automaker. Not only should journalists reject paid assignments from companies they were writing about, they also should not accept the loan of a car so they could join the amateur racing ranks at reduced expense. That was another eye-opener for the average reader.

Jeanes' rules of professional behavior also embraced other journalistic privileges. In addition to being royally feted, writers had become accustomed to souvenirs of their jaunts – driving jackets and sweaters, leather portfolios, even a laptop. Taking aim at the goody-bag largesse, he forbade his staff to accept expensive mementoes. One example at a major launch – a press kit surrounded by an expensive set of luggage placed in each journalist's room.

Jeanes told me:

> There are auto writers out there who will tell you that they live a better life – foreign travel, expensive hotels, big free meals, etc – than they could in another field. These are the ones who actually could not make a real living at what they do without considerable subsidization.

Rolls-Royce has always taken journalists to first-class hotels. It had no option, seeking to create the right ambience for very expensive cars. But the Company was not extravagant with launch mementos. A typical souvenir would be a stainless steel *Spirit of Ecstasy* paper knife or a modestly priced Rolls or Bentley driving jacket worth about a $100. Even a major introduction, as with the Silver Spirit and Spur, was accomplished in a little over twenty-four hours. Journalists from Britain and other European centers were flown to the South of France where a small fleet of cars and maps awaited at Nice airport. They were piloted along the oceanfront and up into the hills, winding up at a fine hotel for a media conference and an excellent dinner. Overnight, engineers checked the cars and the following morning the journalists drove back to the airport, where they handed the cars over to a new group just flying in.

Understandably, journalists do not like to talk about mishaps. One very experienced British national newspaperman, on a trip to France, overshot an intersection. As he turned around he had an argument with a truck. Result: a Bentley Azure became an instant one-third-of-a-million-dollar write-off. Happily, the two occupants were able to walk away.

Though press cars are well maintained, no one knows how much fierce revving beyond the red line they've been subjected to, or how much transmission spooling-up they have suffered. This is where the driver, doing acceleration tests, holds the brake while revving the engine to screaming point – then lets go. Imagine what that does to the power train. These cars often wind up on dealers' lots. I have never seen any advertised as press demonstrators, but they have been known to be presented as 'factory executive cars'. The mileage may be low, but a car might have had a lifetime's thrashing in a few months.

Ready for a smile? Journalists are noted for clever phrasing, but owners, too, can be funny. National Public Radio's *Car Talk* sought votes for the worst cars of the millennium. The *New York Times* published comments about 'The 10 Least Wanted'. First was the Yugo, sold in the United States from 1986–91. The comment was damning:

1. I once test-drove a Yugo, during which the radio fell out, the gearshift knob came off in my hand, and I saw daylight through the strip around the windshield. At least it had a heated rear window so your hands would stay warm while you pushed.

The other nine did not distinguish their makers in Detroit, France, Germany or Italy. Owners listed them thus:

2. Chevrolet Vega (1971–80) 'As near as I could tell, the car was built from compressed rust.' 'My Chevy Vega actually broke in half going over the railroad tracks.'

3. Ford Pinto (1971–80) Remember that great Pinto bumper sticker, 'Hit me and we blow up together? We had an orange Pinto the year that car thieves hit our street. Although a dozen cars were stolen in one night, ours was there the next morning on a strangely empty block.'

4. American Motors Gremlin (1970–78) 'The car had all the quality and safety of a cheap garden tractor. It was possible to read a Russian novel during the pause between stepping on the gas and feeling any semblance of forward motion…'

5. Chevrolet Chevette (1976–87) 'An engine surrounded by four pieces of drywall.'

6. Renault Le Car (1977–83) 'Our car couldn't climb a hill fully loaded so the passengers had to get out and walk. It would put you in mortal danger if you had an accident with anything larger than a croissant.'

7. Plymouth Volare and Dodge Aspen (1976–80) 'After the floorboards rusted out in the rear, they would fill up with water and freeze. I ended up putting soda crates on the floor in the back to keep people from falling under the car. The stalling problem was so bad that I had to take a clockwise route to work, so I could make all right turns and not risk stalling on a left turn in front of oncoming traffic.'

8. Cadillac Cimarron (1982–88) 'GM thought it could take a Chevy Cavalier, slap some Cadillac stuff on it, add an extra $5,000 and sell a bundle. Tragically, they pulled it off for a while.'

9. Renault Dauphine (1957–66) 'Truly unencumbered by the engineering process. From a historical perspective, it is a shame that the French spent their Marshall Plan dollars on automaking.'

10. Volkswagen Bus (1950–79) 'There was no heat – unless the auxiliary gas heater caught fire. The bus blew over in the wind and used the driver's legs as its first line of defense in an accident.'

Journalists also work hard to produce humorous phrases. Marshall Schuon, for many years the *New York Times'* automotive writer, described the Range Rover as 'agricultural machinery at NASA prices'. His other description: 'A Jeep in Jaguar clothing'.

A final word about journalists. Even if you feel you know him/her well and have a rapport, it is prudent never to say anything that you would not want to see in print. The distinctions between off-the-record, non-attributable, and background can become blurred. It is easy for the interviewee to misunderstand the basis on which the interview is being conducted, and the consequences can be severe.

People talking to journalists should proceed on the assumption that they are on the record despite murmurs of reassurance to the contrary. Do not be trusting, especially with television reporters. When contract renewal approaches, they are looking for a big-bang story and can get aggressive.

There is a cautionary tale I heard when I was a young reporter. The Archbishop of Canterbury, on his first visit to the United States, was cautioned by advisers to choose his words carefully when speaking to reporters. They suggested answering a question with a question to gain thinking time. Upon arrival in the Big Apple, he was asked: 'Archbishop, will you visit any nightclubs while you are in New York?' 'Are there any nightclubs in New York?' replied the venerable leader of the Anglican Church. The headline was: 'Are There Any Nightclubs in New York? Archbishop's First Question Here.' It was fairly harmless. The seventy-five-year-old prelate probably had only a vague notion of what a nightclub was, but the lesson is worth keeping in mind.

It is tempting to play the friendly, well-informed guy to help a reporter. But when you turn on the evening news, or open the paper and see your leg lying there, you realize that your mouth drove off before your brain was in gear.

22

THE BENTLEY BOYS AND
THE SILENT SPORTS CAR

It was a stylish party on the Cote d'Azur, playground of well-heeled European playboys who enjoyed an indulgent society life that few ordinary folk dreamed of. Smart black-tie dinners and parties with daughters of wealthy families, just out of finishing school in Switzerland, eager to sip champagne and be paid compliments by raffish young men were a major part of Cannes night life. Being France, the food was superb, as were the wines and the cognac, and the talk got around to fast cars and the best way to travel to London. Somebody mentioned an auto company's claim that one of its cars had outpaced the pride of French railways, the Blue Train express at it roared north.

Among the guests was a millionaire playboy and race-car driver, Woolf Barnato, who had inherited a South African diamond mine and goldfield fortune from his father, and he certainly enjoyed the money. Known as 'Babe', Woolf was decidedly one of a kind. He bred horses, was a good boxer, scratch golfer and a top-class cricketer, drove fast cars and raced speedboats for extra fun. Add that to being a multi-millionaire in London and you might say he lived the sort of life one could only fantasize about.

Three times he had driven for the Bentley team in the famed Le Mans twenty-four-hours race, and each time was first at the finish. His favorite road car of the moment was a Bentley Speed Six, a sporty 6.5-liter coupé with a Gurney Nutting body that within hours of that dinner party in 1930 would write its own page in automotive history and forever be known as 'The Blue Train Bentley'.

Barnato told his fellow guests that merely to go faster than *Le Tren Bleu* was not a particularly notable achievement. A real test would be a long haul, and he wagered a £100 – about $500 – that his Bentley Speed Six would not only outrun the train, but would get him to London before it reached Calais. A friend taking the train, accepted the bet, and lost.

Barnato started out as the train pulled out of the station at 5.50p.m. and driving fast on the indifferent roads grandly called *Routes Nationales*, accomplished his amazing feat despite fog and heavy rain, blowing a tire and having to scour a French town to find a refueling pump in the middle of the night. He caught the mid-morning cross-Channel boat and by 3.20p.m., he and a friend, who had come along as relief driver, were parked at the Conservative Club in London's St James's Street, taking afternoon tea, or perhaps something stronger, four minutes before the train steamed into Calais, and four hours before the man who had taken the bet arrived at Victoria Station.

Barnato's blowing the wheels off *Le Tren Bleu* clearly offended Gallic pride, but the only offence he had committed was perhaps exceeding speed limits a trifle – something that French cars, he and his friends would muse, would not be familiar with. The French Car Manufacturers' Association was so outraged, it was reported, to merriment in London, that it wanted to fine him.

Above: Woolf Barnato's 'Blue Train Bentley,' the Speed Six which offended the French by beating its famous *Tren Bleu* out of sight.

Left: Walter Owen Bentley, whose great engineering achievements earned a special place in automotive and racing history.

With one of their beloved Bentley racers (left to right) Sammy Davis, W.O. Bentley, Frank Clement, Dr J.D. Benjafield, L.G. Callingham and George Duller.

Barnato's 'Blue Train' Speed Six was not the prettiest of cars. Its rather unusual body, which he had sketched out on the back of an envelope, had a steeply sloping back that allowed for only one rear seat fitted crossways. This gave access to the trunk from the inside, along with picnic hampers and two cocktail cabinets – essential accoutrement for serious travelers in those hedonistic days. But the heart of the car was pure Bentley, with a big engine that could take-off in seconds and comfortably go straight to top gear. At Le Mans, Speed Sixes propelled the racers around the Sarthe circuit on the top side of 100mph. *Autocar* magazine observed in September, 1930: 'There is undoubtedly charm in the way in which the big car answers immediately to its driver's control… that suggests the intelligence of an animal and giving just as much response to good treatment.' *Autocar* went on to enthuse that:

> Performance is more than sufficient even for an enthusiast; there is something that makes the Bentley feel that it is entirely under its driver's control with the minimum of effort whatever the speed, and however the road may twist or curve – a mysterious quality that makes one forget it is a machine.

So, what's special about a Bentley? For a start, the drivers are different, if you ignore one thing they and Rolls-Royce owners usually have in common – money! They have always been driving enthusiasts, often younger, wanting a sporty car that they could take to its limits and a bit more adventuresome than Rolls owners in lifestyle and tastes in wine and women. This does not characterize them all, but historically and emotionally, that description applies to the majority of Bentley owners.

Who made the cars bearing the beautiful winged B insignia and where did they fit in with Rolls-Royce? The man whose name they bear, Walter Owen Bentley, was a variant of Henry Royce with skates on. A dedicated and imaginative engineer, and twenty-five years Henry's junior, he got his early technical training, like Royce, as an apprentice in railroad workshops,

The 1930 Le Mans race. The no frills do-it-yourself pit crew, Barnato adds oil and Glen Kidston refuels their winning 6.5-liter Bentley.

which included stints on the footplate shoveling several tons of coal into the firebox on round-trip express runs between Yorkshire and London.

Bentley dreamed of speed and aggressive, snarling racers masquerading as touring cars and left locomotives to go into the automotive business with his brother, designing engines and racing them in hill-climbs and other competitions. Like Henry Royce, Walter Bentley also designed First World War aircraft engines. They also shared a passion for engineering excellence.

Later, when Bentley built the big, lusty cars for which he became famous, the marque spawned a gang of playboy drivers – Woolf Barnato's contemporaries – wealthy, 'let's pack all the living we can into twenty-four hours' young men who forged a legendary reputation as the Bentley Boys and beat the motor-racing daylights out of everything the Germans, Italians, French and other Europeans could throw at them.

Between 1919 and 1931, when the money ran out and the Company was bought by Rolls-Royce, Bentley produced only 3,061 cars, a little more than half powered by 3-liter engines, others 4.5-liter efforts, and eventually a massive 8-liter which offered 100mph, luxury motoring and outperformed the Rolls-Royce Phantom II.

They were robust grand tourers, thundering green road warriors as solid as brick outhouses and they dominated motor racing in the 1920s with the Bentley Boys driving hard races, often after partying all night. They won the grueling Le Mans twenty-four-hours race five years out of six, including finishing first, second, third and fourth in 1929 with strong cars of great speed, strength and endurance that prompted the Italian carmaker Ettore Bugatti to comment laconically: 'Mr Bentley makes the fastest lorries (trucks) in Europe.'

Le Mans, 1930 – Bentleys took first and second.

Trucks or not, Bentleys took on all-comers, and blew them away. The 4.5-liter Bentley was described by journalist L.K. Setright as 'not unlike riding on the footplate of a steam locomotive'.

A dozen young men became known as the Bentley Boys – the motoring rock stars of their day – most of them well-heeled enough to indulge the good life, enjoying partying and plenty of female companionship in London's Mayfair and other night-life Mecca's in Europe. Fast road cars, knotted silk scarves streaming in the breeze and a mistress here and there, added to life's color. They could have stepped out of *Boys' Own Paper* – Sir Henry Birkin, known as Tim, Baron D'Erlanger, Glen Kidston, Bernard Rubin, S.C.H 'Sammy' Davis, who was sports editor of *The Autocar* for twenty-five years and when he died at ninety-four in 1981, had outlived all his comrades; Dr J.D. Benjafield, a London bacteriologist, Herbert Kensington-Moir, Frank Clement, L.G. Callingham, Jean Chassagne, George Duller, J.F. Duff and brothers Jack and Clive Dunfee.

Four of them, Barnato, Birkin, Rubin and Kidston, owned adjoining apartments in Mayfair's Grosvenor Square opposite where the US Embassy has stood for many years. Cab drivers knew the block as 'Bentley Corner'. They behaved like exuberant schoolboys, playing hard and inflicting fearful punishment on the cars. The races were rough and physically demanding, as they pushed to the limits heavy cars with unforgiving suspensions and no power assistance. Little wonder, perhaps, that the Bentley Boys were known to take a shot or two of a strong beverage before the start.

Barnato, the wealthiest and most flamboyant of them, who won the Le Mans twenty-four-hours race three times in 1928, 1929 and 1930, bailed-out the financially ailing Bentley Company. Friends swore that he did it only to ensure a supply of great Bentleys to drive.

'W.O.' as Walter Owen Bentley was known, described Barnato as 'the best driver the team had, and the best British driver of his day'. That Bentley had faith in his engines, the first of which he built just after the First World War, was demonstrated by the fact that each carried a five-year warranty. His cars bore the famous Flying B, which has survived all the mayhem down the years and still proudly adorns the prow.

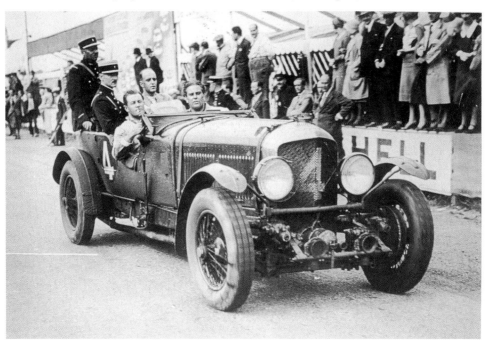

Commander Kidston and Captain Barnato lead the winners' parade. Note the cigarette being smoked by Kidston in those less politically correct days.

Victory at the 1934 Le Mans twenty-four-hours race – W.O. Bentley, J.F. Duff, Frank Clement and a 3-liter Bentley.

A 1929 supercharged 4½-liter Bentley.

He was a brilliant engineer, dedicated to making great cars, and preferred being out on the road testing a prototype and dissecting the car with the engineers at the works at Cricklewood in North London to being a businessman driving a desk. His racing and hands-on engineering experience resulted in road cars that were essentially de-tuned racers.

'W.O.' built memorable cars which today are regarded as automotive gold and keenly pursued when one comes up for sale. These majestic world-beating tourers still turn heads. You may remember the Blower-Bentley (blower being a supercharger fixed to the front) driven by John Steed in *The Avengers* television series.

Like Rolls-Royce, Bentley did not offer customers a complete car. He built the chassis and mechanicals to which some of the finest coachbuilders of the day added their artistry. The huge, bull-nosed tourers in British Racing Green from the early days are, however, the hallmark. But, as befell so many companies over the years, Bentley, even at the height of its Le Mans fame, ran into cash-flow problems.

Racing was expensive and the 1929 depression triggered a disastrous chain of financial events. Barnato became chairman and put in £90,000 – a fortune in those days – driving a hard bargain with shareholders, paying them only about 5 per cent of the face value of their stock. He shrugged off the Jeremiahs who said it was a rash thing to do. But economic reality caught up in 1931, on the heels of Bentley's fifth victory at Le Mans. Large loans were called in which the Company was unable to meet and Barnato declined to be a one-man cavalry for another rescue.

The company was offered for sale and Rolls-Royce stepped up as an immediate buyer. Woolf Barnato reputedly lost his entire initial investment and a lot more than that if you count the additional money he had put in to keep the Company going. But he shrugged it off, observing that he had made more than his total losses on a diamond deal that very week!

Walter Bentley joined Rolls-Royce as part of the purchase-package with much to offer in automotive and aviation engineering expertise, but Henry Royce seemed to resent his engineering credentials. Royce's deteriorating health might have been a factor. He died within two years. Bentley was to an extent a captive employee and was prevented by the deal from

'There is a little square almost in the heart of France that is forever England – in fact now called the W.O. Bentley Square', *The Times* newspaper waxed lyrically in 1993. Mulsanne residents dedicated their square to Walter Owen Bentley to celebrate his cars' famous victories in the twenty-four-hours race. Bentley Continenal R celebated by proudly leading a trio of three legendary 1930s Bentleys around the circuit.

The classic 1950s Bentley R-type Continental.

The beautifully styled 1995 Bentley SI.

working for another engineering company. It was foolish that Rolls-Royce did not capitalize on his enormous talent. The quality of the cars he had produced, their remarkable racing successes and the wonderful contribution he could have made to the design and testing of Rolls-Royce and Bentley models, should have made a leading role for him a no-brainer.

He was more or less left to spin his wheels, wasted on sales meetings in London and other duties that bore little relation to his engineering abilities. In his book *The Cars in my Life*, he wrote regretfully: 'I only met Royce once or twice under rather unhappy circumstances and I wish I had got to know him better.' There has been a strongly held view for many years that Walter Bentley would have been the ideal engineering leader for the Company, and Royce should have made him his successor. That would have been an inspired move. Bentley lived until 1971, when he was eighty-three. Given the chance, he could have given much to Rolls-Royce. Some idea of what Rolls-Royce missed out on can be gained from Bentley's work when he eventually escaped, and moved to Lagonda a couple of years after Royce's death, designing engines for Aston Martins.

'Rolls-Bentleys' as he described the cars bearing his name after the take-over (with the exception of a few like the famed Continental) were Royces sporting a Bentley grille. For decades, aficionados criticized Rolls-Royce for passing Rolls clones off as Bentleys, the grille and badging being the only differences. Bentley versions of the Rolls-Royce Silver Cloud, Shadow, Spirit, Corniche and Seraph were produced, and went some way toward meeting the need of enthusiasts who preferred the understated Bentley name and grille to the higher-profile Rolls-Royce. The 'Bentley pretenders' maintained a presence, providing the nourishment for a resounding resurgence toward the end of the century.

On the way, revered examples of stand-alone Bentleys emerged in the 1950s, the beautifully styled Continental and Flying Spur and convertibles from the Park Ward, H.J. Mulliner &

Named after the famed motor-racing circuit in Surrey, England, where some of the banking survives, even as enthusiasts celebrated its centenary in 2007, a new sporting saloon, the Brooklands, played to Bentley enthusiasts' nostalgia. Seen here with a classic Le Mans Bentley racer of the 1920s, the Brooklands offered virtually everything the Turbo R had (*sans* Turbo) at a considerably lower price. Automatic Ride Control assured tight cornering and a centre console was given a new sports-style gear selector.

James Young coachbuilders, graceful classics that still generate excitement and big bids on the odd occasion that one comes up for sale. The Continental fastback, powered by a tuned version of the 4.75-liter motor car, was the fastest four-seat production sedan in the world and was capable of sustaining 117mph.

An American visitor to the Crewe factory in the early 1980s, when few Bentleys were ordered, spotted one in a crowd of Rolls-Royce models. 'Ah,' he said. 'Bentley… for the man who has won the race, but declines to wear the laurels.'

Cost ruled out a separate Bentley range, but a serious effort began to differentiate Bentleys to attract young entrepreneurs who favored a sporty car suitable to their age group. The revival that became critically important to the Company began with a turbo for the Mulsanne sedan, the Bentley-grilled version of the Silver Spirit. Its performance was exhilarating – a Garrett turbocharger grafted onto the massive 6.75-liter Crewe-built engine, generated acceleration to pin your ears back. But it needed a beefed-up suspension to handle the power. This was a priority for the new director of engineering, Michael Dunn, a gifted engineer who came from Ford in 1983 on the same day, coincidentally, that Peter Ward arrived to head up sales and marketing.

Dunn spearheaded technical improvements that led to a car that would have thrilled the Bentley Boys – the Turbo R – a full-blooded sedan that we joked would blow the doors off most Porsches. Bentley the sleeper was stirring, blossoming into an exciting revival. Mike Dunn developed a car to quicken the pulse and stir the heart, and if it did not, you should know that it was not beating any more!

'The Silent Sports Car' re-emerged as a high-performance luxury car and it was to become the financial savior for Rolls-Royce. Just as Bentley might not have survived without Rolls-Royce back in the 1930s, so Bentley returned the compliment, fifty years on. A concept coupé, Project 90 dubbed 'The Black Rat', gave the first hint of a separate body for a Bentley in 1985. It was a big two door with a long hood and flowing side panels evoking memories of the fabled Bentley Continental of the 1950s, but stubbier. A stalking horse, it did not look bad, and created a buzz. The design was not yet there; nor was the development money, but the Black Rat served a purpose. It suggested Bentleys to come, and Rolls-Royce should be credited for going on to build a number of distinctly different Bentley models in spite of a lack of big investment money. The Bentley springboard was developing in Europe, but the name was a mystery in the United States and without a strong American market, they might as well say goodnight Vienna.

The turbo engine at that time would not meet United States emissions requirements, so a four-stage campaign was devised, starting with the Mulsanne S. a freshened version of the non-turbo Mulsanne and a more affordable sedan, the Eight, as an attractive, sporty Bentley alternatives to a Rolls-Royce.

The next part of the build-up invoked the legendary Brooklands, the cradle of British motor racing and the world's first banked circuit. Brooklands was ideal for the speed-crazy, adventurous Bentley Boys. The birthplace of British aviation, it was there that Alliott Roe made the first flight in a British-made aircraft in 1908 and Tommy Sopwith developed his Pup and Camel planes and where the first airplane to cross the Atlantic non-stop, and the first to fly to Australia, were built. Famous Second World War aircraft like Hawker Hurricane fighters and Wellington bombers were built there and later the Vickers Viscount and VC10 airliners. The sprawling complex, about an hour's drive south-west of Heathrow Airport now has a fine museum chronicling its wonderful motor racing and aviation history.

The Brooklands cockpit – all the instrumentation needed for speedy and comfortable driving, along with the traditional veneer and leather which sets a Bentley apart from other performance saloons.

The Mulsanne Turbo signaled in the early 1980s that performance was stirring again in the world of Bentley.

Bentley himself raced there as a young man in 1909, two years after the track's opening. Many world speed records were set there. In 1926, Woolf Barnato had the stamina and skill to clock 100.23mph for three hours in a 3-liter motor and six years later Bentley Boy Tim Birkin set the lap record, 137.96mph, in a 4.5-liter Bentley Blower.

Also in the Brooklands history mix was Barbara Cartland, aristocrat of the pink bouffant, who authored hundreds of frothy romance novels. Her daughter was later to marry Princess Diana's father, Earl Spencer. As a spirited young woman, she raced cars at Brooklands. As an elderly lady, she returned to open a new ladies lounge and reading room in the clubhouse, and waxed nostalgically about racing in the 1920s and 1930s and the daring young men in leather helmets who blasted around the steep banking at 100mph.

She recalled many famous names like John Cobb and Malcolm Campbell and particularly the Bentley Boys. Why did they have a special place in her memories? 'Because, darling, they danced so divinely,' she smiled. She chose not to elaborate on wild days of partying and *bon vivants*. Bentleys ruled at Brooklands longer than any other marque, dominating distance events like the British Racing Drivers Club 500 miles race, and where every Bentley production model until 1939 was tested and developed.

Sixty years after Birkin's lap record, we marked the track's place in Bentley history with a car bearing its name, the Bentley Brooklands, a luxurious sedan with sharp performance enhanced by a computerized suspension to give sports car-like handling. We told the media: 'Today's Bentley remains a true driver's car, blending advanced technology with peerless hand crafting.' Badging was in British racing green to reinforce the connection with racing heritage.

Most of the old circuit had crumbled away over the years, but a small section of banking survived, and we introduced the car there to journalists from North America and Europe. We drove them up from the club house which enthusiasts regard as Bentley's spiritual home, in a 1920s open-topped London double-decker bus.

In the distance could be heard the approaching thrum of a mighty engine of a long-gone era. Everybody turned toward the trees to the south. The roar became louder and the clock turned back more than half a century as a legendary racer roared into sight – the first 4.5-

Engineering Director Michael Dunn transformed the Mulsanne Turbo into 'Crewe's missile' – a mighty new Bentley flagship, the Turbo R that would move its 2-plus tons from zero to 60mph in six seconds.

liter Bentley which Woolf Barnato nicknamed 'Mother Gun' and in which he and co-driver Bernard Rubin won Le Mans in 1928. This car, which also held the record for the fastest speed over 1,000 miles of any Bentley, was damaged in a multiple shunt during night driving in the 1927 Le Mans, but was rebuilt and won the following year.

For good measure she went into the *Guinness Book of Records*, having been awarded the last 130mph badge, clocking 131.06mph at the final Brooklands race meeting in August 1939. She began life as a four-seat open tourer, was rebodied as a two-seater for Brooklands racing in 1933, then converted the following year to a single-seater and given a 6.5-liter engine.

Now, back at the birthplace of British motor racing, this historic racer proudly led the latest expression of the Silent Sports Car, three Brooklands sedans abreast, steadily holding position on the banking. Even the reporters applauded. Journalists generally do not do that. The car created a stirring in the soul and not just of jaded Bentley owners. One third of buyers of the Brooklands Bentley in the first year of production replaced other luxury cars like Mercedes and BMW.

A top speed of 134mph and acceleration from rest to 60mph in just over nine seconds – pretty quick for such a hefty car – brought a gleam to the eye of the sporty driver money-set. Brooklands was the precursor to the main event, Michael Dunn's 'balls-out' roaring Bentley – the Turbo R – a 2½-ton hot-rod described by one excited journalist as Crewe's missile. A landmark projectile, it was described by *Autocar* as the car that gave Bentley back its dignity. Though it shared the body shell of the Silver Spirit, it bore as much resemblance to a Rolls-Royce in performance terms as the Wright Brothers' Kitty Hawk to a Spitfire.

Piloted by a company test driver, Derek Rowland, around the banked Millbrook circuit in Bedfordshire, the R, from a standing start broke the British international one-hour endurance record and fifteen additional records, covering more than 140 miles in one hour. It beat by eight miles the record held by a Lamborghini Countach despite a bird-strike three minutes from the finish that cracked the windshield, giving the driver a few anxious moments. The unfortunate bird was a pheasant – nothing less would have been appropriate in Bentley terms of course.

Project 90, dubbed 'the Black Rat' in the mid-1980s, caused tremendous excitement among aficionados and, though it did not go into production, heralded Bentleys-to-come with a distinct separation from Rolls-Royce models.

Champagne toast by the Bentley crew when the Turbo R broke sixteen speed records, covering more than 140 miles in one hour at the Millbrook circuit in England.

The Turbo R, a stock model with 30,000 miles on the odometer, had to cover each two-mile lap in less than fifty-two seconds to regain the speed and endurance title that a Bentley set back in 1926. Indeed, 145mph was clocked over the first five kilometers – a record – then the car settled back to maintain 138/140mph for the remainder of the outing. Its turbo-engine, engineers chuckled, generated greater torque output per liter than a Ferrari.

The Bentley Turbo R was pivotal in 'the Big B is back' proclamation. But more was needed to underscore the stylish, high-performance range that the revived Bentley Motors was offering, an array summed up by the Company as 'sporting motor cars for serious drivers who demand performance, space and luxury'. The car that dropped the other shoe, sealing the renaissance, was the Continental R, the first Bentley in forty years not to share a body style with Rolls-Royce. A rakish coupé, its surprise unveiling at the 1991 Geneva Motor Show was a sensation. It was hailed as a 'sporting super car' – big, comfortable and very powerful.

Its spectacular performance covered zero to 60mph in 6.6 seconds and the top speed was governed to be 145mph. A sweeping console with a built in phone (cool, then) extended from the instrument panel to the rear seats, emphasizing the cockpit effect and with a soundsystem that enabled you to sit in the house at night listening to the garage, this most certainly was not your father's Rolls – or even Bentley! The car was greeted as breathtaking and enthusiasts were delirious.

A decade along, when Volkswagen assumed ownership of Bentley, it paid homage to its illustrious history, by producing a brace of sleek racing cars to recall the magic. A Bentley team competed in the Le Mans twenty-four-hours race. At the second attempt, in 2003, the cars in Bentley markings won it. Enthusiasts lauded the feat, putting aside dark thoughts that the only Bentley connections were the 'Flying B' decals decorating the cars and the drivers being described as the New Bentley Boys.

Volkswagen plowed tens of millions into modernizing the Crewe factory, strengthening engineering and design and making Bentley a meaningful player again in the luxury league with highly successful cars invoking famous names from its heritage – a Mulliner Park Ward Arnage sedan, the Continental GT, a low all-wheel-drive sports coupé, and in 2005, a four-door version, the Flying Spur. Then in 2007 a new Brooklands, a rakish two-door to mark the centenary of the famous racing circuit after which it was named. It was propelled by the most powerful V8 engine in Bentley history. Barnato and his racing chums would certainly have approved of that. The Brooklands was followed almost immediately by a stylish convertible, the Continental GTC to note the diamond anniversary of hand-assembled motor cars built at Crewe. Without Volkswagen's huge financial and technical resources, Bentley might not have survived.

Thanks to Volkswagen's tremendous commitment to one of the most revered marques in automotive history, exciting, sporting Bentleys are being built again, and W.O., Wolf Barnato and the Bentley Boys, doubtless, would be very glad about that.

23

EYE OF THE BEHOLDER:
THE MEDIA TAKE

When you get into a Bentley, forget anything to do with money. This is a car for people who
are sick with money; who hold religious services on the steps of the Bank of England. It's a
lifestyle you are buying.

Daily Mail Weekend

Rolls-Royce and Bentley have inspired the full gamut of human emotion: envy, love, criticism,
admiration and much journalistic comment about dedication to excellence and a special
place among coveted possessions. Reality versus myth was an integral part of a reputation-
enhancement program that constantly polished the magic over decades.

One journalist said at a launch: 'I believe that for a long time, Rolls-Royce has sold more
on image than product.' If so, it is not alone. The same can be said about other luxury products
– not just much-vaunted European cars with outrageous price-tags, seducing the wealthy in
Monte Carlo and so many other centers of indulgence like Geneva and Beverly Hills, but
ridiculously priced jewelry, watches, villas and fine wines at $5,000 a bottle and up. Image is
crucial, but without substance, it will usually not get the job done.

For all its breath-catching price, a Rolls-Royce represents tangible value, something you
can touch and experience, beautifully put together, stylish and luxurious and unquestionably
superior in presentation to anything else on the market.

Possession brings immense pride and pleasure but there have been instances of mechanical
problems and it should be acknowledged that Rolls-Royce has produced a few cars that, if
not lemons, had a strong citrus aura. If it became evident that the owner would never be
happy with his car, efforts would be made to get him into another one through a buy-back
transaction. Changing the car was known as a 'policy decision'.

There were occasions when owners with minor complaints demonstrated a high degree
of paranoia, lambasting dealers and service engineers. Some, with more intractable problems
would go to the mat and there were times when the Company would have saved large sums
by settling before the case got to the courthouse.

CAVEAT EMPTOR – OR IS THIS CAR A LEMON?

After the owner of a Silver Spur described a sixteen-month repair nightmare starting on the
day he paid $144,000 for it, a lemon-law arbitration panel in Florida ruled that Rolls-Royce
should pay him $134,000 and take the car back. His lawyer said: 'What amazed me was the
intransigence of the Rolls-Royce people. They kept saying there was no way this could
happen and said he must have played with the fuses.'

Screw magazine publisher Al Goldstein said his Silver Shadow's beautiful interior 'gave off vibrations that flooded my body with post-ejaculatory throbbing' but his mood soured when the car stopped dead on the George Washington Bridge and passing drivers jeered, making him an object of derision.

Red Adair, the oil-well firefighter suffered an extraordinary number of problems. He complained that his new Silver Spur refused to start, the brakes pulled to one side, doors were out of alignment; mineral oil leaked, the driver's door rattled and the interior lights, stereo system and horn did not work. Lawyers for Rod Stewart, the pop singer, sent a strong letter about his $170,000 convertible. They claimed the defects involved virtually every major system including electrical, braking, cooling, steering, suspension, hydraulic and ventilation.

A Rolls-Royce is supposed to be perfect. But it is made up of many thousands more parts than the average car, so the risk of a hiccup is greater and when it happens, owners can invoke colorful rhetoric. One, in Maryland, claimed that his Spur spent 189 days in the repair shop for peeling paint and a transmission that refused to select reverse. This recalled a story – possibly mythical – that quoted Henry Royce as saying that he would not fit a reverse gear on his motor cars because it was not dignified to see a Royce going backwards.

Be that as it may, the attorney/owner pointed out that he also had difficulty going forward. When accelerating from rest, his car suffered a drag effect as though it had dropped anchor. In a letter to a local paper, he said, 'The car is a lemon that leaks money as fast as it leaks oil.' The front number plate of the car proclaimed interestingly: 'I'm spending my kids' inheritance.'

Al Goldstein, famous, or infamous according to your view of racy journalism, for his explicit *Screw* magazine – a publication not generally found in homes for elderly ladies or on hotel coffee tables – had some critical things to say about his Silver Shadow in a *Playboy* article. But he also waxed lyrical about what the car did for his psyche:

The occasional Silver Spur was less than perfect, some owners alleged, and vented their ire through lawyers. Most of the long-wheelbase sedans, the Company was pleased to note, performed as expected, delighting owners who loved the leather, polished walnut and veneered picnic tables. One journalist commented that the Spur did not so much cut through the air as batter it aside.

I was like a kid crowing about his first sexual conquest, I wanted to drive the Rolls past the houses of my two ex-wives, a high school teacher who had said I wouldn't amount to much and a boss who'd fired me a year before I started *Screw* for asking for a $15 raise.

Instead, I settled for going to the homes of about fifty friends and exhausting myself in a frenzy of waving and horn honking. A Rolls-Royce is truly the ultimate show-off car, and as I drove from house to house, I felt like a virtuoso playing a superb musical instrument.

The extraordinary wood paneling, leather upholstery and carpeting gave off vibrations that flooded my body with post-ejaculatory throbbing.

Naturally, I hoped that in addition to impressing everyone, the car would enable me to meet scads of beautiful women. I imagined myself getting laid on the splendid back seat while my chauffeur (which I did not have) piloted the Rolls through envious traffic.

The delirious Mr Goldstein went on to say, however, that his bliss lasted only three days. Disillusionment set in on the way to dinner with his wife. The car stopped dead on the approach to the George Washington Bridge.

I was stunned. What had happened to my beautiful car, the embodiment of my success? People in cars roaring past were giving me the finger. A stranded Rolls-Royce is not an object of universal pity, and though some of the passing throng were riding in hopelessly decrepit wrecks, complete with rhinestone crucifixes and toy dogs with nodding heads – they were suddenly superior because *they were moving!*

The situation was even more dismal than I had thought. Three tow companies refused to even touch so expensive a car. Meanwhile, Gena and I, dressed to the teeth, sat by the side of the road like two refugees from Bloomingdales.

It was the weekend, and Mr Goldstein got the dealer's answering machine. Eventually the Rolls was hauled back into Manhattan on a truck and had to be left on the street until Monday:

> Panicked by visions of my precious jewel's being stripped by scavengers, I spent Saturday and Sunday nights in the Rolls, on guard against predators.
> I started to think of the car as a beautiful woman I had worshipped from afar for years; after finally winning her and savoring her charms for the first time, I hear her whisper, 'I've been a hooker for six years in Bombay.'

Al Goldstein's riveting narrative on Rolls-Royce ownership went on to describe how the snooty dealer always responded to his complaints by saying that he must have done something to cause the problem.

'About 300 miles after an engine replacement, the car developed leprosy. On each outing some part would fall off, polluting the streets of New York with the world's most expensive litter.' The final outrage, he said, was the car's overheating on the way to La Guardia airport one blazing July afternoon:

> I had not used it in a while but as I gazed at it in the garage, I was seduced again by its shimmering beauty and my desire to show off. About a mile from the airport the fan belt broke while the temperature gauges lit up like Times Square on New Year's Eve. The Rolls stopped, victim of heat prostration.

Of the arrival of the Silver Spirit, the distinguished journalist Don Vorderman wrote: 'Here is a thoroughbred with an incomparable history that the new Spirit can only enhance.'

Rushing for his plane, bags in hand and drenched with sweat, he knew it was the end:

> If the Rolls were a failure as transportation, it was even worse as an aphrodisiac. Beautiful women gathered around the car like moths, but invariably, the beauty of my choice turned out to have some mental or social aberration that made sexual conquest impossible. I never seemed to drive more than two or three blocks before I had to mumble some excuse and let the girl out of the car.
>
> On the few occasions that I met someone who was not deranged or too dull to chew gum and fake orgasm at the same time, I was so nervous about the car that I couldn't concentrate on the fine points of seduction. For all the money the Rolls cost, I got laid more often on foot or in my Jeep.

Whether the flamboyant Al applied journalistic license to his experiences, I do not know, but even half the problems he described would be exceptional, as many owners will tell you. Very few journalists own a Rolls, and if they do – to the Company's relief – they have not had Goldstein's experience. The media take on Rolls-Royce has generally been objective, and the Corniche convertible has provided many examples of lyrical writing.

The Corniche is a glorious example of styling and craftsmanship, striking testimony to the craftsmen and women at Mulliner Park Ward who sculpted the metal and wood and tailored leather and wool into cars that dreams are made of. It is a motor car of exquisite beauty, and despite the occasional problem, I have always felt it worth every penny for the pleasure it gives.

Marshall Schuon of the *New York Times* and noted for his dry humor, wrote: 'A Rolls convertible is a state of mind. It is ego and fun and the most outrageous sort of conspicuous consumption. Life is more interesting because such a car exists.'

In an earlier feature article he said: 'These cars, whose prices sometimes sound like the annual budgets of developing nations, are continuing to sell as if this were the golden age of the automobile.' About the tendency of passersby to leave fingerprints on the paint, he observed: 'A Rolls is just not parkable; it needs human companionship at all times.'

Harper's Bazaar advised readers: 'For some, it is Beluga caviar or a chateau. But for status with an English accent, the only symbol is a Rolls-Royce. Chauffeur-driven or drive-it-yourself, it is the best advertisement money can buy.'

Paul Dean of the *Los Angeles Times* came up with a beauty about the Bentley Azure. Of a convertible version of the Continental R coupé, he observed laconically: 'This has to be the most expensive decapitation since Mary Queen of Scots.' A syndicated automotive editor, Al Haas, of *The Philadelphia Inquirer*, described a test drive as almost eerie; so quiet and restful 'you find yourself wondering if you are in a car or a closed casket'.

For the better part of a century, Rolls-Royce refused to disclose the brake horsepower, describing it as 'sufficient'. Henry Royce addressed the question thus: 'My motor cars are built to transport four people in supreme comfort and safety and at high speeds if demanded, and how that performance is achieved is irrelevant.' This missive by the great man himself was usually enough to put the impertinent questioner in his place, and was the main line of defense for decades. Before we eventually made the great revelation in 1995, we would dance around the subject of horsepower, feeding speculation that had fascinated journalists and owners for decades.

Launching the Turbo R, with a stunning power curve for such a hefty car, the Company agonized over whether to break with tradition. The torque and the horsepower were so prodigious, there was a compelling PR reason to trumpet the numbers, if only to stick it to Messrs Mercedes, BMW, Porsche and Ferrari. But the boardroom grey-beards prevailed and the magical figures that would have generated a terrific buzz among owners and in the automotive community remained sealed. However, we did turn a publicity trick with it. Asked about the power output, we reminded journalists of Sir Henry's position on such a delicate matter, but conceded, 'The brake-horsepower of the Bentley Turbo is sufficient – plus 50 per cent!'

In the early 1980s, about ninety-five Rolls-Royce were built for every five Bentleys. Within a few years, Bentley had overtaken Rolls, and by the 1990s accounted for 80 per cent of production. A *Financial Times* writer noted:

> Ownership of a Rolls-Royce is regarded by some as a statement of brash vulgarity, which is a tragedy as they are special cars of which Britain should be proud. Anyone who has ridden in one and watched the sunlight glinting off that long bonnet with the little winged radiator mascot dancing along the road ahead, enjoys the noblest prospect in motoring.

The point has often been made that Rolls-Royce has never been concerned about being on the leading edge of technology, preferring to stick to creating beautiful, smooth machines to cosset the body and please the soul. Phillip Bingham, a British journalist writing about the Silver Spur III for America's *Motor Trend*, debunked 'the myth that Rolls-Royce makes the best cars in the world'. He acknowledged:

> It's unique. For interior ambience and exterior presence, there's nothing quite like it. One thing that hasn't changed is the prestige of the Rolls-Royce name, enhanced by the exclusivity of the product. Rolls-Royce builds fewer cars in a year, Bentleys included, than Mercedes makes S-Class sedans and coupés in a week.
>
> Perhaps that's why there's a sense of occasion every time you slide onto one of those wide, overstuffed leather seats and look down on the world. Inhaling the rich aromas of shiny hide, polished wood and fluffy lambswool carpets – the unmistakable smell of money – you are gently persuaded to cast aside rational value judgments. To best enjoy this regal carriage, heart must be allowed to rule head. And it can, for the Rolls stirs surprisingly strong emotions.

Commenting on the Spur's massive, solid body, Bingham wrote: 'The overall effect is not one of automotive styling, but of architecture – and Palladian at that. This is at the expense of aerodynamic efficiency and handling. The Spur doesn't so much as cut through the air as batter it aside.' If the Rolls still drank heavily, he noted, it staggered and swayed less due to firmer suspension damper settings and other technical improvements:

> But it is unlikely their Lord and Ladyships will mind that it takes around 10 seconds to reach 60mph. And they'll worry not a jot about its running costs or gas-guzzling. The V8's thirst is amply justified by its dignity, its inaudibility at tick over, its mellifluous growl at medium operating speeds, and its aloof refusal to rev any higher.

Don Vorderman, who for many years brought outstanding literary style to automotive writing in America's *Town & Country* magazine, was probably more aware than most of just what a Rolls-Royce is and its place in the transportation firmament. Of the Silver Spirit, the first new body-style in a decade and a half, he noted:

> When the most prestigious of all the world's car manufacturers presents a new model, it is a rare, genuine event. The last time it happened, the Green Bay Packers were still the best pro football team in the nation, and everybody was humming tunes from *The Sound of Music*.
>
> It could be argued that this is one car maker that exists outside of time, in a sort of fourth dimension where time passes at a different rate and the real world never intrudes.
>
> Just as we are being urged to reduce our consumption of energy, and generally mend our wasteful ways, here comes the new Silver Spirit, a big, lusty, thirsty, capacious, exquisitely finished motor car that will quietly, effortlessly run the legs off many of today's sports cars. Rolls-Royce is still building Rolls-Royces, thank heavens.

It was, he said, a glory to drive:

> The ride, handling and braking are all or more than any luxury car buyer could expect, and probably of a higher order than most drivers have ever experienced.
>
> Here is a thoroughbred, with an awesome reputation and an incomparable history behind it that the new Spirit can only enhance.

This accolade, by one of the most knowledgeable and respected automotive journalists was critically important, for many of his readers had an ability to sign a big check without blinking.

Co-existing with distinguished writers like Vorderman and colleagues at other sober publications are the fleet-of-foot tabloid reporters. Catering to short-attention-span readers who would much prefer to view shapely nymphs than shapely cars, they have to come up with sharp, to the point words and pictures to grab attention. And if it is a Rolls-Royce or the Germans caught in an embarrassing situation, that is okay too.

When BMW was testing its first Royce Phantom in 2002, and, horror, it broke down near Munich, the London tabloids used a photograph of the stranded car with the headline: 'The Picture the Germans Do Not Want You to See.' They went on to chortle that the conked-out limousine was 'towed home by a new model that BMW was also trying to keep under wraps.' They published a picture of that too.

The finest exponents of the tabloid art are to be found in London – I have worked alongside many of them – and though some celebrities and others they have pilloried might not agree, their numbers include some very good journalists as perceptive and nimble as any reporters you are likely to meet. Likeable bar raconteurs and fun to be with, most could easily hold down jobs on papers whose standards require less sensational news reporting. But they prefer the freedom and excitement of going after stories about models with rich, overweight, heavy-breathing suitors in tow, erring clergymen, and tell-all political insiders. Also to be factored in are very good salaries and generous expense accounts.

British tabloid graduates were recruited to teach America what bare-knuckle journalism is about and have found fame with flag-wavers of the genre like the *National Inquirer*, the *Globe* and the *Star*. These quick-on-the-phrase guys specialize in stories surrounding royal family scandal or establishment figures fathering children with women who are not their wives… celebrities made pregnant by Martian invaders… miracle cures achieved by eating carrots… transvestite members of parliament with unusual tastes in sex.

Day after day they produce glitzy screamers to win the circulation game by titillating a public open to being persuaded that the wealthy and the famous are alcoholics, deviates or simply coke-sniffing sex maniacs. Tabloid journalists should never be under-estimated. They are smart operators who thrive on their special type of journalism. Rupert Murdoch's News Corporation has profited hugely by tapping public taste for sensation on several continents.

It was one of Murdoch's bright journalists on the *New York Post* who crafted one of the truly great headlines following a violent altercation between a bartender, a customer and a couple of ladies in the small hours in a Queens drinking establishment. The fabled streamer on page one, bawled: 'Headless Body in Topless Bar.' A classic indeed. He went on to write for *Medical Economics*, would you believe, and when I met him was just about to enroll in law school. The tabloid boys never cease to amaze. I wonder how Al Goldstein would have fared at the *New York Post*, or Murdoch's *Sun* in the United Kingdom – pretty successfully, I suspect.

24

ROLLS-ROYCE GOES BUST, BUT 'MR PICKWICK' FINDS A WAY TO KEEP ON DRIVING

It takes something cataclysmic to put the English off their morning tea but that something happened with chilling suddenness one Thursday morning in February 1971. A shockwave swept the country. Rolls-Royce, 'Pride of Britain' and 'Envy of the World' as publicists had propagated for decades, had gone under… into receivership… bankrupt … bust. The culprit was not the fabled motor car, it was the dominant aerospace division whose ambitious project to make the world's most advanced engine for the Lockheed Tri-Star had hit the wall. The money had run out and in British law, if you can't meet the payroll, you have to stop everything and call in a receiver.

Pushed by the Labor government, which promised stage payments, they had bet the farm on beating American competition to the prize of being the sole engine supplier to Lockheed's new big, wide-body passenger jet. Development costs were huge, but Rolls-Royce had to get the multi-million dollar contract and had cut its price to the bone. Too much, it turned out.

The first whiff of the crisis floated into the newsroom at the BBC Television Centre in London the previous evening, as I was finishing up a story on the main evening television news about a fight between the Post Office Corporation and its unions. It was a Press Association flash: 'Heavy after-hours trading in Rolls-Royce stock knocks millions off the value of the Company.' I called a Rolls-Royce board member at home and when he answered, he sounded 'tired and relaxed' as the newspapers describe someone who might have had a glass or two. But this was no party night. There was anxiety and depression in his voice. I asked what was happening. Why the flurry of activity in the shares?

'Can't tell you a thing,' he said, enunciating carefully. 'Can't because you do not know, or because there's a big problem and it is going to hit the fan in the morning?' I pressed. 'Can't tell you – just can't say,' he almost mumbled. Something certainly was up. But I was no further along the trail to finding out. Since the early days of broadcasting, the inviolate principles of BBC News have been drummed into every reporter. Try to be first, but never at the expense of accuracy. Speculation was not encouraged and as the BBC's industry correspondent, I could not go on the air and suggest that Rolls-Royce might be on the verge of going bust without something more solid. People relied on BBC News for accurate and balanced reporting, not just in Britain, but in many countries. Many religiously listened to the BBC World Service and were known to say: 'I heard it on the BBC. It must be right.' More substance was needed for a story for the late television and radio newscasts. I could not report that a sudden wave of selling of stock in Britain's most revered company had clipped a big chunk of its value without giving a reason.

With little to go on, I painted in the background for the network news – how Rolls-Royce was fighting to stay in the big league and compete with the United States jet-engine manufacturers, General Electric and Pratt & Whitney, and that the new engine, the RB 211,

Dennis Miller-Williams (at the wheel), one of the few men trusted to drive the Silver Ghost, and colleague Reg Abbiss, took the priceless motor car on a tour of major Australian cities. Enroute, they called at Sydney International Airport where, alongside a Rolls-Royce-powered Qantas Boeing 747, they celebrated eighty years of Rolls-Royce technology. Reg stands in the air-intake of the RB-211 jet engine to give an idea of its enormity.

vital to its future, was draining finances to the point where it needed cash and quickly. It was a sort of forewarning for listeners of serious trouble at Rolls-Royce. The following morning, dealing in Rolls-Royce stock was suspended just before the Company issued a terse statement: A receiver and manager had been called in. That's legalese for 'we've gone bust'.

Within an hour or so the locks at the factory were being changed, delivery of materials stopped, even food for the cafeterias, and the receiver was now in charge. In effect, he owned Rolls-Royce, and in his hands was an industrial dynasty and the jobs of 80,000 people. Dazed would be a fair description of the staff at Rolls-Royce who stuck mechanically to the one paragraph statement. A cynical paraphrase fitted the situation: 'If you can keep your head when all around you are losing theirs – then brother – you haven't heard the news!'

As the story spread that Rolls-Royce was bankrupt, it was likened to the Bank of England closing its doors. People who had never ridden in a Rolls-Royce, but were proud of its stellar reputation were appalled. Even the City of London, home of the banks and financial markets, accustomed for centuries to absorbing shock, was in something of a tiz. Rolls-Royce was not a particularly large firm with clout, but it was more than a company in the psyche of the British. Its cars, aircraft engines and industrial power turbines were British icons. This was the dynasty of world-class engineers that had built Frank Whittle's first jet engines; that powered the de-Havilland Comet, the world's first commercial jetliner and designed and built the Merlin that gave the legendary Spitfire and Hurricane Second World War fighters the muscle to defeat the Luftwaffe in the Battle of Britain.

And it had been crafting magnificent motor cars for nearly seventy years. Even cynical city traders metaphorically took off their bowlers and shook their heads as they sipped their midday claret in the pubs around Threadneedle Street. I thought of the inspiring stained-glass Battle of Britain memorial window in the main hall at the Derby factory depicting a young airman in leather jacket and flying boots, holding his helmet and standing atop the front of a Merlin engine. The moving inscription reads: 'This window commemorates the pilots of the Royal Air Force who in the Battle of Britain turned the work of our hands into the salvation of our country.'

In my piece that led the BBC's national *One O'Clock News* I reported: 'The enormous cost of developing jet engines, particularly the advanced technology of the RB 211 has brought Rolls-Royce to its knees.' Almost bitterly, the directors said this morning that the Company had received none of the £60 million of aid arranged three months ago when their financial situation was raised in Parliament. The money from the government and banks was subject to a satisfactory report by independent accountants, whose work is not yet finished:

> Originally the Company estimated the cost of developing the RB 211 at a hundred million pounds, and took on a fixed price contract to supply engines for the Lockheed Tri-Star.
>
> Last November, costs had risen by a third – they're still climbing – and now the problems are much worse than forecast – heavy additional liabilities well beyond their financial resources.
>
> The Board says it had no alternative but to call in a receiver and manager.

It was a tragic event for British industry and a blow to national self-esteem. But in the payoff to the piece there was a wry smile here and there when I reported, deadpan: 'When I told Lockheed's London office of today's developments, an official there said dryly "If it is true, then we've got the biggest fleet of gliders in aviation history."'

I learned later that while I was covering the developing story that had stunned the nation, Dennis Miller-Williams, the London PR manager, a kindly and cultured man who could accurately have been described as 'the conscience of Rolls-Royce', was taking speedy measures to ensure the safety of the Silver Ghost, the most famous and most valuable Rolls-Royce ever built. He went quickly to the Hythe Road works in West London where the Ghost was garaged and drove to a secret and safe place in London 'to prevent its falling into the hands of the ungodly!' as he told me months afterward. When the dust settled, and Dennis was satisfied that there were no proposals to dispose of the venerable old lady, he returned the car to her home, safe and sound.

On the television newscasts, I outlined the devastation that had overwhelmed Rolls-Royce on several fronts – soaring costs and a serious technical setback to do with carbon fiber, a lightweight material stronger than steel, for the main fan blade of the massive engine. The blade shattered during bird-strike impact testing. This major problem delayed the program, causing concern to Lockheed and the airlines. The engineers switched to Titanium which added nearly half a ton to the weight of the Tri-Star's three engines. Difficulties multiplied and huge cost overruns were inevitable. Rolls engineers needed more time and money. Behind schedule and with Lockheed already building the planes, they had too little of either.

In my lead story on the BBC Television *Newsroom* program, I focused on the human problem – the enormous job losses everybody feared while news was awaited as to whether the new Conservative government would come through with financing. Pink slips looked like going to at least 20,000 people, a quarter of the workforce, and I quoted a union man at the main Derby factory: 'We've always tended to think of Rolls-Royce as something that has always been there and always will. Maybe that's been the trouble.'

Rupert Nicholson, the receiver, a senior partner in the international accountancy firm Peat Marwick Mitchell, was a dead ringer for Mr Pickwick. A stocky, bespectacled man suddenly thrust into an unwelcome national spotlight, he was more comfortable with numbers than television cameras and the oft double-edged questions of devious journalists 'the reptiles' as Margaret Thatcher's husband, Denis, was fond of describing reporters. In the face of enormous media coverage and speculation, he recognized the need to say something about the uncertainty and the work he had to do and a few days after the crash, agreed to meet journalists at the Conduit Street offices in Mayfair. This building with its impressive oak-paneled street-level showrooms was where Charles Rolls started his car-importing business in 1902 and was the Rolls-Royce Motor Cars London headquarters to the end of the century.

After the press conference, my colleague from ITN and I escorted Nicholson to an adjoining room where our camera crews were set up. 'The chair' under lights, must have looked to him like the electric version awaiting the condemned on the last mile at Sing Sing. I sensed that already he was regretting having agreed to answer questions for television and radio where, if trying to parry a question seeking to extract more information than you are willing to give, you can tend to come off as evasive, even shifty. Despite his vast experience, this distinguished gentleman was uncomfortable and feeling out of his milieu in a media-manufactured time warp. I needed him to say succinctly what he had been reluctantly skirting around with print journalists and also to relax him. But both ITN and I were bumping up against deadline and we had to work quickly.

It was already the wrong side of 7p.m. and I had to get the interview done, drive through London traffic to the Television Centre in West London, write a script, incorporating interview sound bites, and do it all before 8.50p.m.

I put the mike on the floor, leaned forward and said gently: 'It's good to meet you Mr Nicholson. You've been in the news so much this past week, but I've not met anybody who's seen you, and we were beginning to suspect you did not exist.' He smiled. I went on:

> I know this is a strange experience – all this media stuff and lights, when all you want to do is do is concentrate on pressing matters a lot more important than this. I'm not here to try to get you to say something you would rather not go into. But this interview for our main news gives you the chance to address the concerns of many families whose lives are directly affected by what's happening at Rolls-Royce.

Journalists generally do not provide notice of questions. But this was more than a run-of the-mill news interview and it was essential to put Rupert Nicholson at ease; assure him that I was not there to ambush him, rather genuinely seeking answers to two or three important questions.

I told him:

> There's really only one issue worrying people – how many jobs do you believe you can save at Rolls-Royce? And of course, tied in there – can you tell us if work on the RB 211 engine will continue, and realistically, can Rolls-Royce survive as a world-class engine maker?

He nodded. 'I'll do my best, but you'll understand that I can't say a lot at this stage.' I did understand. He came across with quiet honesty. The government would underwrite the RB 211 engine for the next month, but a new deal would have to be negotiated with Lockheed if the project was to have a future. He would do everything he could to preserve jobs and salvage the RB 211 program and also secure a future for the car and diesel divisions at Rolls-Royce. Before he could chart any sort of way forward, however, he had to contend with the inertia-machine called government while ensuring that the struggling company stayed alive.

Shortly before the collapse, Ted Heath's government – sending a message to companies that might look for taxpayer help – indicated that the next industrial lame duck to come to Downing Street with the begging bowl would be sent packing. The next duck was Rolls-Royce. The timing, as the English would say, was unfortunate. The previous government, recognizing that Rolls-Royce did not have the funds to underwrite the huge development costs of the new engine, had committed to stage payments. This had been done before, and the loans repaid when engines began to earn revenues. Four months before the crash, the Conservative government was warned of the cost overruns and a danger of Rolls-Royce going under without a big cash injection. It said okay to $120,000 of public and private financing subject to a satisfactory report by independent accountants.

Less than two weeks before the collapse, the government was told that the situation was critical and the engines could be up to one year late. But the politicians feared that if they rushed to take the strain, the government might be exposed to hundreds of millions of debt as well as huge claims from Lockheed and airlines. Cynics speculated that if Rolls-Royce were allowed to slide into bankruptcy, the heavy late delivery penalties due to Lockheed would fall off the cliff with it.

Lockheed too was cash-strapped, and sought help from the United States government. It was not practical to try to switch to another engine. The Rolls-Royce RB 211 had already flown in the prototype Tri-Star, and ten had been delivered. Within three months of the crash. Receiver Nicholson divided Rolls-Royce into two companies. The biggest chunk, the aerospace marine and industrial turbine divisions which made engines not only for jetliners and military aircraft, but ships, nuclear submarines, power stations and oilfield pipelines was sold to the government for £1 as a package.

This ensured a life-saving flow of cash; saved many thousands of jobs, kept Britain in the world aerospace league and reassured governments and commercial customers all over the world that Rolls-Royce would be there to meet its commitments to their air forces and navies, airlines and power generation. The new company was named Rolls-Royce (1971) Ltd to differentiate from the original. The car and diesel divisions of the old company were spun off and called Rolls-Royce Motors Holdings, whose fortunes we shall look at in the next chapter.

Most remaining clouds cleared when Lockheed secured loan guarantees from Washington, and the British government came up with financing for the RB 211. Parliament was told this would assure the jobs of 30,000 more workers at Rolls-Royce and its suppliers.

Rupert Nicholson's accomplishments on behalf of Rolls-Royce were outstanding and became what many regarded as a receivership classic. When he started sorting out the corporate wreckage, the shares stood at about 14¢, and virtually worthless, except to sentimentalists buying a few of the ornate share certificates to frame. He set the aerospace company on course into a profitable new era and secured a bright future for Rolls-Royce Motor Cars, which was floated on the stock exchange just over two years after the crash. And for the original stockholders he achieved a payout of 58 pence – nearly $1 per share. It was a remarkable feat. How many stockholders, skewered when a firm goes bankrupt, wind up with anything?

'Mr Pickwick', the creative accountant, saved many thousands of jobs and skillfully mapped out an assured future for not one, but two firms bearing the most illustrious name in engineering. In 1979, as guest of honor, he was gratefully recognized when Rolls-Royce Motors held a lunch at the Midland Hotel in Manchester to mark a milestone anniversary of the historic meeting of Charles Rolls and Henry Royce in the very same dining room seventy-five years before. Rupert Nicholson beamed. Accountancy could border on the exciting after all!

IRONIC FOOTNOTE

The RB 211 engine that brought Rolls-Royce down in 1971 had enormous potential. Its performance was enhanced over the following thirty years to generate a mighty thrust of more than 100,000lb – two and a half times the original design power output. Arguably the outstanding jumbo jet power plant of the twentieth century, its technology was the genesis of the huge Trent 900 engine built by Rolls-Royce for the gigantic double-deck Airbus A380 that went into service in 2007.

25

GANGBUSTER EIGHTIES BUT DRIVING TOWARD THE FALL

We've punched every button, pulled ever lever, and only two things can knock this for six – the California earthquake, or if somebody does something weird like taking a shot at Reagan.

I made this comment to my colleagues as we finalized details of a critically important upcoming event. New models from Rolls-Royce did not come along too often, but when they did, it was a major occasion and a much-needed fillip to the cash flow. We were about to unveil the first new sedans in fifteen years in a beautiful setting in New York's Central Park, at the Tavern on the Green, which is about the only place you can park a string of cars in Manhattan without getting towed.

A full range of media was expected, broadcasters having the opportunity to crawl all over the cars and do their interviews and stand-ups before the print journalists rolled up. We had a whiz-bang start lined up with ABC's *Good Morning America* arranging to open the leading morning television show against a backdrop of several-million-dollars-worth of Rolls-Royce motor cars.

The program embraced test drives through the park, presentations, interviews, breakfast and lunch, and the signs were that journalists were eager to see and sample the new cars. Alas my prescience was spooky. On the day before the launch, George Lewis, president of Rolls-Royce Motors International, was at the Plaza Hotel discussing the new models and market development strategy with *Forbes* magazine when a colleague came in and whispered to me: 'Some lunatic has just shot the president.'

How bad was it? Would this blow our program to pieces? How could we launch the most expensive cars in America, talking up the good life and all, against a mournful, all-pervading news event like the president, in critical condition, having bullets taken out of him? That evening we were to hold a reception and viewing of the Silver Spirit and long-wheelbase Silver Spur, with the Bentley version, the Mulsanne, at the posh Park Ward showrooms in Manhattan. The guests included bankers whose right side we had to stay on.

We just had to go with it. It was too late to cancel and though the atmosphere was a bit somber, George Lewis, a master at judging a situation, acknowledged everybody's concern about the president, while skillfully conveying our commercial message to the financial community. Meanwhile I monitored the news from Washington and talked to television network planners, trying to make judgments about the launch in the morning. It was impossible to gauge media attendance or how disastrous the event would be if the post-surgery news about the president was not good. ABC felt that it would not be appropriate for *Good Morning America* to be waltzing around luxury cars. Thanks, however, to the skills of surgeons at the George Washington hospital and the toughness of the old Gipper, everything turned out okay.

To counter unofficial 'Rolls-Royce limousines' produced by cutting a Rolls-Royce sedan car in two and adding a section, Rolls-Royce decided to build its own for 1986, by stretching the Silver Spur. Further work on its proportions was clearly needed and work began on a successor.

Above and opposite: Though the exterior might have been slightly out of proportion, the interior delivered Rolls-Royce luxury as expected, along with an entertainment system, cocktail requisites and a refrigerator concealed by the armrest. Coming in at under $200,000 it was an appealing head-turner.

Early the following day, as we drove to Central Park, Chief Executive George Fenn and Engineering Director John Hollings, who had flown from England to take part in the media interviews, asked what the turnout would be. 'Impossible to say,' I replied. 'We're in uncharted waters. It could be a bust. Or it might work because Reagan seems to be holding his own.' It was about 7 o'clock on a beautiful spring morning. The cars, looking magnificent in the sun were lined up outside the Tavern, breakfast was laid out just inside, the press kits were on display and we were ready for the media. The question was: would there be any media?

It was a relief to see Ian Hargreaves of *The Financial Times* jump out of a cab. Soon after, the first television crews arrived from CBS, NBC and ABC, then the AP, UPI, Reuters and a string of print reporters and we were off. The news about the president was encouraging, news desks relaxed, deciding there were other stories out there today, and the coverage of the new cars was extensive on radio, television and in the papers.

That evening, we flew to Los Angeles for the western states launch the following morning at the Bel Air Hotel, a swish watering hole, where, my Los Angeles friends aver, even the busboys insist on their cars being valet parked. The news about President Reagan continued to be encouraging, and the Los Angeles media arrived in spades to photograph, talk and write about a bunch of cars making a bow in what many saw as their natural habitat. California accounted for more than one-in-three of all the Rolls-Royce cars sold in the United States and its evening newscasts carried stories about the latest must-have automotive baubles.

Where ever you can smell the money, you will find Rolls-Royce. And you do not sense it any stronger than in the exclusive, wall-to-wall cash enclave they call Bel Air and a rich streak of real estate embracing Beverly Hills, Malibu, Pasadena, and Newport Beach. In the evening we held a reception in the courtyard at the Sunset Boulevard home of the author, Sidney Sheldon. Again it was a big media turnout to view the cars and mingle with Roger

The Bentley Eight was lauded as 'a driver's car', having virtually all the characteristics and opulence of the Mulsanne but at a more affordable price, and opened up the exclusive club to more buyers. A wire-mesh grille was a reminder of the glory days of Le Mans.

Though fitted with less expensive straight-grain walnut veneer and durable carpeting *sans* lambswool rugs, virtually all the luxury was there in the Bentley Eight. It was good value and succeeded in attracting new customers.

Moore, Jaclyn Smith, and others with the financial heft to buy a Rolls-Royce and perhaps a private jet or two.

The Silver Shadow range had lasted well and four-year-old models were fetching much of their original purchase price, but they were suffering styling fatigue and the new cars arrived non-too-soon. Though the order book was strong, David Plastow realized that limited resources made it increasingly difficult to go it alone. He skillfully engineered a marriage with the Vickers engineering group, giving Rolls access to much-needed funding, and Vickers a wider industrial base with a world-famous product. It also got Plastow the role as chief executive of the expanded group, a sharp young businessman to inject energy into the old leviathan.

Famous for its guns, tanks, warships and aircraft, Vickers had made healthy profits for more than a hundred years, selling armaments to the British government and any other nation or faction that sought weapons for an aggressive initiative. Indeed few conflicts were waged on any continent without Vickers shipping arms to the combatants, often happily supplying both sides. Vickers and Rolls-Royce went back a long way together – to the first non-stop flight across the Atlantic in 1919 by a Rolls-Royce-powered Vickers bomber and of course the legendary Merlin engines that powered the fighters and bombers in the Second World War.

The Press greeted the merger with some cynicism. One paper likened it to 'two drunken Earls, black ties askew after a jolly good night out, holding on to each other for support as they staggered up the steps of *Annabel's* Mayfair nightclub'. But the merger brought benefits to both companies with the 1980s turning into record-setting years for Rolls-Royce, and the start of a Bentley revival program.

The Silver Spirit was pitched as the self-drive Rolls-Royce, and the Silver Spur, with additional legroom for rear passengers, positioned as 'eminently suitable for formal business use with a chauffeur, or for the enjoyment of the owner wishing to drive himself'.

The Bentley version, the Mulsanne, recalling racing history, was publicized as a performance sedan of impeccable road manners, fastidious attention to detail, silence and comfort, coming together in the newest of an historic line of fine motor cars that had made Bentley a by-word among enthusiasts for more than half a century. But again, it was a Rolls under the skin, so any inference that it zipped along more sportingly than a Rolls, was illusory. The Spirit and Spur were a little wider and lower than their predecessors to make them contemporary and, hopefully, a little more aerodynamically efficient, yet retaining sophisticated Rolls-Royce elegance. The proclaimed better aerodynamics was stretching it a bit. Rolls products were always regarded as having the drag coefficient of a brick, and the wind resistance of the Hoover dam.

Missing from the lineup was a limousine. Enterprising body-shops had jumped in with Silver Spur conversions, extending them by several feet and we were concerned about the safety aspect and product liability. If one of the 'chop-jobs', as they were known, disintegrated in an accident, the world would think it was a Rolls-Royce that had come apart.

It was decided to take the converters on by putting genuine Rolls-Royce limousines on the market and they began to appear in the mid-1980s. The Mulliner Park Ward coach- building division did the work, adding more than 3ft to the length, creating a luxurious chariot for the captain of industry or the pop star, complete with entertainment system and cocktail cabinets that would have added grace to a London club. Priced at $185,000, it was a seven-seater, equipped in typical Park Ward style with a burl walnut console housing television, video and stereo, crystal decanters and tumblers recessed into each side of the car and a refrigerator in the armrest. An option was a flag mast.

Though a splendid road cruiser, it looked a bit sausage-like because there was no proportional adjustment to height or width. This was addressed in a later version, which was given a raised roof to make the dimensions more normal. We introduced this behemoth at the Los Angeles Auto Show – not in, but outside the show so that journalists could take a trip around downtown Los Angeles.

An example of 'badge engineering', the Mulsanne bore a Bentley grille but was a Rolls-Royce Silver Spirit in most respects. It was hailed as 'the return of the silent sports car' and aimed at motorists who wanted a sporting driving-machine image, yet still enjoy the quality and luxury of a Royce. A version called the Mulsanne S was produced for the United States to lay the ground for a Bentley power programme. Identified by powerful circular headlights and a deep airdam, the Mulsanne S offered an 18 per cent power increase over the Mulsanne and promised buyers 'performance, spirited driving with automatic ride control, sure-footed handling'.

They enjoyed the chance to ride around like millionaires, and the huge car generated more coverage on the evening newscasts and in the papers than anything else in the auto show – galling for carmakers that had spent millions of dollars on their exhibits and publicity.

About mid-morning, however, we lost the media for a while. A gangland killing behind the convention center diverted the television crews. When they returned with obligatory coverage of the sheet over the victim on the pavement and soundbites from an L.A.P.D. detective describing an anti-social individual with a Smith & Wesson, with whom he was keen to have a dialogue, one enterprising reporter asked if we would run him with his tape back to his studio to get a start on the competition. 'Certainly,' I said: 'Jump in.'

The Spur sedan got even more attention later in 1985, when it became the 100,000th car to be produced since Henry Royce put his first 10hp vehicle together eighty-one years before. It was celebrated in style with a pageant in front of the factory. The entire workforce turned out to admire their handiwork and that of their predecessors of many years gone by, as a cavalcade of classic Rolls-Royce and Bentleys purred along in colorful procession. A Centenary Silver Spur was produced to mark the milestone and was kept by the Company – an instant classic that collectors would give their eye-teeth for. Also built were twenty-five replicas, a nod to owners' desires for significant niche models. All the expertise of the skilled artisans of Rolls-Royce was crafted into these special motor cars – many exclusive features like monogrammed waist rails on the door cappings, silver-inlaid picnic tables and a commemorative plaque in the glove box.

The Company had been blessed with loyal, highly skilled workers, most of whom, during many years of service, never had the opportunity of even riding in one of the magnificent carriages they helped to create. Managing director, Dick Perry saw a way of putting this right, with the proud 100,000th car milestone as the peg. A former Navy pilot, and one of the most popular and respected CEOs, Perry would start each day with an 8a.m. walk through the factory, during which he greeted workers by their first names. He said: 'Everyone at Rolls-Royce is part of the same team and should experience and enjoy at first hand the excellent motor cars we produce.'

Over the following year, retired test drivers came back to take old colleagues in the workforce on a sixty-mile cruise through the Cheshire countryside and over the months more than 4,000 people enjoyed the experience of being chauffeured in the luxury and comfort of the world's finest motor cars.

For much of the 1980s, Rolls-Royce was the cash cow for Vickers which kept the pressure on to rack up production and generate more revenue even though Rolls already contributed the sparkle to the group's balance sheet. If the factory had been less labor-intensive, a call for greater output might have been taken in stride. But it was not canning baked beans as some seemed to think. There was not even a moving production line in the conventional sense. Workers would push a partially completed car to the next stage. Handcrafting and a build-process often involving simple, traditional tools were time-consuming tasks and not conducive to hurrying. This was the essence of Rolls-Royce, the commitment to doing the job right, and

Rolls-Royce capitalized on heritage with an exclusive Bentley version of the Corniche, bringing back a great name, the Continental.

Michael Dunn (right), Rolls-Royce & Bentley Motor Cars engineering director, here at the induction of Sir Henry Royce into the Automative Hall of Fame. Dunn inspired the Bentley renaissance, developing the Mulsanne Turbo into the Turbo R, and used this as the springboard to develop more scalding performance Bentley models that restored pride in a beloved nameplate. The Bentley development programme turned into the Rolls-Royce Company's breadwinner.

that was what the customer was buying, fastidiousness and workmanship that could be found nowhere else in the building of a motor car.

The philosophy was summed up by a guide who smilingly welcomed a group of visiting journalists to the Mulliner Park Ward coach-building works in London: 'As you pass through these doors, put your watch back 100 years.' The attractions of factory antiquity, however, masked serious engineering and investment issues. This was recognized by the new engineering director, Michael Dunn, who found himself in an engineering time warp compared to the systems he had left at Ford.

He was concerned to update systems and improve the product. His mild manner belied a determination to get things right even though it might cause some bruising. He told the board that tapping into the mainstream motor industry was crucial to the future and he began to extend co-operative engineering links with BMW. He saw that having not kept pace with technology and new features or getting costs down, the Company was unable to sell at a volume and price to be profitable. Survival was doubtful unless Rolls-Royce partnered with a top-class major car manufacturer. His was probably the most prescient thinking on the board.

How could they expand without diluting exclusivity and offending owners? There were people who could afford a Rolls, but saw it as being too stately or conservative. Younger than the average Rolls-Royce buyer, they wanted a luxurious car that was also sporty and fun to drive. The answer, clearly, was Bentley which had been allowed almost to hibernate for twenty years. Its heritage fitted the need perfectly. A start had been made toward restoring the marque's individuality by turning the Mulsanne into a formidable luxury express with a turbo. The Bentley Eight, with a wire-mesh grille to recall the glory racing days was less expensive than the Mulsanne and minus a few luxuries, but a ticket into the super-sporting car club and a bargain. It offered all the handcrafting and engineering for less than $100,000.

Then came the Brooklands, the Turbo R, the stunningly responsive road warrior, and Continental R, fulfilling the commitment to developing a separate, full-blooded Bentley range – cars generating speeds to expose you to a 'Good morning officer' greeting. Bentley sales soared fivefold from 212 in 1984 to 1,049 in 1988 and two years later, overtook Rolls-Royce. The rush of Bentleys surprised and intrigued the car world. Suddenly there was interest in a fast, stylish new toy for modern wannabee Bentley Boys.

Bentley had really taken off in the United States, and was outselling Rolls-Royce in Britain. Sales went up by 70 per cent in Japan where the deputy prime minister bought one and the Japanese ambassador in London followed his example. Vickers, recognizing that investment was necessary if the golden goose was to continue to deliver, provided $600 million for improved production facilities.

Amid the build-up of an exciting new Bentley range, Rolls-Royce was also boosted with model variants. The Corniche convertible II of which 1,226 were built and was a darling of the showbiz set, was made exclusively for the United States in 1987, followed by Marks III and IV, the same classic shape, but offering more creature comforts like heated seats with lumbar support and a ten-speaker stereo system. These elegant models, with flawless fit and finish, were striking testimony to the skills of the craftsmen and women at Mulliner Park Ward, who sculpted the metal and wood and tailored leather and wool. The flurry of model variations in the late 1980s included a Silver Spirit and Silver Spur II and sales reached more than 3,200 – a near record.

It was a gangbuster of a decade, with the most extensive range of models ever offered. Confidence was high, but like the *Titanic*'s crew, nobody dreamed that they were heading for the wall. Rolls-Royce was about to destabilize. The economies of Europe, North America and the Far East dived into recession together, an unprecedented triple whammy, and as they have said for years in the state of Washington, 'When Boeing coughs, Seattle gets the 'flu.'

Now it was 'When the markets are tanking, even the mega-rich draw in their horns,' and a new Rolls or Bentley is not on the front burner. It was cataclysmic news for people selling high-ticket items and a watershed for Rolls-Royce.

26

WHEN THE WHEELS CAME OFF

Vickers now knows what it is like to be buried in a Rolls. Alive! Rolls-Royce has become a cataclysmic millstone.

The Institutional Investor

Rolls-Royce has often been likened to a swan, serene on the surface but paddling like hell underneath. To stay in business it had to and like a nimble-footed feline with nine lives would squeak through when trouble turned to crisis, managing to survive several heart-stopping brushes with financial disaster. But a confluence of events headed by global recession engulfed the carmaker in the early 1990s, took the wheels off and almost brought down the Vickers group. Reeling from catastrophic blows, the old dowager lurched into freefall, underscoring that apart from boutique specialists like Morgan; building a few cars a week for a niche clientele aiming to recapture dreams of youth; little firms do not have the heft to compete with the international goliaths. Small production numbers cannot generate anything like enough development cash to stay abreast and Rolls Royce had to resort to squeezing the last drop from what it had, along with skilful marketing to stay in the game. Jaguar and Aston Martin survived, thanks to Ford money and vast engineering resources; and Ferrari and Saab operated astride the broad shoulders of Fiat and General Motors and Lotus survived too, under wealthy Malaysian ownership.

The realists recognized signs in the 1980s that Rolls-Royce would need to find a well-heeled suitor. Under pressure from Vickers, however, the focus was on producing as many cars as possible and sales were riding high as the decade ended. But you can not dwell in the world of Lewis Carroll forever. Within a few rocky years, German raiders would charge in, first BMW, who tried to get Rolls-Royce for a song and then launched a second foray, pitching its financial cavalry against the Volkswagen panzer.

The roots of the crisis that overtook Rolls-Royce lay in a number of critical areas – high production costs, lack of money to advance the cars technically and fewer *nouveau riche* feeling the urge for the ultimate status symbol. A history of waiting lists had led Rolls management to believe that no matter how inhospitable the economic climate, there would always be a couple of thousand people out there keen to own the most prestigious motor car of all, and for decades this was true.

Rolls-Royce was to some degree a prisoner of ageing technology and time-consuming ways of doing things. Many technical improvements were of course introduced to freshen the cars and occasionally there would be a quantum leap such as in the case of the computer-controlled suspension in 1989 which gave the range of heavy sedans – never noted for wondrous handling characteristics – the cornering attributes of many sports cars. Much is to be said for the American philosophy 'if it ain't broke, don't fix it', and for the wisdom of keeping well-

'A sporting supercar, ideal for the driver who can no longer squeeze into his Porsche!' joked Peter Ward, CEO of Rolls Royce & Bentley Motor Cars, describing the Continental R, the first Bentley in forty years not to share a body-style with a Rolls-Royce. The beautifully contoured coupe was a sensation and stole the 1991 Geneva Motor Show. Powerful and exclusive, it had the rich salivating.

The Continental R did more to separate Bentley from Rolls-Royce than any other model in the marque and though costing more than $300,000 with taxes, was probably the most desired two-door on the market.

The Continental R interior was marked by a sweeping console that ran from the instrument panel to the rear seats.

proven components. That Rolls-Royce was not in the vanguard of frequent change did not much bother most owners who disliked the idea of frequent changes. Ingrained in the culture was a conviction that a gentleman's club on wheels was not required to be on the leading edge of the technology race. Let the other fellows fight it out with electronic dashboards, tilt steering wheels and traction control.

The slow pace of change extended model life. To the question 'What do you drive?', where the reply might be 'I have a Seven Series' or an 'S Class', a Rolls owner had only to say 'A Rolls-Royce.' It was and still is, unnecessary to identify the model. So there was some benefit from graceful ageing, but the auto industry had made technological strides at an unprecedented pace; impressive luxury cars of high quality were coming from Germany and Japan, and while Rolls owners adored the superb appointments and supremely satisfying motoring experience, a string of frequent price increases tested their stamina. A buyers' rebellion and signs of international recession came together as sales peaked in 1990.

Few in management seemed to comprehend that the light in the tunnel was a locomotive thundering toward them that would take the Company into the buffers inflicting grievous damage that would forever change it. As the new year dawned, economic problems spread across all markets, hitting discretionary purchases, embracing yachts, private planes and luxury cars. And the United States, for many years the most fertile trading area, introduced a luxury tax targeting mostly European imports, on a sliding scale above $30,000. The wealthy reacted negatively, objecting to effectively being taxed twice. Detroit escaped unscathed; testament to the power of the 'Gucci-gulch' lobbyists of Capitol Hill.

Rolls sales plunged 70 per cent to 408 in North America, and worldwide to 1,378, the lowest for twenty-three years. They continued into the basement and 1990's handsome $50 million profit turned south at supersonic speed. The view that Rolls-Royce and its owners were recession-proof melted away. Previous downturns had been nowhere near as deadly. If business fell off in one part of the world, other markets usually compensated. This financial

The kite-flyer Java, a compact Bentley four-seat roadster, was unveiled at the Geneva Motor Show to test public reaction. It was sleek, had a Cosworth turbo engine and public reaction was ecstatic.

Java had a removable roof to give the owner a coupe/convertible, but despite positive reaction from enthusiasts in Japan, the United States and Britain, the concept car went on the shelf. It was put aside so engineering effort would not be diverted from new Rolls-Royce and Bentley models planned for the late 1990s.

twister, however, was worldwide; customers evaporated, and the Company without automotive rival when disposable income was being apportioned, began to stare economic Armageddon in the face.

With thousands of dollars being lost on every car sold, pink slips went out cutting the workforce from 5,000 to 2,100. Cash flow was so poor there was hardly enough to keep the business running. Losses in 1991 ran to $90 million and a further $40 million-worth of red ink followed in 1992. Loose change for Detroit, but Chapter Eleven numbers for a small company. A need for new models also had to be faced, particularly a convertible to replace the Corniche that had lasted well, about 5,700 including 526 Bentleys being sold over a quarter-of-a-century production run. But the price had become very steep – $269,000 which, with $24,000 luxury and other taxes, took the sticker well over $300,000 and demand was falling off.

Another round of cost-cutting was essential as consultants came in to produce a survival plan. Vickers, its main cash generator underwater, was in a vice. The cost of putting the lights out at Rolls-Royce, analysts calculated, would destroy the whole group. Restructuring ran to nearly $50 million in the first year, with critics saying that Rolls would have been in better shape to take the heat had it not been constantly milked since the merger in 1980. Vickers had a hotchpotch of businesses in seventeen countries, alloys, ceramics, marine engineering, printing and medical diagnostic equipment; tanks that few governments outside Britain wanted to know about and Riva, an Italian luxury yacht builder, which like Rolls-Royce, was poleaxed by the recession. Vickers also owned Cosworth, famous for race engines.

Rolls-Royce had been the group's star performer for a decade and Vickers, keen to bolster the group stock-price, sucked out the money. Analysts slammed them for failing to nurture the golden goose with profits from the sale of the printing subsidiary and for splashing out millions to buy Riva and an aerospace alloys company, right at the top and poised to nosedive into loss. In December 1991 merchant-banker Warburg Securities said Rolls-Royce had become a financial drag on Vickers, whose shares had plunged 40 per cent in a year, and should be sold.

The *Institutional Investor* observed:

> According to automotive lore, one Rolls-Royce owner was so fond of his Silver Shadow he had himself buried in it. With Rolls-Royce colliding head-on with the recession, and losing a staggering $25,000 on every car sold, Vickers also knows what it is like to be buried in a Rolls.

Societe Generale Strauss Turnbull Securities, also bluntly critical, said Rolls had failed to ensure an up-to-date product line and anticipate the large sales decline. Vickers had failed to nurture its main cash cow and fund the development of a credible new model range. It was now in a bind. *The Times* of London, the 'Old Thunderer', warned: 'If Rolls-Royce is not to sink into the twilight as a mobile tourist attraction of Old England, it will need to produce cars that the wealthy will buy for their fitness of purpose, not for their name.'

As the board was going through cerebral gymnastics about what to do, I was invited with two communications colleagues to lunch at the Millbank Tower headquarters where Sir Colin Chandler, the group chief executive casually asked: 'How do you think it would play if we sold Rolls-Royce to BMW?'

Nearly stabbing myself in the chin with my fork, I replied:

> The tabloids would probably make a big fuss, shouting something like 'The Germans are doing with their checkbook what they failed to do with their bombs'. But if you told 5,000 families in the Crewe area that it was either German ownership or closing the factory, they would probably ask how highly polished would you like the boots to be?

Chandler smiled. 'Did you ever work for the tabloids?' Indeed, I did. Before going all respectable and joining the BBC, I spent a few happy freewheeling years reporting for the racy

Above and below: Money and engineering resourses were found, however, for a glamorous high-performance Bentley, the Azure, the most expensive convertible the company had ever produced.

Introduction of the Bentley Azure in Scottsdale, Arizona. The famed 'Flying Dutchman' racing driver and Indy 500 winner, Arie Luyendyk, came along to try the fastest Bentley convertible ever brought to the United States. Reg Abbiss is trying to explain to Arie how the Azure should be driven. Oh yes!

Sundays and other large circulation nationals where the rewards came from titillating, risqué stories with wonderfully provocative headlines like: 'His Lordship claims girl in love nest said she was sixteen' or 'Bigamist pensioner says he can't believe bride is preacher's wife on the run' – the sort of frothy journalism that sends a shudder through neoconservative territory.

I wondered if Chandler recalled my knee-jerk forecast when six months later, in December 1991, The *Daily Mirror* reacted with an outraged leader to report that Vickers was about to sell Rolls-Royce to BMW. Headed: 'Hans-off,' the *Mirror* noted disparagingly that 'BMW makes cars that companies give to senior executives who are not worthy of a Mercedes' and went on to describe Rolls-Royce as a national institution – as British as the bulldog and roast beef:

> They have a better pedigree than the aristocracy and are a damn sight more useful. They are more than the vehicles of the royals and the rich. They are a matter of pride for us all in the skill and beauty of superb craftsmanship.
>
> What the Germans failed to do to our country in two world wars, they could soon be doing to our finest limousines. What a sorry end if the bulldog was crossed with the dachshund.

Rolls, with sales in the tank and frantically undergoing major restructuring and short time working, was a basket case and was being hawked. Vickers announced it was reviewing all options – a euphemism for 'let's get the hell out of this and fast'. There was shock in London when the chairman of Toyota revealed at a Tokyo press conference that he had been asked if he was interested in buying Rolls-Royce Motor Cars, but had turned Vickers down because they demanded a quick decision – quick as in 'over the weekend'. General Motors, still smarting over being pipped at the Jaguar post by Ford, also cautiously dipped a toe in the water, but nothing came of it. BMW emerged as a possible buyer but kept on denying it.

Bernd Pischetsrieder, chairman of BMW, an anglophile, who ultimately was torpedoed by his multi-billion-dollar fiasco at Britain's Rover Group, made the first of two attempts to take Rolls-Royce into the BMW stable. His first low-ball overture, offering a price tantamount to grand theft auto, was made in late 1991 as Rolls was heading fast for the rocks. The Vickers board, though desperate to sell, balked at Pischetsrieder's fire-sale chutzpah.

Vickers annual stockholders' meeting attracted a larger than usual attendance spiked with principled, determined elderly English gentlemen affronted by the very idea that Rolls-Royce could fall into the hands of a country they had fought in a bitter war. Emotion was evident at the Millbank Tower headquarters, ironically less than a mile from Parliament Square where the Churchill statue is a constant reminder of the mighty fight against the Germans. I was called to London 'to handle the American press'. The *New York Times* and the *Wall Street Journal*, two of a handful of American newspapers that acknowledge that there is news beyond Nantucket, had begun to take an interest in the possible sale of Rolls-Royce to the old enemy.

The conference hall was packed. A huge press gang turned out for what was usually a small gathering of shareholders who traditionally murmured approval of the annual report, re-elected the directors, then enjoyed a lunchtime glass of sherry with canapés before catching the 3.30 to Chalfont St Giles or Stow-on-the-Wold, arriving home in time to switch on the BBC *Six O'Clock News*. Only in England, one might sigh.

Not today. There were feisty stockholders of mature years filling the seats and they had something to say. Old colleagues of mine from BBC News were there, along with ITN and

A 'Rolls-Royce bargain'. The Silver Dawn, produced in 1996 to attract American owners of top-line European cars who secretly lusted for a Rolls, but found the stickers a little too rich, was pitched at $154,000, $22,500 lower than the Silver Spur. A full-size long-wheelbase sedan, it enjoyed the latest technical improvements like a new engine management system and greater performance, but lacked some of the Spur's interior refinements (read 'synthetic leather' in part of the upholstery). The synthetic leather was so good, the average person would have had no idea.

Above and below: A new flagship for the 1990s, the Silver Spur touring limousine, had a raised roofline and sophisticated engineering advances to complement the luxury built in by the craftsmen of Mulliner Park Ward. It was an opulent and impressive carriage with the rear compartment 2ft longer than the Silver Spur II, the model on which it was based.

The fastest and most powerful Rolls-Royce sedan in the Company's ninety-year history. The 6.75-liter turbo-charged Flying Spur was decidedly not your father's Rolls. With automatic-suspension damping giving the heavy car exceptional handling and acceleration (0–60mph in under seven seconds) the Flying Spur was 'a sleeper'. That is until it showed its rear bumper as it took off at the lights.

business writers from the nationals. One of the most perceptive journalists roaming around, observing every nuance, was a reporter from the *Wall Street Journal*. He was meticulous in his probing; establishing shareholder views that Vickers, focused on its thirty pieces of silver, would 'sell out to the Nazis'. He reported:

> Staring up at the podium, Basil Scott's voice rises with the emotion of someone speaking out for queen and country, or in this case, something just as precious to the British soul. 'Rolls-Royce,' intones the elderly gentleman, 'must remain British.'
> Approving nods and shouts of 'Hear! Hear!' rise from the sea of gray hair and tweed packed into the meeting hall. For many of those gathered, this was a last-ditch attempt to avert the unthinkable.

The chairman, Sir David Plastow, faced a barrage of pleas not to sell. Some Second World War veterans, implored 'certainly not to the Germans'. He sympathized, while pointing out that the board had a duty to realize maximum value from its investments. But he promised that shareholders would be consulted before any sale.

Plastow loved Rolls-Royce. He had worked his way up from a regional sales representative to CEO and had steered the Company through the rough days following the 1971 bankruptcy, leading to almost two decades of sales increases and profits. He was bothered by the prospect of selling Rolls-Royce to a foreign company and some speculated privately that the high price he demanded was designed to push BMW into walking away. Whatever his reasons, motivated also perhaps by not wishing his legacy to be the man who sold Britain's industrial crown jewel to the Germans, Plastow's case for holding on was vindicated several years later. His standing firm changed the dynamics; the board provided funding to modernize production systems and give Rolls a chance to engineer new models and get back into the game. And of course, it was investment that would make the Company more attractive to a buyer. The money was used well. A slew of model enhancements transformed the product line.

Six years after that critical shareholder meeting, and after Plastow's retirement, Vickers made a handsome profit on the sale of Rolls-Royce & Bentley Motor Cars. The buyers were indeed the Germans, and the deal was somewhat acrimonious, of which more later.

27

ROLLERCOASTER RIDE BACK

Tumultuous… customer defections… political infighting… all washed over Rolls-Royce in the 1990s. It was a wild ride encompassing severe labor cut-backs, a desperate effort to stay independent, a cavalcade of freshened and new cars and ended with the Germans marching into the factory on which they had dropped bombs in the Second World War.

Vickers' major rainmaker was now its greatest liability. Costs had to be cut and more efficient production methods found. No longer could 'striving for perfection' be allowed to take three leisurely months to build each car.

Massive cash injections were needed for Rolls to stay in business. Vickers concluded it had to do whatever it took to get it back in shape, and then unload it.

For half a century, the town and surrounding villages in the Cheshire countryside had provided the sinews and skilled hands that had made the Merlin aero engine, and after the war, the motor cars. The forced unemployment caused hardships in many communities. In some Rolls-Royce departments fathers and sons worked alongside each other, and in the street, if you asked somebody where he worked, he would tell you proudly, 'I work at Royce's'. Royce was the engineer and he was the man they identified with.

Facing one of the most critical periods in its history, Rolls-Royce had to try to maintain the confidence of a range of constituencies, and in May 1991, I wrote a blunt communications strategy paper for Vickers' managing director, Sir Colin Chandler:

> Vickers is perceived among key audiences to be a very troubled company, indulging in 'obfuscation-speak' about the future ownership of Rolls-Royce – it may sell it, it may keep it, it is undecided. There are new rumors almost daily about possible buyers and those saying 'no thanks'. Vickers responds with the bromide 'keeping options open', but does not take a firm stance or reassure owners or investors.
>
> With heavy losses there are growing doubts about the Company's ability to survive. We have to get out there quickly with positive messages to the media, owners, the financial community and the public whose perceptions of Rolls-Royce are important to those who buy the car.

I listed public relations assets. Rolls-Royce still held the high ground, possessing reputation and goodwill. On the down side it was no longer seen as the unchallenged leader of the luxury market, and even the *nouveau riche* were backing away from flaunting their affluence.

I urged Vickers to project the message that Rolls-Royce was staying in business, and regardless of ownership would remain at the pinnacle of handcrafted excellence. Sir Colin Chandler should come to New York to brief journalists on his plans and vision for Rolls-Royce. Then to Detroit to lay it out for the automotive media, and Los Angeles to reassure

A car for those who, in the Company's words, 'require the highest levels of personal protection' – an armoured Phantom. Engineered to VR7 level, the highest international protection rating, the car's 'ballistic security', involving special steel and thickened glass, adds weight, but, customers are assured, provides the same 453bhp performance and refinement as the standard Phantom. The armouring process is done 'off-site' by a specialist firm.

the important West Coast market. It was essential to raise visibility in the United States and project an image of confidence, a company in for the long haul.

Colin suggested we discuss strategies in London the following month. Vickers management, however, was fighting fires all over the place, and the discussion didn't materialize.

Meanwhile, the consultants were at work – teams of management gurus who spoke a language somewhat distant from everyday dialogue. I heard a consultant once described as someone who knows all the positions, but doesn't know any women, and I have heard PR people described as failed journalists, and failed PR people, management consultants.

Both descriptions are harsh on most consultants and PR people, but when your company, losing its shirt, spends many months with advisers in talking shops that do not appear to be producing answers to pressing problems – like generating life-giving sales – one might be forgiven for wondering what the hell was going on.

The consultants' brief, in August 1991 was to chart a way out of the mess, create a leaner organization, cut costs and increase output. After all the talk and the meetings, and critical path analyses, and bills running into millions, an action plan emerged. Workers were reorganized into efficient production teams, systems were streamlined, cutting the time needed to make a car by one third to about eight weeks, and the break-even point was halved to 1,300 cars. It was a terrific achievement.

Losses were reversed, and the business was back in profit by 1993. Vickers, with the eagerness of a virginal missionary venturing into a bar filled with happy pot-smokers and Hells Angels on a 'tribute to Elvis' night out, produced cash for redesign and technical enhancement, and the focus sharpened on the whole model range, playing especially to the strengths of the revitalized Bentley.

Two blockbuster events at the world's leading motor show, Geneva, boosted momentum. Bentley was the name on the cars, the turbo-charged Continental R coupe, in 1991, and in 1995 a sibling, the Azure, one of the most stylish convertibles the company had ever produced.

The high performance Continental R, the most significant Bentley to be built since the Second World War, was priced at a quarter of a million dollars and was pivotal. It was profitable – and a scorching companion to the Turbo R sedan, which made for a happy dilemma for serious Bentley drivers.

Work was stepped up on development of new sedans to be called the Rolls-Royce Silver Seraph and Bentley Arnage. The venerable 6.75-liter V8 engine was partially redesigned to increase power by 20 per cent, and an impressive array of luxury and performance models, both Rolls and Bentley, began to reinvigorate the business.

New models kept coming – a long-wheelbase Bentley Turbo R and a companion souped-up sedan, the Turbo-charged Flying Spur, the fastest Rolls-Royce ever built. Priced in the US at $225,000, it could better 60mph in less than seven seconds – quite a performance for a car weighing 5,440lb.

Michael Dunn the engineering force driving the team that injected life into the product range, a tall, quietly spoken man, looked as though he would be more at home in a bank than devising how to wring enormous power out of car engines. He loved speed like a Schumacher, and was known to take a Turbo R close to its limits on a test track.

His courteous manner masked a no-argument call for a speedy solution when a problem was defined. A shockwave ran through the engineering department when soon after joining Rolls-Royce, Dunn determined that a little re-engineering would make the seating mechanism work more smoothly. He startled colleagues who then were still in 'everything in due time' mode by setting a deadline for the fix, saying smilingly: 'Shall we say next Thursday, gentlemen?'

The factory worked flat-out on model variants, one a special edition turbocharged Corniche S, the 'fastest-ever Rolls-Royce convertible'. Twenty were made, and then production of the most glamorous convertible ever built by the Company ended. The Corniche S thrilled California devotees who regarded the classic ragtop as the Malibu Ford Escort.

It was becoming increasingly clear that a new engine was needed. But development money wasn't there. Dunn and his engineers identified three companies – Mercedes-Benz, BMW and General Motors – to explore using one of their engines, with Rolls engineering input, for new generation Rolls and Bentleys.

Analysis at Crewe determined that a powerful Mercedes engine was superior to BMW's offering, and in December 1994, newspapers reported that Rolls-Royce expected to do a deal for a Mercedes 6-liter V12 engine before year's end.

The Rolls-Royce board and Vickers unanimously voted for the Mercedes, and Peter Ward shook hands on the deal with Helmut Werner, head of Mercedes-Benz, and an announcement was drafted.

Then came the flip-flop. BMW, confidently expecting the nod, heard about this upsetting turn of events, and went into a spasm. Its chairman, Bernd Pischetsrieder, called for the intervention of Sir Ralph Robins, chairman of Rolls-Royce Aerospace, with whom BMW had a jet engine collaboration.

Robins had the power to withdraw permission for Rolls-Royce Motor Cars to use the name and badge and threatened to do just that. Within days, Vickers caved, and Ward had to tell Mercedes that the deal was off.

Pischetsrieder, who had bought the Rover group earlier that year, came up with a guffaw-generating quote: 'We are now a British car maker, so we thought it only natural that we should help another British car maker.'

Ward felt that Vickers' reneging on the Mercedes agreement made his position impossible and he resigned. There was speculation that it wouldn't be long before the Germans would be in charge. It was right on the money.

Earlier, when Peter Ward sought a public relations view, I told him there was a risk of adverse reaction from potential buyers if a bought-in German engine came in a box and was just dropped into the car. There would be a better chance of its being accepted if the engine was assembled at Crewe.

In the event, it did come in a crate, along with a German transmission.

It should be acknowledged however, that regardless of which German company Rolls-Royce got into bed with, the contract provided for essential components as well as an engine. Technically and financially, it was the only game in town.

Classic post-Second World War Bentley Continental styling, admired the world over, inspired the drawing-board musings of modern-day Bentley stylists.

For the indulgent, an extended wheelbase Phantom emerged in 2006 10in longer than the standard version and a European sticker within hailing distance of a quarter of a million pounds. The Company noted that the extra space 'lends itself perfectly to the addition of bespoke features, limited only by the imagination of the customer'.

Who are the people who will pay a fortune for a car? Research pointed to most Rolls-Royce and Bentley owners having more than one home, owning five or six cars, liked the arts, cruises, tennis, golf, car racing and wine tasting. Casino gambling, horse racing, polo, sailing and skiing were also well up the list.

In the US, nearly one third of Bentley owners were company presidents and one fifth CEOs. Six per cent were doctors and 9 per cent retired. Found mostly in New York, Florida and California, they had a net worth of about $16 million and were about fifty. Many convertible drivers were in the retail business and real estate and their favorite colors were black, peacock, arctic white, British racing green and red pearl.

In the changed market conditions as the company slowly recovered, owners' views were sought, to help freshen the range. The sedans became slightly more rounded. Interiors were redesigned with comfier seats, a sweeping center console and more headroom.

New electronics gave the engine quicker acceleration, and profits were starting to come again. Overall sales reached 1,414 in 1994 and two years later were 1,675. The climb back continued in 1997 with Bentley outselling Rolls by three to one, then faltered to less than 1,400 in 1999 — almost where they were seven years before.

The Silver Seraph and Bentley Arnage, the last sedans styled by Graham Hull and his team at Crewe, arrived in 1998 and would have made the old stylist Fritz Feller proud. With flowing waistlines, they were elegant — even sexy — successors to the Spirit and Turbo R, and the only reservations aficionados had about them were the BMW engines.

Unquestionably they were the best-looking sedans the Company had produced since the Silver Cloud, whose sweeping lines provided many styling cues. Hull's task was 'to give the cars classic lines, presence and grace'. He did all that and in remarkably quick time. The car took only four years from concept to production, a record for a new Rolls-Royce.

The sticker said $216,400, but behind it were intriguing and expensive extras for the indulgent. A dual paint scheme would set the buyer back $2,725 and paint matched to his own specification, $3,000. A GPS navigation system, integrated with an audible/video monitor reversing aid came in at a hefty $10,000 but you could save $3,000 if you didn't need a TV picture of what was behind you. You could also blow $9,000 on a video system giving a choice of picture in screens in the front headrests, or projected onto the ceiling.

Other extras to make life on the move more agreeable included a $6,000 cocktail cabinet; document stowage compartment, $4,400; refrigeration in the center armrest $5,750; curtains to the rear $2,850 and $2,700 for a rear center cushion stowage compartment. A silver flask with three nip glasses put another $3,800 on the bill. Fitted luggage carried an eye-rolling $7,500 tag.

Rolls-Royce had had a switchback ride in the nineties, but it hadn't forgotten how to charge breath-catching premiums for additions to make your motor car even more special. Having said that, the workmanship involved in integrating the extras was magnificent, and if you had the loot, why not?

Silver Seraph – what does that mean? The Company offered journalists the *Oxford Dictionary* definition: 'Seraph – a celestial being of the highest order, associated especially with light, ardour and purity.'

Notwithstanding any transcendental attributes the car might have, it was deemed to be prudent to hedge against a lukewarm reception – not unprecedented when Rolls-Royce came out with a new model. A last hurrah was given to the Silver Spur. Seventy remaining Spur body shells parked in the factory yards were brought inside and built with a number of special features. They were released as 'the last of a great line...' and were keenly pursued by Rolls enthusiasts in the US.

They became classics in the eyes of Rolls-lovers who saw them as the last true Rolls-Royce sedans to be built at Crewe. The reason – their engines, the much-loved 6.75-liter that had powered Rolls and Bentleys for decades, were built in Britain. They were Rolls-Royce. The real deal.

But time was running out for the Company's independence. The rules of economics ushered in the inevitable – takeover by the Germans. But not without protest.

28

TEUTONIC SLUGFEST

As Winston Churchill warned of Hitler's war aspirations, Rolls-Royce, in the summer of 1938, raced to build an aero-engine plant on farmland in the Cheshire countryside about 200 miles north of London. The factory, on the outskirts of the industrial town of Crewe, was to be pivotal in ensuring that in later years, I and my schoolmates in England would not grow up speaking German.

In just under fourteen weeks, even as engineering shops were still being built, parts were being made for Merlin engines to power Spitfire and Hurricane fighters. There was urgent need for thousands of engines for the Royal Air Force, and the factory's 10,000 workers played a key role in pounding Germany's mighty war machine.

It was in full production in December 1940 when it was bombed by a Junkers 88, despite an anti-aircraft barrage balloon and light gun defenses. A machine shop was destroyed, sixteen people were killed and many injured. Even today you will see faded camouflage on some buildings.

Over the course of the Second World War, Rolls-Royce engineers and technicians produced 26,000 engines that turned back the Luftwaffe as it tried to soften England up for the invasion and powered the Lancaster, Wellington and Halifax bombers that took the war to the heart of Germany, as well as the American Mustang fighter. It was said that the famed aerial battles over south-east England were not so much between Spitfires, Hurricanes, Messerschmitts and Heinkels, as the engines of Rolls-Royce and Mercedes-Benz.

The factory switched to making Rolls-Royce and Bentley motor cars after the war, but it always acknowledged its history, revering the engineers who built the Merlins from a basic Henry Royce design and continually developed ever greater power curves to out-maneuver the German fighters. To note the proud heritage, two Merlins were permanently displayed in the main engine-assembly hall with pictures of aerial dogfights to chronicle wartime achievements.

This flag-waving tribute to the crucial role Rolls-Royce had played in beating hell out of the Luftwaffe caused the board a twinge of anxiety in the early 1990s when preparing for a visit by a group of BMW executives. To spare the feelings of the German visitors, should they be sensitive about previous hostilities, somebody suggested that the engines and pictures of British fighters shooting the Luftwaffe out of the sky should be removed. It was feared that a gnarled old engineer would glare at the BMW chairman, Eberhard von Kuenheim, jerk his thumb toward a Merlin-powered Spitfire and impolitely growl: 'Now, you bugger – do you recognize that from your rear view mirror?' Despite apprehensions, the exhibit stayed, and the German industrialists, courteous and appreciative of fine engineering, admired the workmanship – if a trifle ruefully.

It's a fair bet that no one in Britain ever dreamed that the legendary Rolls-Royce factory, whose products were indeed the pride of Britain, would one day fall into German ownership.

Graham Morris, Rolls-Royce chief executive, here with the new Silver Seraph, who was blind-sided by back-room ownership negotiations between BMW and Volkswagen which destroyed the unified basis upon which Rolls-Royce and Bentley were to go forward together at Crewe. A surprise deal split the company, destroying Morris's assurance to the workforce that the future of Rolls-Royce and Bentley production would continue at Crewe. Morris, disgusted by the whole episode, resigned on principle.

It is a supreme irony that the factory built to make the engines that had a big hand in defeating Germany is now owned by the Germans. But it did not happen without a corporate brawl between two high-profile chairmen, Ferdinand Piech of Volkswagen and Bernd Pischetsrieder of BMW, who squared off like kids in a schoolyard struggle to grab all the marbles.

Vickers, the parent group, still reeling from the huge cost of putting Rolls-Royce back into saleable shape, was actively looking for a suitor, and in October 1997 announced that Rolls-Royce Motor Cars was for sale. Who should reappear, shrugging off the rejection of his overture a few years previously, but BMW's resilient Pischetsrieder. This time, however, he was not stalking alone. Ferdinand Piech also had designs

The Germans went to the mat for the world's most illustrious engineering name. Pischetsrieder failed to anticipate Piech galloping up on the rails to stage a grandstand finish and outbid him by a generous nose. What a fuss that started!

Initially it was a knuckle-fest between a pair of Teutonic protagonists with Vickers hovering nervously in the bleachers. Lurking in the skybox, with a metaphorical .44 Magnum in its hip pocket, was the other Rolls-Royce, the aerospace company, owners of the golden trademarks – the name and the RR badge. Pischetsrieder assumed BMW had the inside track not only because of a close European aero-engine manufacturing relationship with that company since 1990 but also being the engine supplier for the new Rolls and Bentley sedans. Notwithstanding, Volkswagen's Piech, a street-scrapper when necessary and obsessed with getting Rolls-Royce,

The Rolls-Royce factory at Crewe. Built at record speed in 1938 to make the famed Merlin engine which defeated the Luftwaffe in the Battle of Britain and turned to making motor cars after the Second World War. Ironically, the Germans dropped bombs on the factory and many years later, used a different technique, the check-book, to take ownership.

upped the stakes. Pischetsrieder was just as determined to get Rolls-Royce, while shrugging off years of disastrous losses at the British Rover group, which for BMW had become the financial equivalent of a plane crash.

A bruising donnybrook marked this unseemly chapter in Rolls-Royce history, fuelled by egos, petulance, and infighting among chairmen in Wolfsburg, Munich and London. At one point, Daimler Benz, Mercedes-Benz parent, was interested in buying Rolls-Royce but would not get into a battle over it. Even the controversial owner of Harrods, Mohamed Al Fayed, while fighting the British government over its refusal to grant him citizenship, was prepared to throw his hat into the ring.

BMW made a low-ball offer – a ludicrous £150 million – $225 million at that time. As Volkswagen sniffed around, BMW more than doubled its offer to $568 million in spring 1998, and Vickers accepted with a thirty-day negotiation period. A month later, on 29 April, Vickers said okay; there was an agreement. But the mercurial Piech decided to be the skunk at the picnic. He shocked BMW by topping its offer. Within a week of getting into bed with BMW, Vickers smiled at the new suitor and accepted a $710 million offer from Volkswagen – ultimately increased to $790 million after some serious revaluation discussions. Volkswagen said it would also pay $194 million for Cosworth Engineering.

Volkswagen's Panzer attack rocked the not-so-merry men of Munich, throwing a wrench into BMW's spokes much to the bitter amusement of English observers to whom the prospect

The classic Silver Cloud provided many styling cues for the Silver Seraph and Bentley Arnage, the last sedans to be designed at Crewe before new owners moved in.

The long-awaited Silver Seraph.

of German owners marching triumphantly into the Crewe factory was anathema. Vickers called a special stockholders' meeting in London for 5 June 1998, to rubber stamp the deal, as another sortie to rescue Rolls and keep it in British hands was trying to get traction. A group of enthusiasts led by Michael Shrimpton, a Bentley-owning lawyer protested that Rolls-Royce must stay British. The group could not raise enough money from Rolls and Bentley owners in time to make a realistic counter-offer and failed in a last-minute appeal to Vickers to adjourn the stockholders' meeting.

Sir Colin Chandler, who had succeeded Sir David Plastow as chairman, put the proceedings on hold for half an hour while he met with the group, but concluded that it had not got its financial act sufficiently together; the meeting restarted, and approved the Volkswagen bid. The explanation for sweeping the patriotic, well-intentioned dreamers out of court was that the board had doubts about their ability to cobble together the money necessary to trump Volkswagen's bid already on the table.

It was a raucous gathering, erupting at times in nationalistic fervor. Small shareholders packing the hall berated the directors for selling Rolls-Royce to a foreign company. One pointedly proclaimed that as the allies had given Volkswagen its factory back at the end of the Second World War, the Germans should return the favor and leave Rolls-Royce in British ownership. *The Financial Times* described the stormy meeting as 'a smoldering mix of petty jingoism, big cars and rampant corporate egos making for a gripping auction'.

The approval of Volkswagen's offer however, was far from the end of the issue. The deal began to unravel. Pischetsrieder played his 'If I am not the captain, I am taking my ball home' card, by threatening to stop supplying BMW engines for the new Rolls-Royce Silver Seraph and Bentley Arnage, unless he acquired Rolls-Royce. He gave notice of intention to cancel the engine deal. That would leave Volkswagen in the unique position of offering the world's most silent and fuel-efficient motor cars due to an unfortunate handicap – no means of

Silver Seraph's graceful lines from the rear.

propulsion. With all Volkswagen's engineering resources, it would take more than a year to produce a replacement engine – unacceptable in financial and image terms for the two great marques.

Pischetsrieder showed no concern that cutting off critically important components would close down the Rolls-Royce factory and possibly harm his own reputation. I could see the tabloid-splash subeditors sharpening their metaphorical pencils, producing one-liners like 'German Assassin Torpedoes Rolls'. In the event, Pischetsrieder was not put to the test because Volkswagen, it turned out, had shot itself in the foot with a gaffe of gargantuan proportions that turned the whole bizarre episode into farce.

In its eagerness to deal a knockout blow, it omitted to nail down the legal right to use the Rolls-Royce name on the cars it would be making. Volkswagen had assumed that the purchase of Rolls-Royce Motor Cars from Vickers carried 'all the rights and privileges appertaining thereto' as college degrees aver. Not so, it turned out. BMW, seeing the prize slipping away, played an ace – calling up one of the Queen's trusty knights, the bat-wielding trademark custodian, Sir Ralph Robins, chairman of Rolls-Royce Plc aerospace. A distinguished, impeccably tailored white-haired gentleman, right out of central-casting, Robins perfectly fitted the picture of leader of such a famous company. He was softly spoken, but carried a big stick – the power to determine just who could put the Rolls-Royce name on their product.

He had a track record for putting the bite on Vickers. Four years earlier, he had barged in on BMW's behalf to dismantle a deal to use Mercedes engines in Rolls and Bentleys. Robins again stepped up to hit a home run for BMW, reprising his earlier reminder that no one could use the Rolls-Royce name or the RR badge without his permission and implying that unless they saw it his way, he could tear up the license under which Rolls-Royce Motor Cars Ltd used the name and the badge. He did not just hold the marbles, his fingers were gripping every player's spherical accoutrement. His veto would prevent Volkswagen from marketing any cars bearing the name Rolls-Royce. Vickers, anxious to get its money, got a legal opinion that challenged the validity of Robins's case and threatened to take Rolls-Royce Plc to the European Court of Human Rights if it blocked the deal.

A nasty legal fight risked further alienating Rolls-Royce enthusiasts in Britain and overseas, already distressed by the struggle for control by the Germans and wishing a plague on all their houses. Also, Vickers wanted just to grab the money and beat it. After Robins had delivered his version of the Sermon on the Mount, the backbiting between the warring chairmen became pointless. On 28 July, less than two months after Volkswagen thought everything was tied up, it reluctantly faced the fact that it had to give ground if its huge investment in Rolls-Royce was not to blow up in its face.

The two German adversaries met several times to seek an answer to the impasse, but could not agree. Eventually they held a secret summit at a country club, a short drive from Munich. The gathering was overseen by a bunch of political heavyweights, putting on the pressure to settle the spat and avoid unpleasant lawsuits. In BMW's corner was Bavaria's state premier. Volkswagen brought along his opposite number from Lower Saxony, Gerhard Schröder, an influential member of its supervisory board. Later, as German Chancellor, he had a public row with the media over reports that he colored his hair, and a few years down the line, along with Jacques Chirac, took strong issue with the Bush administration over the Iraq invasion.

Piech's position had become untenable. Threatened with having to make a car without an engine and with Sir Ralph Robins's trademark cudgel that had all the subtlety of a six-inch nail going through his hands, the only choice was to settle for Bentley and the Crewe factory and agree to hand over the Rolls-Royce name to BMW in 2003. In the event, he probably got the best of the bargain as Bentley flourished, though he might have had a few twinges of doubt at the time.

He and Pischetsrieder sought to craft a veneer of believability over a shabby compromise. They flew to London to announce the agreement hoping that everybody would accept that both sides had won. With a beaming Robins the enforcer, Pischetsrieder and Piech, wearing a

The Bentley Arnage.

thin smile, the handshake photograph could have been captioned: 'Ever heard *Auld Lang Syne* sung through clenched teeth?'

Under the heading 'BMW Wins Rolls in Corporate Coup with Volkswagen', Reuters reported the latest twist in the Rolls saga: 'As Alice in Wonderland would say: This deal gets curiouser and curiouser.' BMW effectively got the right to make Rolls-Royce cars without paying a penny to Volkswagen and analysts said that while BMW had lost the takeover battle for Rolls-Royce Motor Cars the previous month, it had clearly won the war.

Britain's largest engineering union reacted angrily to the deal, critical that Rolls-Royce at Crewe would produce only Bentleys, complaining: 'It is absolutely disgraceful; nothing short of a complete betrayal of trust by Volkswagen.' This posture ignored the fact that Volkswagen had secured hundreds of jobs and a strong base from which to grow a good business. It was unfair to load culpability on Piech. The union would have been nearer the mark highlighting the handiwork of Pischetsrieder and Robins, along with the vacillating rubber-legged Vickers people.

After the strained *entente-cordiale* posing, Pischetsrieder lambasted Vickers for the way it had handled the sale. If anything was distasteful, he said, it was Vickers' auction process, selling the prestigious Rolls-Royce brand 'like fake Persian carpets manufactured in India'.

He also criticized its failing to reach agreement on the name issue with the trademark owners. 'Vickers sold something as an entity that it did not wholly own,' he said. Vickers' position was that it did not accept Rolls-Royce Plc's rights to the name. Volkswagen's Piech explained that Volkswagen's long-term interest lay in developing Bentley and rejected suggestions that it had overpaid. The cost of BMW shutting off the supply of engines and other parts, plus the cost of paying Rolls-Royce Plc for the brand would have been too much to risk. 'We went for a peaceful solution rather than a long legal battle.' He added a trifle sadly, 'I would have preferred to keep both brands.'

ROLLS-ROYCE CONVERTIBLES

1910 ROLLS-ROYCE SILVER GHOST. BY BARKER

1933 ROLLS-ROYCE PHANTOM 11. BY JAMES YOUNG

1960 ROLLS-ROYCE SILVER CLOUD. BY H. J. MULLINER

1971 ROLLS-ROYCE CORNICHE

2000 ROLLS-ROYCE CORNICHE

Graham Hull, the talented Rolls-Royce chief stylist who led the design team for the Silver Seraph, Bentley Arnage and the exquisitely styled 2000 convertible – the reborn Corniche – created this montage of the evolution of the classic convertible. The 2000 Corniche was the last new Royce model to be built at Crewe before BMW assumed the name and produced its own version of a Rolls-Royce.

BMW announced it had acquired the Rolls-Royce name for £40 million, about $65 million but would permit Volkswagen to produce Rolls-Royce alongside Bentley for a little under five years at Crewe. Then BMW would assume ownership and manufacturing of Rolls-Royce. Volkswagen would keep Bentley and the Crewe factory. Ironically, the acquisition cost BMW nothing. Rolls-Royce Plc invested its $65 million fee for granting it the right to make cars bearing the Rolls-Royce name in the new BMW company in return for a board seat. And who slid into the seat? Sir Ralph Robins.

What Robins could not deliver, however, were two trademarks of great importance – the classic radiator grille and Flying Lady mascot – the most recognizable symbols of a Rolls-Royce motor car. These registered designs, owned by the car company, were graciously passed to BMW. By locking them away Volkswagen could have done a tit-for-tat on Pischetsrieder's dog-in-the-manger act. Piech had been skewered, but he was magnanimous and emerged as the only class act in a sorry affair.

Ian Norris, a leading British automotive journalist, observed in a piece in *The Car Connection* in the United States: 'In a gesture much more worthy of an English gentleman than the mean-spirited action of Rolls-Royce Plc, Dr Ferdinand Piech, Volkswagen's boss, handed them both over to BMW.' It was indeed a generous gesture, for without the *Spirit of Ecstasy* and the famous radiator shape, the BMW-produced Rolls-Royce which came along in 2003 might have suffered a serious identity crisis, the only indication that it was a Rolls-Royce being the small RR badging.

A generally held view in the international automotive industry was that Volkswagen had been shafted, but that it was partly its own fault for not securing the right to legally use the name Rolls-Royce in its eagerness to sign a check. Conversely, it was not unreasonable for Ferdinand Piech to assume that the right to use the Rolls-Royce name and badge on the product was automatic if Vickers was selling the Company as a going concern.

The real victim, however, was Rolls-Royce Motor Cars, fighting to operate in an atmosphere of uncertainty as the Germans fought over its future. Not only were there no means of determining its own affairs or being able to map a way forward, it suffered a mighty blow with the loss of a man with the talent and drive to take it through a renaissance. The recently arrived chief executive, Graham Morris, a highly regarded manager in the car industry, quit in disgust at the backroom horse-trading between Vickers, BMW and the Rolls-Royce aerospace company.

A former senior United Kingdom and United States Rover executive, who later ran international sales and marketing at Volkswagen/Audi where he was an Audi board member, Morris had taken the helm at Rolls-Royce a little over a year earlier. Pleased with the prospect of much-needed investment from his old company, along with more engineering depth, he told the workforce that Volkswagen would give Rolls and Bentley a stable future and an assurance that both would continue to be made there. His confidence about a key part of the scenario was misplaced.

Astonishingly, Morris was kept in the dark about the row between the chiefs of Volkswagen and BMW, and the meetings going on in London, Munich and Wolfsburg. He was away on a wedding anniversary cruise when he heard about the BMW/Volkswagen deal and having assured employees that Rolls-Royce production would remain at Crewe, his position was not just undermined – it was impossible. Rolls-Royce moving away from the factory that had been its home for more than half a century would result in many people who had given years of skilled and faithful service losing their jobs. He resigned and told me afterward when we talked at his home in Cheshire: 'I had no alternative. I'd given my word and turned round to find decisions being taken that would mean just the opposite.'

Piech, who had great respect for Morris, asked him to fly to Germany to see if he could be persuaded to stay. Morris went, but would not change his mind about resigning. He would stay a while until a successor was appointed. Several months later, at Christmas 1998, Tony Gott, a senior Rolls-Royce engineer who had headed the Silver Seraph new model project,

Designer dreams. Graham Hull's 1977 design for a possible Rolls-Royce of the future.

was made acting CEO and, in April 1999, was confirmed as chief executive. Gott inherited an immediate problem. He was in charge of a business that was losing customers. Potential buyers and Rolls-Royce lovers, disturbed by the uncertainties and whether Rolls would have engine-less orphans next year, did not know what to think about the Company's prospects and where it was going. Also there was concern that BMW power trains and so much German componentry in the cars would dilute their character and exclusivity. Suspicion about a German car in a Rolls-Royce skin depressed sales just when they should have been going in the other direction.

Would the new models hold their value? Though Rolls-Royce engineers had worked on the engines, the perception was that basically they were BMW and that, in the view of the diehards, did not make them Rolls-Royce. In the United States, there was also reluctance to pay well over $200,000 for a Rolls powered by an engine suspected to be quite similar to that in the much cheaper BMW 750.

With the Silver Seraph and Bentley Arnage, the first new sedans for eighteen years, having been launched in March 1998, the Company was looking for sales of about 2,500. But poor market appeal caused estimates to be revised downward several times. What should have been a banner year and the largest profit in a decade turned into disaster. Within weeks of the new models arriving, some dealers, particularly non-franchised traders in Florida, were advertising late Spurs as 'the last genuine British-built Rolls-Royces with a Rolls-built engine'. In the *Luxury Media Showcase* – a glossy companion to the *Robb Report*, a magazine for the rich whose readers awaken each morning asking 'How can I spend a lot of money today?' – a telling advertisement for a 1999 Silver Spur was headlined: 'Your Last Chance to Purchase the Last Real Rolls-Royce. Traditional Styling with a Rolls-Royce Engine.' Not Pulitzer Prize-winning copy, but sending a message. It was placed by a dealer who was also under factory pressure, of course, to take the new Seraph and Arnage models.

As with any new Rolls or Bentley, the diehards had reservations about the styling. I think they were being over-sensitive. Designed at Crewe, they were contemporary, yet clearly identifiable as being of the Rolls-Royce/Bentley family – always a paramount requirement but not easy to accomplish. The stylists moved some distance from the Spirit and Spur, softening the lines and addressing the need for graceful models that were a creditable progression of the heritage. But, while the appearance, leather, veneers and carpeting were classic Rolls-Royce, much beneath the skin had changed, with a large engineering content from Germany.

BMW engines and other components were now being shipped from Munich instead of being assembled by hand by Rolls-Royce engineers. It would have been a shock to many to learn that not only did Rolls-Royce not have a director of engineering, the Company hailed throughout the world for its engineering no longer had an engine-building shop and was making less and less of the car itself. It was tantamount to a hospital telling patients that half its operating rooms were closed and surgery was being outsourced. BMW was supplying a 5.4-liter 322hp V12 for the Silver Seraph, and a 350hp 4.5-liter V8 turbocharged unit for the Bentley Arnage, which took its name from one of the most challenging bends on the Le Mans circuit. The Bentley Turbo R – now called the RT – retained its shape and power-base, but its 6.75-liter 400hp V8 was built by Cosworth.

Nonetheless, Volkswagen sprang for a huge investment program. New engineering and design resources at Crewe began planning a stylish twin-turbo sports coupé, a 550hp to which a much-loved name would be attached – the Bentley Continental. The letters GT were added and hundreds of orders came in from customers who had not even seen it. A volume car by historical Bentley standards, sights were set on annual production of about 7,000. With almost everything riding on this new flagship due in 2004, and no inclination to nurture the other part of the business that was due to go away, little attention was given to Rolls-Royce which was left to slumber along, awaiting a transfusion from BMW in 2003. It was tantamount to denying sustenance to a member of the family on life-support and an ignominious end to a century of distinction and achievement.

The Teutonic slugfest ended with an ironic twist. Bernd Pischetsrieder, the BMW chairman who had gone to such lengths to get his hands on Rolls-Royce, never got to lord it over the world's most famous motor car after all. His devotion to the British Rover company, a corporate fiasco of nerve-jangling proportions, in which more than $3 billion of BMW money was lost on the poor-performing British auto group, cost him his job after a tumultuous board meeting in early 1999.

Piech then made a surprising move considering Pischetsrieder's hard-ball tactics in the battle they had fought. He hired him to run Volkswagen's Spanish subsidiary. And, when Piech retired, who should succeed him as Volkswagen chief but Pischetsrieder. He inherited Bentley, but not Rolls-Royce to which he had committed so much energy to acquire and which generated so much fighting. Considering the lukewarm reception given to the Rolls-Royce Phantom produced by his his former colleagues at BMW and the potential rising profit curve Bentley offered to the Volkswagen group, he probably thanked a lucky star or two, and maybe appreciatively tipped his hat to Dr Piech.

29

WHAT FUTURE FOR LUXURIOUS DINOSAURS?

BMW suddenly became the 800lb gorilla ringing the doorbell at the House of Lords when a deal was struck in 1998, giving it the right four years down the road to make cars bearing the name Rolls-Royce. It was inheriting a unique dynasty, 'The Rolls-Royce of automobiles' as some journalists have described it; a revered name towering above all others, viewed worldwide for close to a century as a benchmark of excellence and quintessentially English.

A task force was put together to work out how to reconcile a confluence of pressures. There were three immediate issues: the design of a flagship to take the Rolls-Royce marque into its second century; infuse engineering heft, and provide a big chunk of development cash.

Hovering over the task was a realization that BMW must approach the sea change with a sensitive appreciation of what had been entrusted to its care; do nothing to contaminate a unique DNA. Meddling with the heritage or a perceived dilution of the 'Englishness' could destroy the essence. Rolls and Bentley enthusiasts had already given the thumbs down to BMW engines in the Rolls-Royce Seraph and Bentley Arnage sedans whose dismal sales sired the Bentley Red Label – a hastily concocted revision of the Arnage, powered by the venerable British-built 6.75-liter engine.

Ford had already negotiated the delicate road of foreign ownership of a British icon when it acquired the ailing Jaguar, a staggering financial disaster that was close to going under. It took years of intense rehabilitation, the application of Yankee engineering know-how and tons of money to cover losses running into hundreds of millions, and fashion a future for a much-loved name that for so long had been the despair of long-suffering, yet forgiving owners. The grunt work was done expertly beneath the stage, while the front office maintained the classic sporty image and Englishness of the brand.

BMW concluded that a Rolls-Royce makeover was necessary, fresh styling and new technology, and there was a feeling in Munich that new ownership should be emphasized. The lines to be walked were fine ones, so a study to determine what to do began with an international design team based in London. They set up shop in a bank building near Marble Arch, making daily pilgrimages to Mayfair to observe the traffic, particularly Rolls-Royce and their owners, as they sought to get a handle on what sort of car they should make. Rolls-Royce watchers forecast that they would produce a large 7-Series BMW. This they were determined not to do and went to inordinate lengths to make a car far removed from the Munich flag-carrier.

What they came up with in early 2003 was a large car fronted by an enormous grille that you could almost see from across town and it was named Phantom. The profile however, was graceful and cues from notable Royce coachwork of the past were evident in an understated way.

Over the previous seventy-five years there had been six Rolls-Royce Phantom models, each bearing a number – P I through P VI, in Rolls parlance. The new one, with the name but

The Bentley State Limousine presented to Queen Elizabeth II after Volkswagen took over Bentley manufacturing at Crewe.

no number, was praised by journalists for comfort, tremendous performance, handling and technical excellence, but given a less than ecstatic reception for its looks.

Nineteen feet long and weighing 5,478lb, it was a superbly engineered, powerful and easy car to drive and so potent, it would leap from rest to 60mph in 5.7 seconds with hardly a sound. The makers, however, were not able to resist fitting a version of BMW's notoriously complex I-Drive system controller to comprehend which, critics suggested, a degree in applied sciences could be useful.

Unquestionably, the new Phantom was the most technologically advanced Rolls-Royce to carry the illustrious name in half a century, but the media was far from complementary about the front-end appearance. Some journalistic judgments probably put the BMW apparatchiks off their bratwurst for the day. 'A Camargue on steroids' was one view. *Automobile Magazine* described it as 'a caricature of a Rolls-Royce, the front seeming not to go with the back end'.

It got worse. When you are making a car costing more than many people pay for a house, *Wall Street Journal* readers are among your prime demographics, so a knock in the weekend section causes palpitations, especially if it is in a feature called 'The Ugly Cars' and headed: 'The new BMW Rolls-Royce. The goal: Timeless British elegance. "A Soviet staff car" – Panel verdict.' It was a first for any car bearing the Rolls-Royce name. In its century-long history, I do not believe Rolls-Royce was ever accused of building an ugly car. BMW achieved that regrettable distinction before its offering even got to the showroom starting blocks.

A *Journal* panel of car experts, pronouncing on which new designs were daring and which were duds, observed:

> Its boxy shape has jarred some longtime fans. It's hard to miss the huge grille, which one of our panelists compared to a jack-o'-lantern. A transportation design instructor at Art Center College of Design in Pasadena described it as 'quite vulgar'. Criticism aside, our panelists agreed its presence makes a statement. 'It's the difference between arriving and just showing

The new face of Bentley.

up,' says Leslie Kendall, the Petersen Automotive Museum curator. Bottom line: If it doesn't look like a Rolls can it still be a status symbol?

The respected journalist Phil Llewellin wrote: 'I gasped "Miss Piggy" as the luxo-barge was revealed. The colossal radiator grille and tiny headlights created an impression of the prima donna porker's snout and eyes.' Llewellyn was kinder about Volkswagen's first foray into the world of Bentley, its Continental GT, coming to market at less than half the Phantom's price and, like the Phantom, drawing its name from the marque's glorious past. The new Bentley *wunderwagen* was a technological tour de force and represented terrific value for money at the big-bucks end of the market. It looked muscular and purposeful.

Rich Taylor noted in the *New York Times* that the Phantom's engine stemmed from BMW's 6-liter V12 and most of the running gear was derived or borrowed from the BMW 7-Series. 'The only really controversial part of the Phantom,' he wrote, 'is the awkward styling of the nose. The classic Rolls-Royce grille has been widened into a caricature. Rectangular headlights and a protruding jaw do not help.'

Andrew English in the London *Daily Telegraph* observed that the stately car was put together with 2,500 separate parts made by BMW in Germany:

> However much BMW says it has kept 'The project' at arm's length, is this new Phantom anything more than just an exorbitant BMW limousine with the National Gallery pop-riveted on the front (the grille) and topped by a silly flying fairy? Is Eleanor Thornton, the model for the *Spirit of Ecstasy*, blushing with embarrassment, or soaring with, well, ecstasy?

He described the front bumper as a barely concealed square bar that looked like something brutally welded on by Mr T in between takes for the *A Team*. English recalled that Sir Henry Royce once said: 'It is either right or it is not.' The journalist added: 'That bumper is not.' I sense he did not care for the car.

Above and opposite: The Flying Spur and the Continental GT coupe which immediately generated a two-year order book.

Nor did *Automobile*'s design editor, Robert Cumberford, who opined:

> The body color bumper looks cheap, as though BMW got a deal on surplus truck parts. The BMW-built Rolls-Royce Phantom doesn't look completely right to me. It is incongruously gigantic, and mounted on brutal wheels that could have come from a *Wehrmacht* vehicle, it is certainly a bit bizarre for what traditionally has been an understated and subtly elegant marque.

The auto-buff book sage David E. Davis, Jr, whose opinions have been listened to industry-wide for many years, advised: 'Look for a rationalized second-generation Rolls-Royce Phantom that comes together better – that looks less like a caricature and more like the Rolls-Royce of our dreams.'

Paul Eisenstein, the syndicated automotive writer and one of the best journalists around, liked it. 'The Rolls-Royce Phantom may look like the locomotive driving the Twentieth Century Ltd' he said, 'but it drives much smaller, and with 75 per cent of the power available at 1,000rpm, has plenty of giddy-up and makes 100mph feel more like 55mph.' The Phantom did not disguise its opulence, he said, but made a strong and commendable effort to deliver a car serious drivers could take a pride in. Whether there was a market for such a car in the extremely crowded luxury car market remained to be seen. One thousand sales a year was the original target but the early going was tough, and it took three years, to the spring of 2006, before sales in North America reached that figure.

Keith Martin in the *New York Times* liked the Phantom's effortless performance, but found the body leaned noticeably on corners. The rival Mercedes Maybach was the better car, he thought, but the Phantom the more striking statement of success. Overall verdict: 'Majesty without subtlety.' Asked by *The Times* for her opinion, Jean Jennings, editor-in-chief of *Automobile Magazine* said the Rolls-Royce was clearly a driver's car, a rocket ship, and no longer a Zsa-Zsa-mobile. 'The Maybach is for quiche-eating layabouts,' she merrily quipped.

Prestley Blake, well-known for his twenty-plus Rolls-Royce collection told me he ordered a new Phantom, and then cancelled when he saw it up close. He later confided to a Bentley

executive: 'I wouldn't pay a Rolls-Royce price for a Hummer in a tux.' A couple of years later, in 2005, he changed his mind and bought one and told me he was delighted with it.

It is a pity that the new custodians of the marque, aiming to produce a high-tech British luxury car should clothe it in a jacket that triggered such critical reaction. The Phantom, carrying a revered name, could do without references to ugliness and Kremlin staff cars. The shape was some way from the lines of the Silver Cloud, which set the bar decades earlier for classic Rolls-Royce styling. And that is a shame because a Rolls-Royce is expected to have a gracious appearance that stands out and is admired. It could only be a Rolls-Royce. As David Davis suggested, 'Maybe they will get it right next time.'

The former Rolls and Bentley CEO, Tony Gott, who was hired by BMW as chairman and chief executive of the new Rolls-Royce Motor Cars Ltd, was quoted by Paul Eisenstein: 'The task at hand is to get Rolls Royce taken seriously again.' Speaking more frankly than any Rolls executive in memory, Gott lashed out at previous managements of which he had twenty years' experience. Neglect by Vickers over the eighteen years that it owned Rolls-Royce and Bentley; the four years under Volkswagen ownership, and years of financial chaos before Vickers bought it, 'was something well short of Rolls-Royce's finest era. We had nothing to work with. Very little in resources.' Under Vickers' watch, he said, strategy shifted in 1989 to building up Bentley, effectively turning the Company upside down from Rolls-dominated, to one dominated by Bentley cars. Gott criticized compromises made to Rolls-Royce suspension, quality and craftsmanship during the previous decade when the cars got smaller, especially inside, to meet the proportional needs of the Bentleys.

There is no question that BMW inherited a marque suffering profile malnutrition, despite the recent introduction of a beautiful successor to the Corniche convertible that had been in the works for several years and turned out to be the valedictory contribution of Graham Hull and his colleagues in the Crewe styling department. As Volkswagen busied itself with all things Bentley, Rolls-Royce, for four years, suffered atrophy, hibernation, neglect, and debilitation – call it what you will. Starved of attention, marketing and publicity, the marque disappeared from public consciousness as Volkswagen, with the split coming up, focused resources and energies on Bentley. BMW was prevented by the purchase agreement from mounting any Rolls-Royce publicity before 1 January 2003 and had to stand by helplessly as the brand

The head-turning Continental GTC.

A new Bentley Brooklands in 2007 – the second model to bear the name of the famous racing circuit.

languished in a visibility vacuum. It was noticeable at the New York Auto Show in 2002 that the Rolls-Royce brand was still in the wilderness, that the Company exhibit was dominated by Bentleys in the front, while a lone Rolls was stuck at the back, as if an illegitimate son was being kept out of the way.

After the in-fighting between Wolfsburg and Munich to wrest control of the Company, BMW's moving Rolls-Royce out of the Crewe factory seemed to be a classic case of cutting off its nose. Enthusiasts and many in the Crewe area speculated that a way might be found to continue building both marques there. Why walk away from the skilled craftsmen and women who knew better than any labor force anywhere how to create Rolls-Royce and Bentley motor cars? And why not take advantage of the many millions Volkswagen was spending on new production facilities?

An economics degree was unnecessary to deduce that with a sales target of about twenty Rolls-Royce cars a week and expensive, time-consuming interior work, BMW would hardly expect to make a profit. It would surely be more cost-efficient to take space at Crewe. But, the depth of obstinacy, and perhaps pride, between the German titans ruled out a strategy from which everybody would come out a winner.

BMW struck a deal to build a plant on the Earl of March's estate, close to the Goodwood racing circuit in West Sussex, just a few miles from the house at West Wittering where Henry Royce spent the evening of his life. To appease local environmentalists who would not be thrilled to see a car factory silhouetted in an area of pastoral splendor, much of the building was constructed underground, attracting journalistic observations about hunkering down in the bunker. About 350 people, including some Germans and craftsmen from the yacht-building industry, were hired to assemble the car.

The aluminum-frame body shells and most components were shipped from Germany and a spokesman used an unfortunate phrase that caused much headshaking among Royce aficionados.

The Arnage – a different car when the BMW engine was abandoned and the venerable 6¾-liter Crewe-built engine was substituted.

The highly skilled craftsmen and women of Crewe still make what most people would say are the finest interiors in the world.

'It will take about three weeks to give the car its Englishness,' a journalist reported. Brigadier-Generals and the tweed jacketed 'Tory-set' in the shires were said to have spluttered that no matter how long they took about it, a car put together mostly of German bits, even well-engineered bits, could not truly claim to be a Rolls-Royce which had always been essentially British in design and crafting. Time may soften that and sales will perhaps determine acceptability.

BMW clearly put enormous effort and care into making a Rolls-Royce worthy of the name. Around launch time, Tony Gott spoke about the ideology and aspirations that had driven the team to make a car 'that will bring about a renaissance of the Rolls-Royce marque and secure its future'. The legacy was remarkably rich and the designers, he said, took inspiration from famed models like the Phantom, Silver Cloud and Silver Shadow. They sought elegance and perfect proportions with a modern look. And of course, peerless engineering. Gott recalled that in the late 1920s and early 1930s, toward the end of Sir Henry Royce's life, his motor cars reached a pinnacle, being renowned as the finest in the world. That was the underlying goal of the new Rolls-Royce Company; committed to producing a car to recreate the legend. Tony Gott did not stay as long as he might have liked. In May 2004, a few weeks after the Rolls-Royce Centenary celebrations, he abruptly resigned as chairman and CEO. Personal reasons were cited, but executives in Munich were reported by *The Financial Times* as talking of disagreement over strategy and strained relations with BMW chairman, Helmut Panke.

Karl-Heinz Kalbfell, a long time BMW executive who had supervised the Phantom project from the start in 1998, overseeing design and development before returning to Germany, was parachuted in to take charge. Both Rolls-Royce and Bentley now had Germans in the driving seat. A prominent British automotive guru, Professor Garel Rhys, director of the Centre for Automotive Studies at Cardiff University, said Kalbfell's appointment as chairman and CEO strengthened the umbilical cord with BMW: 'The car is assembled in Germany; they put it in a crate and it is reassembled in Britain. Rolls-Royce knows now in no uncertain terms who the master is.' Rhys attached no blame to Tony Gott, noting that BMW showed sensitivity by

The Rolls-Royce Phantom, the first car to be produced under BMW's stewardship. A majestic behemoth with much more agility than its bulk would suggest.

making him chief executive: 'But after launch, you move to the production phase, then the corporate phase, and the Germans want people imbued in BMW culture.'

Financial analysts, who are a bit like sophisticated bookmakers and can sniff concerns before even the bulls and bears, called for more Brits on the board 'to stop it becoming like an American interpretation of a British pub'. Aside from perception issues, BMW had to grapple with another problem as it geared up for the Phantom launch in January 2003. It came into a world where it was no longer okay to show off your wealth. The timing of the re-introduction of the Rolls-Royce name could have been better.

The Gulf war was brewing, America was rocking from a sagging economy and corporate scandals. Ostentation was not the flavor of the year. Even investment bankers were drawing in their horns, balking at Concorde's $12,000 round-trip fare between New York and Europe, and British Airways and Air France retired their supersonic fleets before year's end.

The landscape had changed since the feel-good halcyon days when Rolls-Royce could barely keep pace with demand in a stratospheric price field that it dominated. Despite questions about the acceptability of cars that epitomized conspicuous consumption, optimistic manufacturers refused to believe there was not a market for luxurious dinosaurs and several very pricey and exotic models began to crowd a tiny plateau at the top of the pyramid.

Interlopers competed to seize the high ground that had been owned by Rolls-Royce for many decades – Daimler-Benz, with its $400,000 behemoth, the Maybach, Volkswagen's luxurious Phaeton that did not sell and quietly disappeared from the United States within a couple of years; Audi with a street version of its Le Mans winning RS 6 racer; ultra-expensive Ferraris and Lamborghinis and, of course, Volkswagen's Bentleys, whose entry level Continental GT, with taxes, left little change from $200,000. An extended wheelbase version of the Phantom arrived in 2006 – an impressive, luxurious land yacht weighing in at 5,866lb. This was followed in 2007 by a drophead coupé bringing the Rolls-Royce stable to three models.

Above and below: The new Phantom is exported to more then fifty countries, sales in 2006 totalling 805, and production ramped up as demand increased with the launch of a convertible in 2007. The USA was the leading Rolls-Royce market, followed by Britain and China. The top five dealers were in Beverley Hills, Tokyo, London, Dubai and New York.

Above and below: The spacious and beautifully fashioned Phantom interior.

Above and below: The Phantom drophead coupe, which for 2008 carried a price tag of $407,000, 'flaunts an open-topped invitation to car-jackers and it is like waving a bag of cocaine under the noses of Customs officers', wrote Neil Lyndon in the London *Sunday Telegraph*. He added: 'Its rearward-opening coach doors are so long and heavy they can hardly be reached from the seats or pulled by hand, and hydraulic motors are needed to push them closed.' After listing technical shortcomings, he queried: 'What justification can there be for paying £300,000 for a car that doesn't work faultlessly?'

Above: A 2007 Phantom silently speeds into the night, 'not so much cutting through the air as battering it aside', as one British automative writer observed about Rolls-Royce styling. But, of course, doing it with panache and serenity.

The Continental GTC, one of the most stunning performance Bentleys of the new era. With a prodigious 552bhp propelling it from zero to 60mph in 4.8 seconds, and capable of covering more than three miles a minute, its driver can make frequent acquaintance with humorless people driving cars with flashing lights – if they can keep up, that is!

Meanwhile, the Bentley market gathered momentum, with sales achieving 8,000 annually by 2007 – outselling Rolls-Royce by about eight to one. The arrival in 2005 of the 195mph four-door Continental Flying Spur triggered an order book stretching two years out and, with other high performance luxury Bentley projectiles on the way, the factory worked flat out.

The Flying Spur, however, while eulogized by most journalists, did not entirely escape the lash that had thrashed the Phantom. 'Not much more than a Volkswagen with pretensions,' reckoned Michael Booth of *The Independent*: 'Bentley's German masters have gone to great lengths to make this feel like a "proper Bentley", classic organ-stop air-vent controls, rich walnut paneling and heavy carpeting… determined to inject the essence of Bentleyness into what is essentially, a tarted-up Phaeton.'

Notwithstanding a barb or two, Volkswagen's Bentleys were doing well with the order book, while BMW's Phantom struggled for sales momentum. The rival Mercedes Maybach wallowed in the same waters and its sales director conceded that 1,000 cars a year was unrealistic and Maybach would not be expected to make money for a decade.

An automotive research center pinpointed the problems facing BMW and Mercedes with their flagship land yachts: 'Stately vehicles are driven by fairly conservative people who are increasingly reluctant to flash their wealth because of concerns about crime and terrorism.'

A few weeks after the Phantom was introduced, Bentley's marketing director, who seemed to be one of the few realists around, said there were not enough customers willing to spend $250,000 and more to support planned increases in luxury car production. The Bentley chairman and CEO, Franz-Josef Paefgen, warned that decisions to invest heavily in new top-of-the-range cars were taken 'under the influence of the bubble economy'. But the limited number of people ready to make a public statement with a very expensive car was shrinking because the social environment was changing. In Europe, people wanted a socially acceptable car. This was a frank statement from a company that continued to invest hundreds of millions of dollars despite the business climate and was gearing up to crank out more Bentleys priced to give them a greater chance of success than the behemoths.

The old money was evaporating and corporate earnings, the wellspring that fed the high-ticket market, was fluctuating. Against Wall Street travails and the WorldCom/Tyco/Enron scandals, caution became the prudent course. There was unwelcome focus on corporate plunder; the multi-million dollar rewards and huge stock options taken by CEOs and senior acolytes even when the share price had tanked. It got worse when business leaders were hauled up to answer charges of corporate malfeasance and collected hefty jail time.

Given all that, there will probably always be successful people around who desire a Rolls-Royce or Bentley, whose presence, opulence and beautifully crafted interior are in a realm of their own. And those two marques possess the most magical names you can conjure. Some, reaching to fulfill the dream, will produce the heavy money to make a statement with what for a century has been the king of status symbols. But the number feeling the urge to drive a high profile, tangible demonstration of success that some now regard as excess, has diminished.

Regardless of huffing and puffing by the PR spinners and lyrical brochure copy extolling the charms of the new 'ultimate cars for the wealthy', I cannot help but feel that if you own a Rolls-Royce built before 1998 by British engineers and craftsmen and women, you should hang on to it. You have the genuine article – a car possessing the heart and soul and true essence, of a Rolls-Royce.

Apart from its beauty and the pleasure it gives, it will increase in value if you look after it well and will become an heirloom to be treasured and handed on to your children and their children.

Henry Royce, I do believe, would find that quite satisfying.

Strive for perfection in everything you do.
Take the best that exists and make it better.
When it does not exist, design it.
Accept nothing nearly right or good enough.

Frederick Henry Royce
Mechanic

INDEX

If you are interested in purchasing other books published by Tempus,
or in case you have difficulty finding any Tempus books in your local bookshop,
you can also place orders directly through our website

www.tempus-publishing.com